Buffy THE VAMPIRE SLAYER™

VIVA LAS BUFFY!

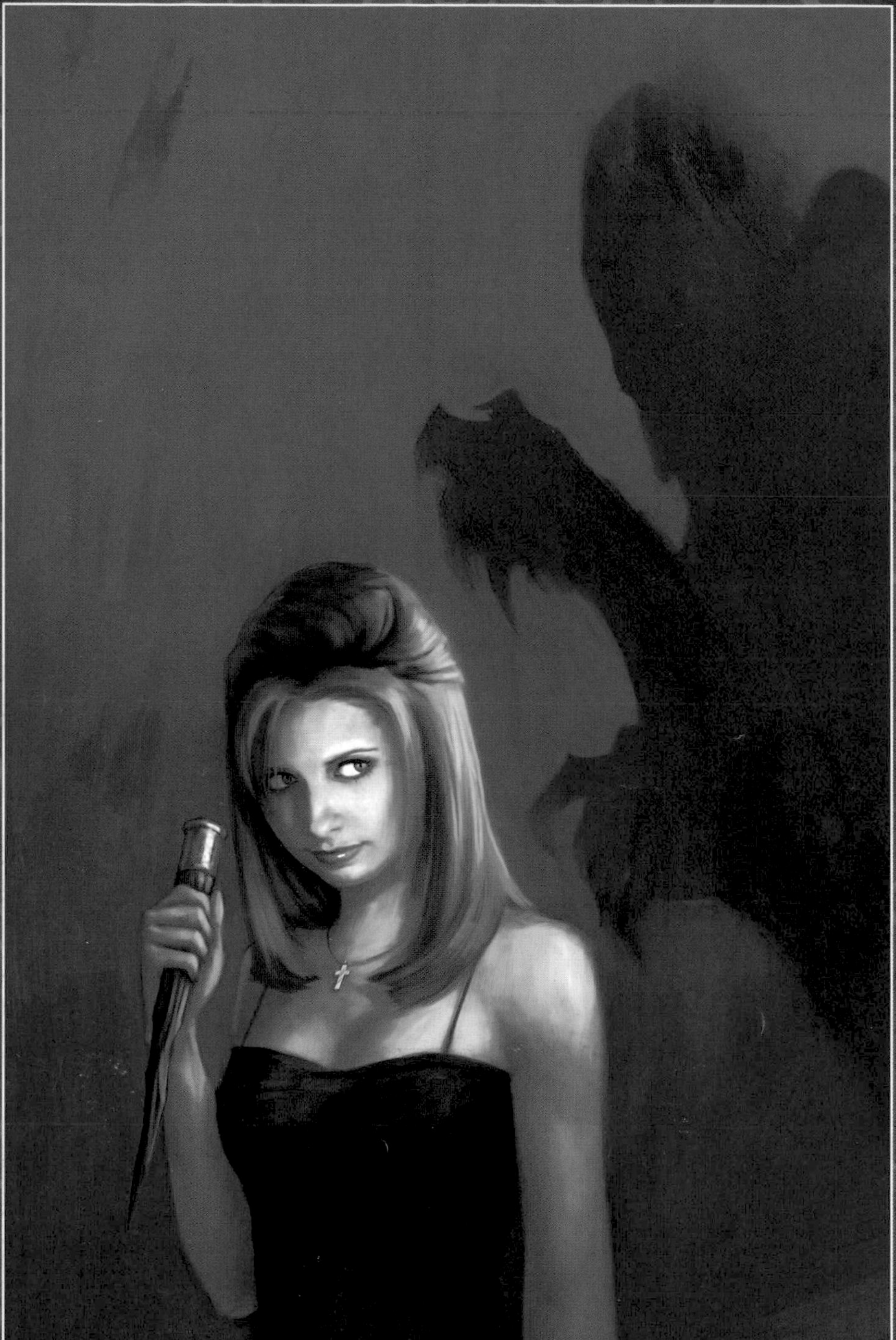

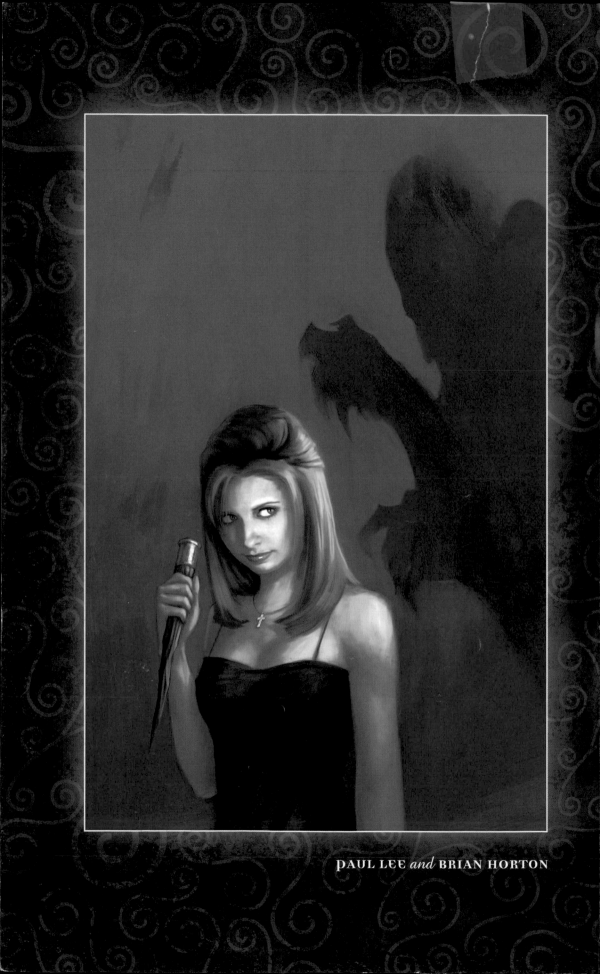

PAUL LEE *and* BRIAN HORTON

Buffy the Vampire Slayer™

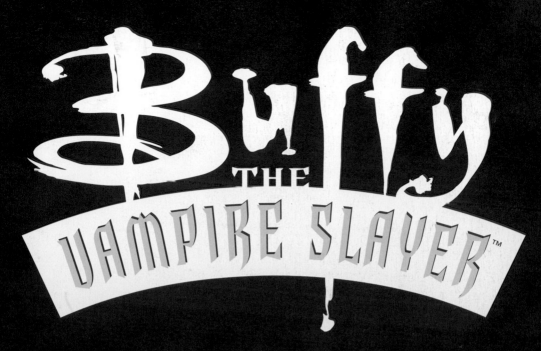

Viva Las Buffy!

based on the television series created by
JOSS WHEDON

writers SCOTT LOBDELL & FABIAN NICIEZA

penciller CLIFF RICHARDS

inker WILL CONRAD

colorists DAVE MCCAIG & LISA GONZALES

letterer CLEM ROBINS

cover art PAUL LEE & BRIAN HORTON

This story takes place before Buffy the Vampire Slayer's first season.

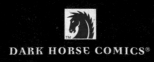

DARK HORSE COMICS®

publisher
MIKE RICHARDSON

editor
SCOTT ALLIE
with MATT DRYER

designer
LANI SCHREIBSTEIN

art director
MARK COX

special thanks to
DEBBIE OLSHAN AT FOX LICENSING
AND DAVID CAMPITI AT GLASS HOUSE GRAPHICS

PUBLISHED BY
DARK HORSE COMICS, INC.
10956 SE MAIN STREET
MILWAUKIE, OR 97222

FIRST EDITION
JULY 2003
ISBN: 1 - 56971 - 980 - 2

INTRODUCTION

Los Angeles high school freshman Buffy Summers shouldered an overwhelming burden, what with worrying about boys, cheerleading, and coordinating shoes, who could deal?

Then a mysterious man named Merrick came to her. Told her he was a Watcher. Said she was the Chosen One. Called her The Slayer, humanity's protector from the forces of darkness.

"Yeah, right," she thought. Then she encountered her first vampire. And her second. And a lot more. As Buffy began to train for her destiny, a vampiric overlord named Lothos infiltrated the underground of Los Angeles. With the help of a high school slacker named Pike, Buffy stopped Lothos, but at the cost of Merrick's life, her high school social status, and her criminal record.

Because the gymnasium burned down during the vampire attack, Buffy has been suspended from school pending expulsion hearings. Her parents are having marital problems. And she's a fifteen-year-old Slayer without a Watcher.

The end of the original motion picture was just the beginning of her story...

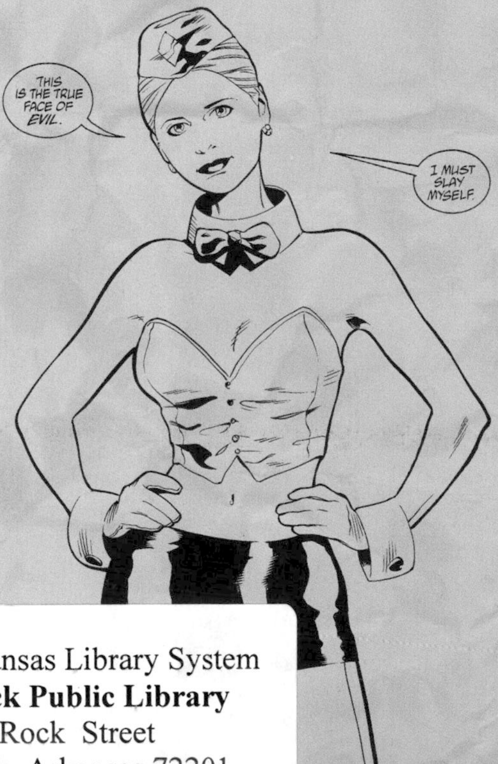
THIS IS THE TRUE FACE OF EVIL.
I MUST SLAY MYSELF.

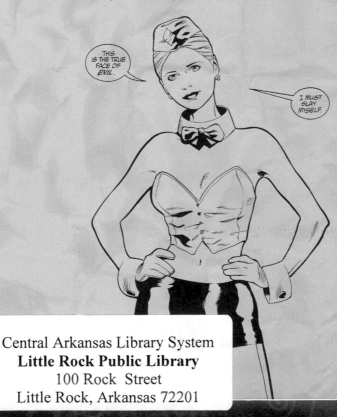

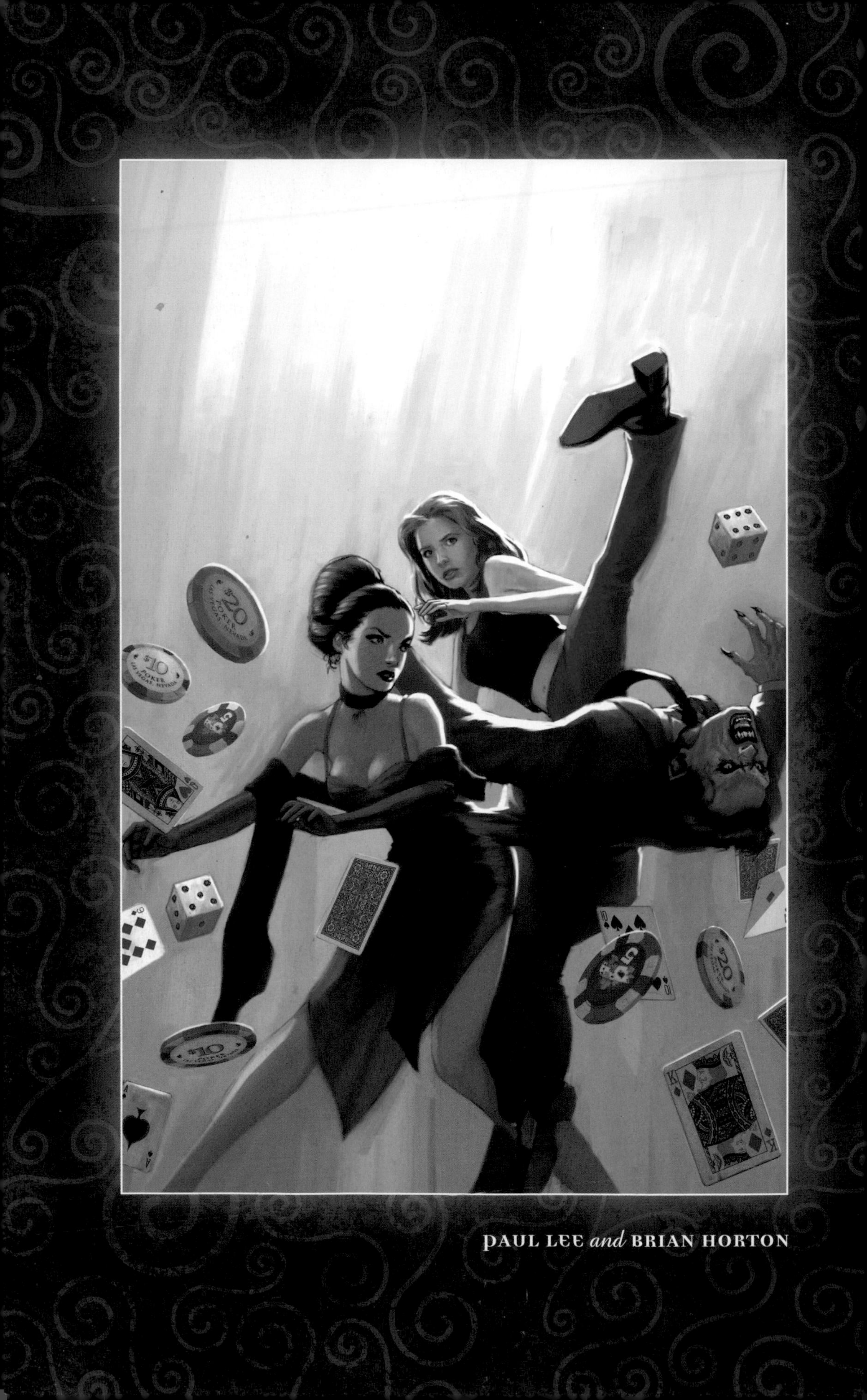

PAUL LEE *and* BRIAN HORTON

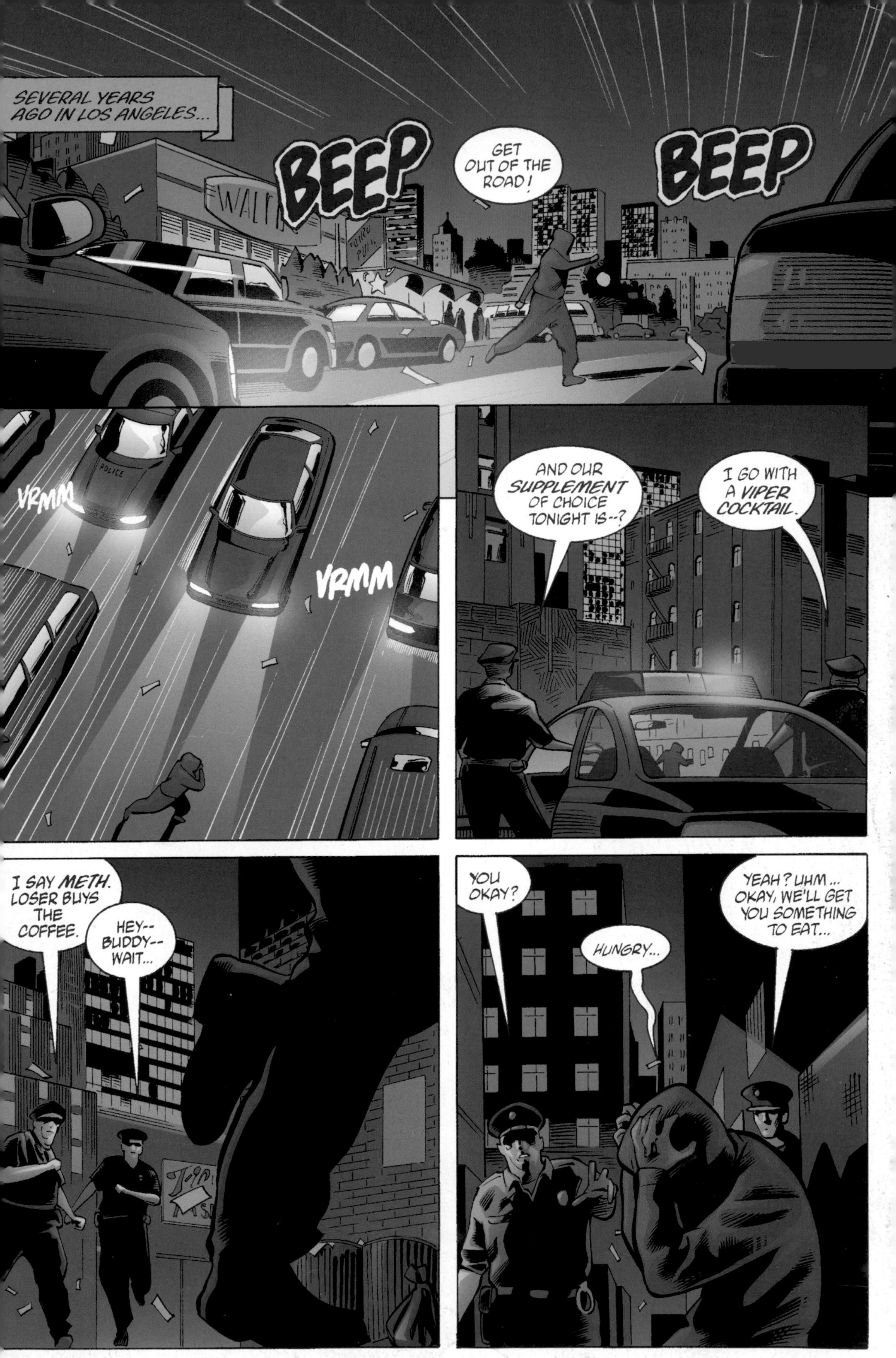
SEVERAL YEARS AGO IN LOS ANGELES...
BEEP
GET OUT OF THE ROAD!
BEEP
VRMM
VRMM
AND OUR SUPPLEMENT OF CHOICE TONIGHT IS--?
I GO WITH A VIPER COCKTAIL.
I SAY METH. LOSER BUYS THE COFFEE.
HEY-- BUDDY-- WAIT...
YOU OKAY?
HUNGRY...
YEAH? UHM... OKAY, WE'LL GET YOU SOMETHING TO EAT...

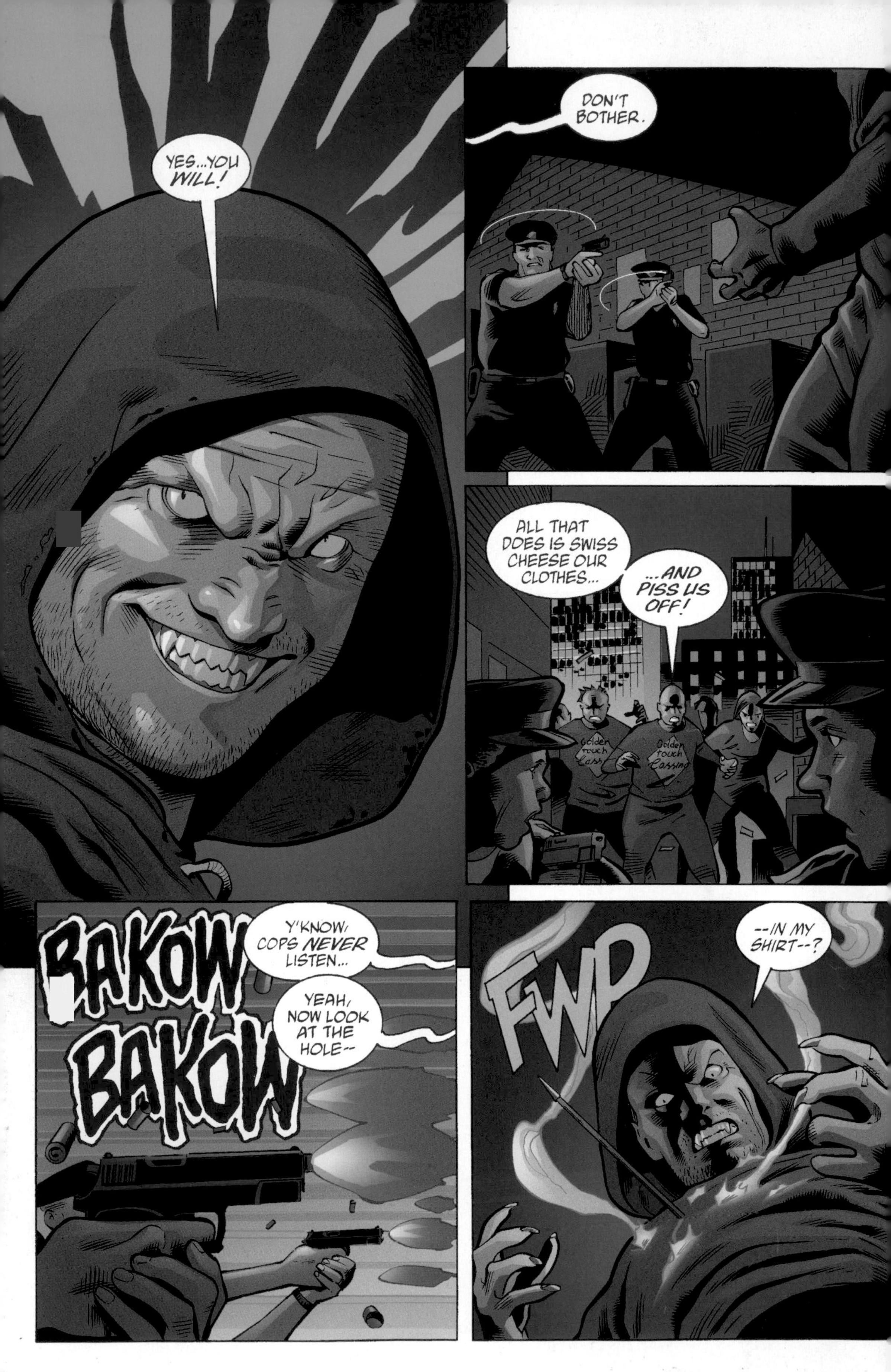
YES...YOU WILL!
DON'T BOTHER.
ALL THAT DOES IS SWISS CHEESE OUR CLOTHES...
...AND PISS US OFF!
BAKOW
BAKOW
Y'KNOW, COPS NEVER LISTEN...
YEAH, NOW LOOK AT THE HOLE--
FWP
--IN MY SHIRT--?

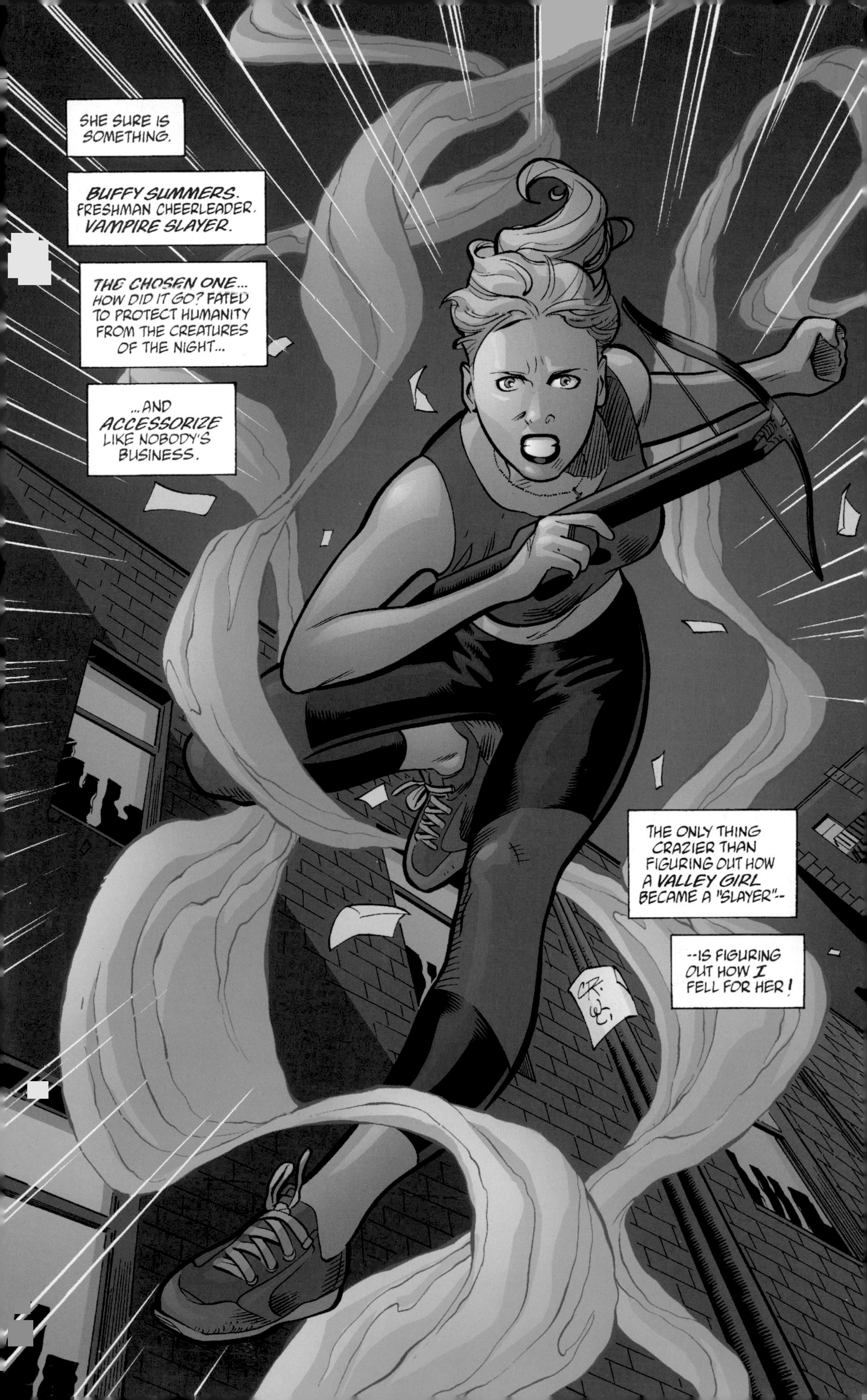
SHE SURE IS SOMETHING.
BUFFY SUMMERS. FRESHMAN CHEERLEADER. VAMPIRE SLAYER.
THE CHOSEN ONE... HOW DID IT GO? FATED TO PROTECT HUMANITY FROM THE CREATURES OF THE NIGHT...
...AND ACCESSORIZE LIKE NOBODY'S BUSINESS.
THE ONLY THING CRAZIER THAN FIGURING OUT HOW A VALLEY GIRL BECAME A "SLAYER"--
--IS FIGURING OUT HOW I FELL FOR HER!

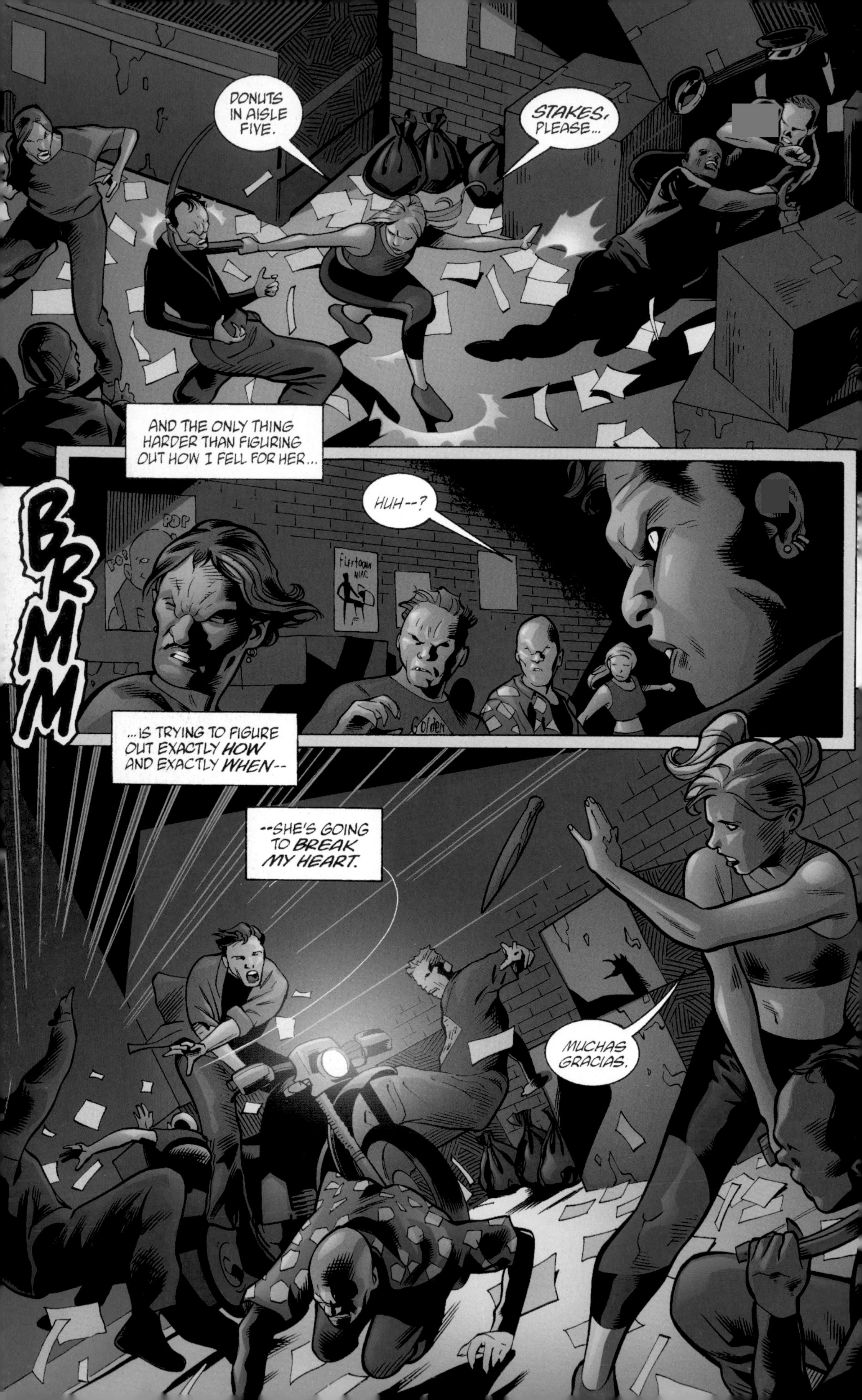
DONUTS IN AISLE FIVE.
STAKES, PLEASE...
AND THE ONLY THING HARDER THAN FIGURING OUT HOW I FELL FOR HER...
BRMMM
HUH--?
...IS TRYING TO FIGURE OUT EXACTLY HOW AND EXACTLY WHEN--
--SHE'S GOING TO BREAK MY HEART.
MUCHAS GRACIAS.

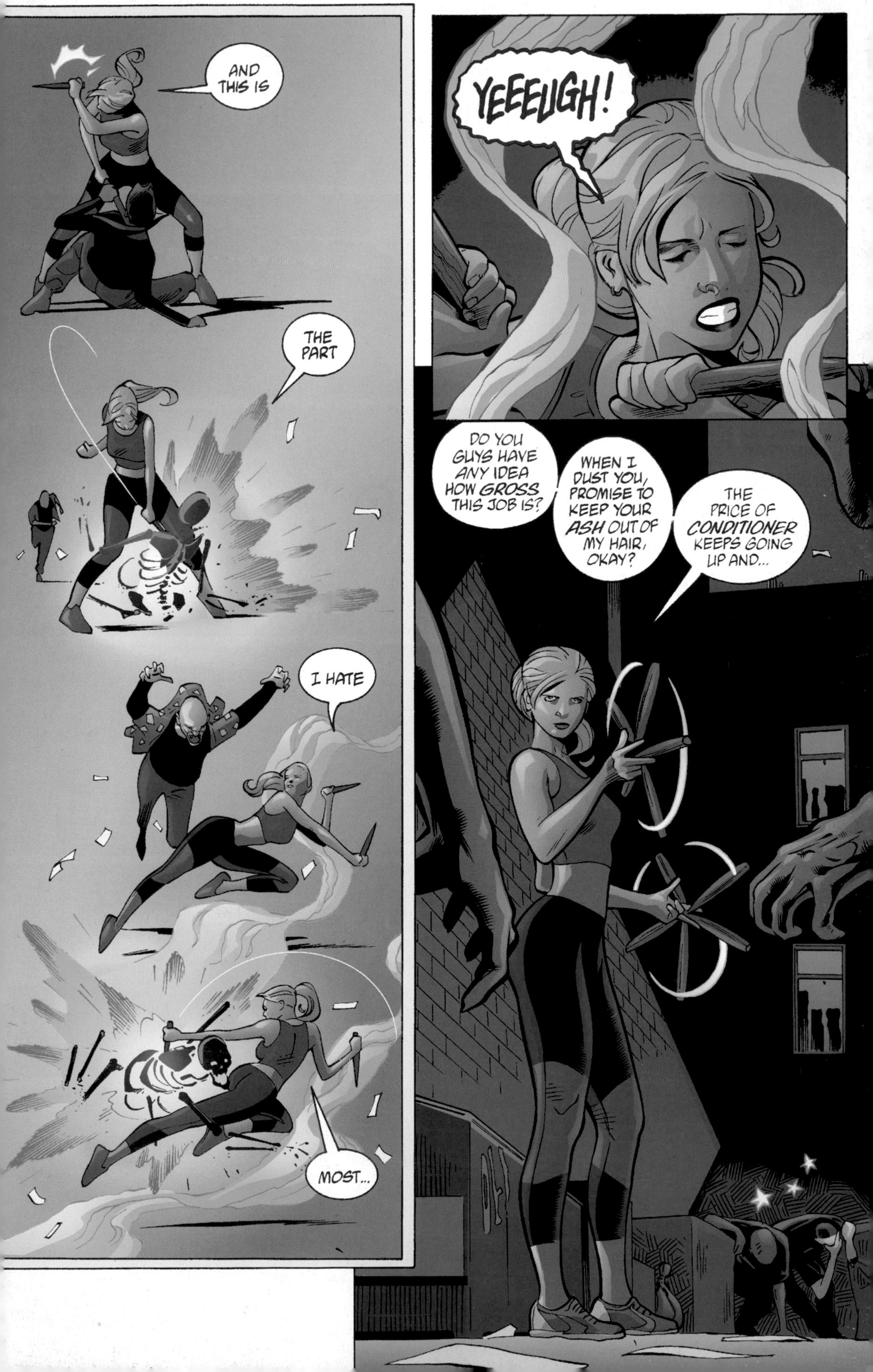
AND THIS IS
THE PART
I HATE
MOST...
YEEEUGH!
DO YOU GUYS HAVE ANY IDEA HOW GROSS THIS JOB IS?
WHEN I DUST YOU, PROMISE TO KEEP YOUR ASH OUT OF MY HAIR, OKAY?
THE PRICE OF CONDITIONER KEEPS GOING UP AND...

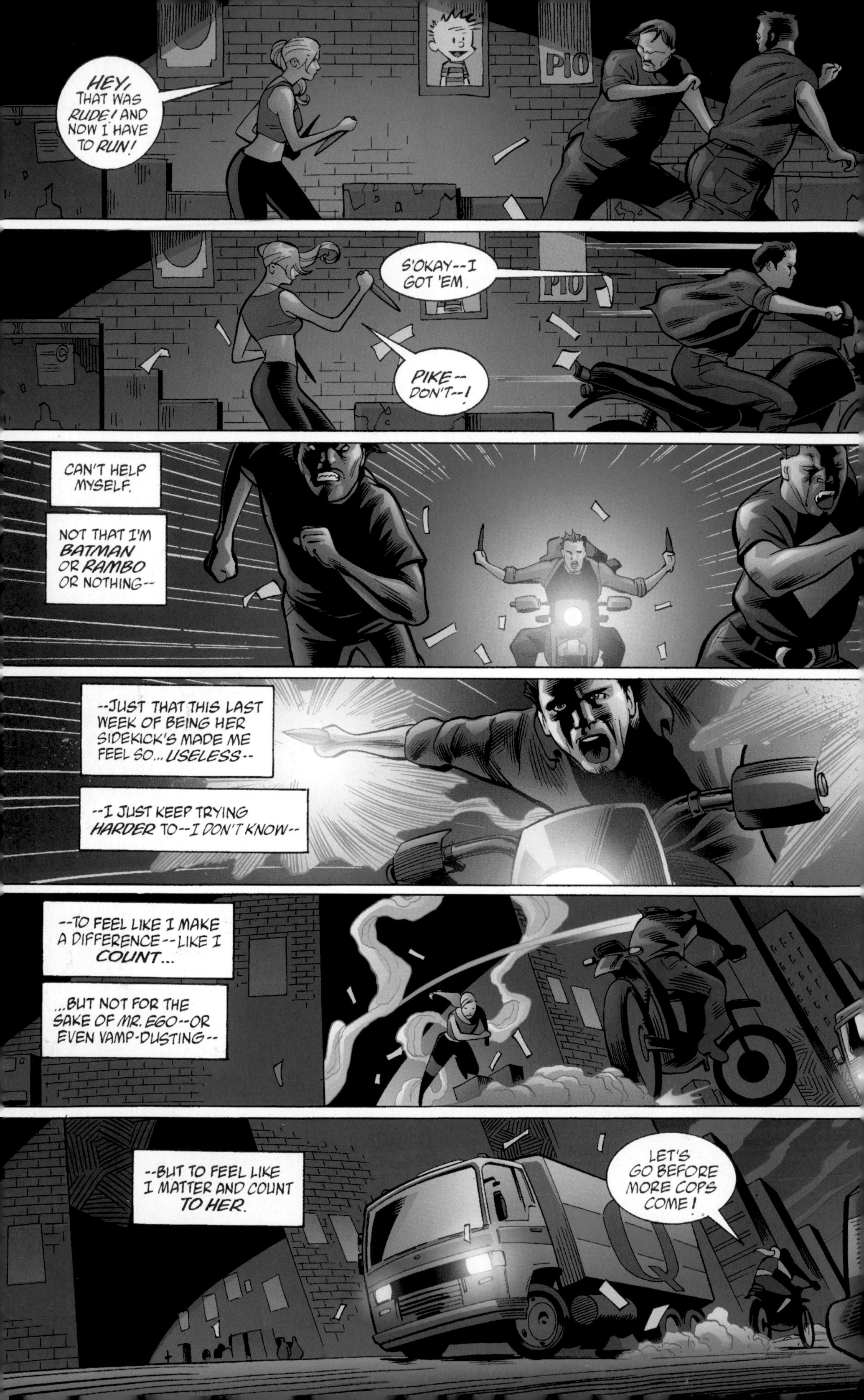
HEY, THAT WAS RUDE! AND NOW I HAVE TO RUN!
PIO
S'OKAY--I GOT 'EM.
PIKE--DON'T--!
PIO
CAN'T HELP MYSELF.
NOT THAT I'M BATMAN OR RAMBO OR NOTHING--
--JUST THAT THIS LAST WEEK OF BEING HER SIDEKICK'S MADE ME FEEL SO... USELESS--
--I JUST KEEP TRYING HARDER TO--I DON'T KNOW--
--TO FEEL LIKE I MAKE A DIFFERENCE--LIKE I COUNT...
...BUT NOT FOR THE SAKE OF MR. EGO--OR EVEN VAMP-DUSTING--
--BUT TO FEEL LIKE I MATTER AND COUNT TO HER.
LET'S GO BEFORE MORE COPS COME!

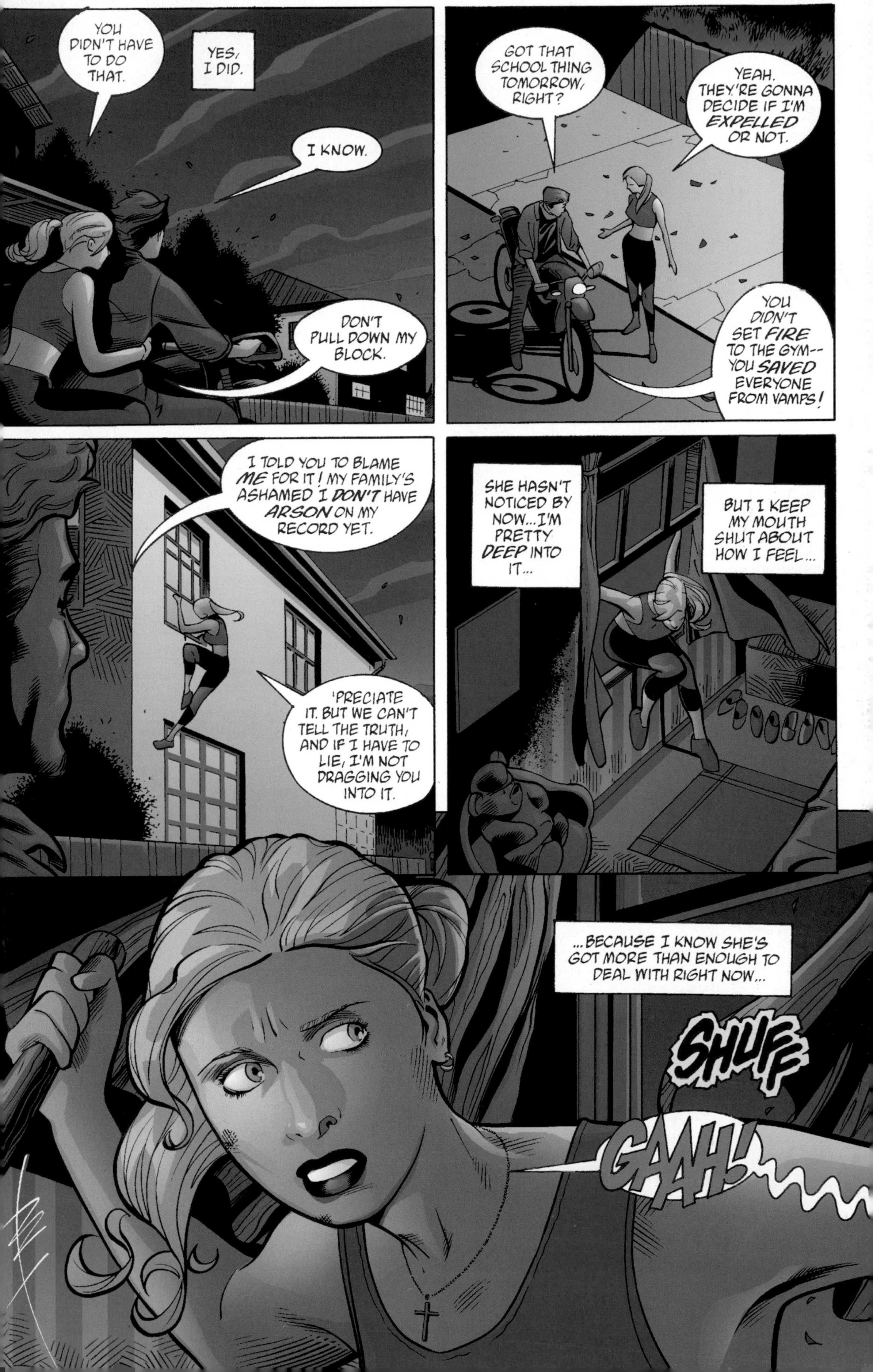
YOU DIDN'T HAVE TO DO THAT.
YES, I DID.
I KNOW.
DON'T PULL DOWN MY BLOCK.
GOT THAT SCHOOL THING TOMORROW, RIGHT?
YEAH. THEY'RE GONNA DECIDE IF I'M EXPELLED OR NOT.
YOU DIDN'T SET FIRE TO THE GYM-- YOU SAVED EVERYONE FROM VAMPS!
I TOLD YOU TO BLAME ME FOR IT! MY FAMILY'S ASHAMED I DON'T HAVE ARSON ON MY RECORD YET.
'PRECIATE IT. BUT WE CAN'T TELL THE TRUTH, AND IF I HAVE TO LIE, I'M NOT DRAGGING YOU INTO IT.
SHE HASN'T NOTICED BY NOW...I'M PRETTY DEEP INTO IT...
BUT I KEEP MY MOUTH SHUT ABOUT HOW I FEEL...
...BECAUSE I KNOW SHE'S GOT MORE THAN ENOUGH TO DEAL WITH RIGHT NOW...
SHUFF
GAAH!

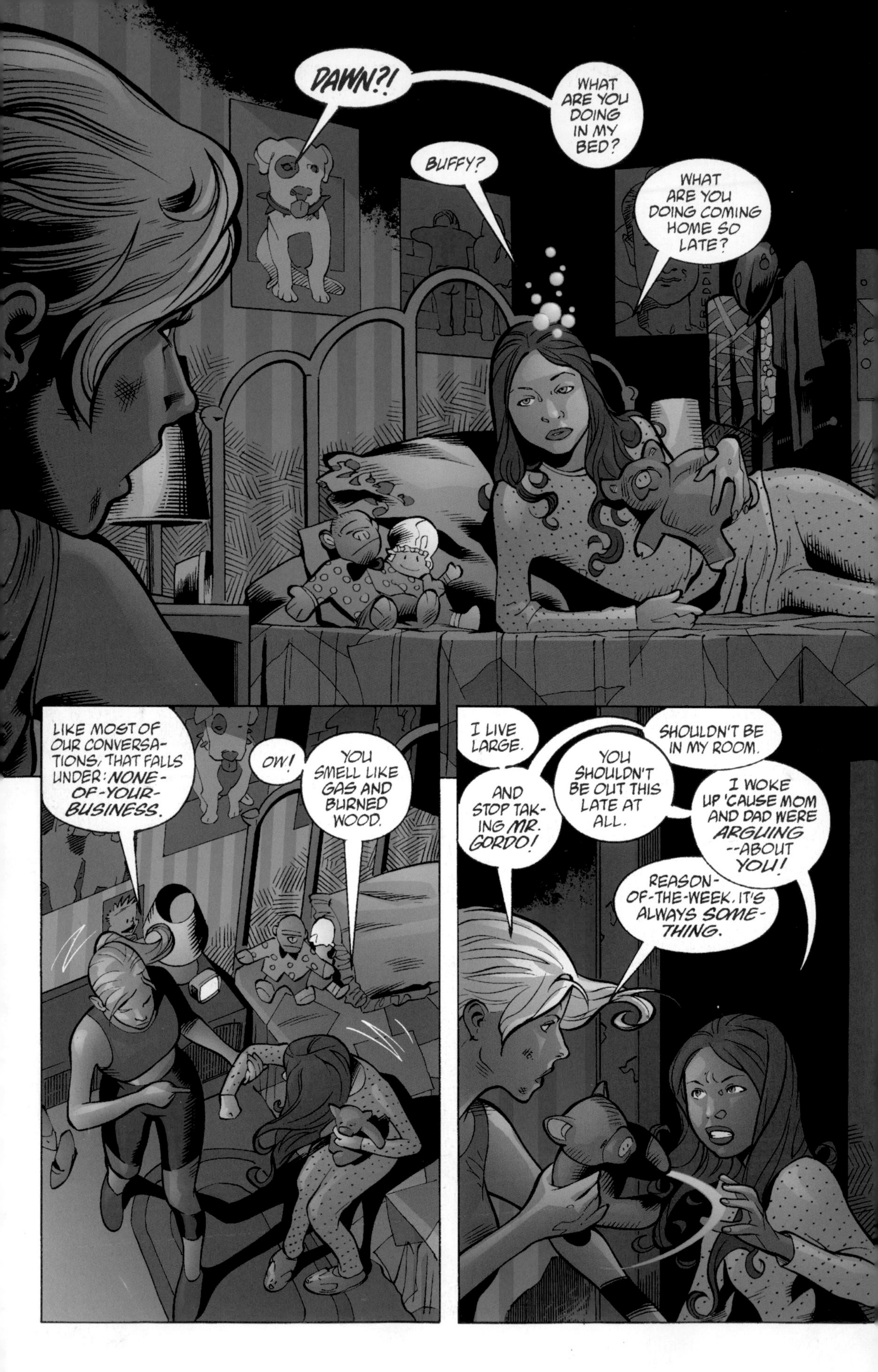
DAWN?!
WHAT ARE YOU DOING IN MY BED?
BUFFY?
WHAT ARE YOU DOING COMING HOME SO LATE?
LIKE MOST OF OUR CONVERSATIONS, THAT FALLS UNDER: NONE-OF-YOUR-BUSINESS.
OW!
YOU SMELL LIKE GAS AND BURNED WOOD.
I LIVE LARGE.
SHOULDN'T BE IN MY ROOM.
AND STOP TAKING MR. GORDO!
YOU SHOULDN'T BE OUT THIS LATE AT ALL.
I WOKE UP 'CAUSE MOM AND DAD WERE ARGUING--ABOUT YOU!
REASON-OF-THE-WEEK. IT'S ALWAYS SOMETHING.

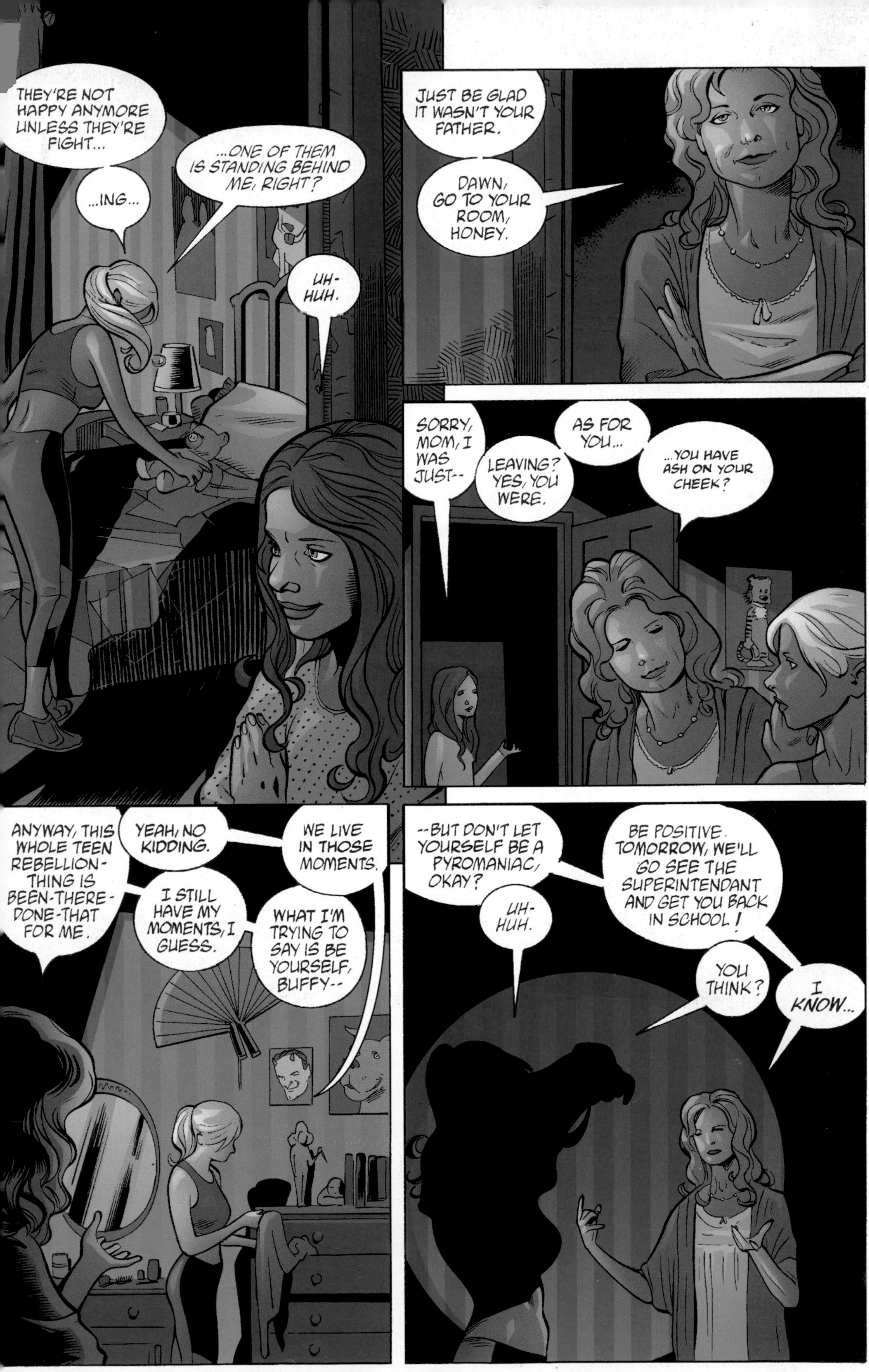
THEY'RE NOT HAPPY ANYMORE UNLESS THEY'RE FIGHT...
...ING...
...ONE OF THEM IS STANDING BEHIND ME, RIGHT?
UH-HUH.
JUST BE GLAD IT WASN'T YOUR FATHER.
DAWN, GO TO YOUR ROOM, HONEY.
SORRY, MOM, I WAS JUST--
LEAVING? YES, YOU WERE.
AS FOR YOU...
...YOU HAVE ASH ON YOUR CHEEK?
ANYWAY, THIS WHOLE TEEN REBELLION-THING IS BEEN-THERE-DONE-THAT FOR ME.
YEAH, NO KIDDING.
I STILL HAVE MY MOMENTS, I GUESS.
WE LIVE IN THOSE MOMENTS.
WHAT I'M TRYING TO SAY IS BE YOURSELF, BUFFY--
--BUT DON'T LET YOURSELF BE A PYROMANIAC, OKAY?
UH-HUH.
BE POSITIVE. TOMORROW, WE'LL GO SEE THE SUPERINTENDANT AND GET YOU BACK IN SCHOOL!
YOU THINK?
I KNOW...

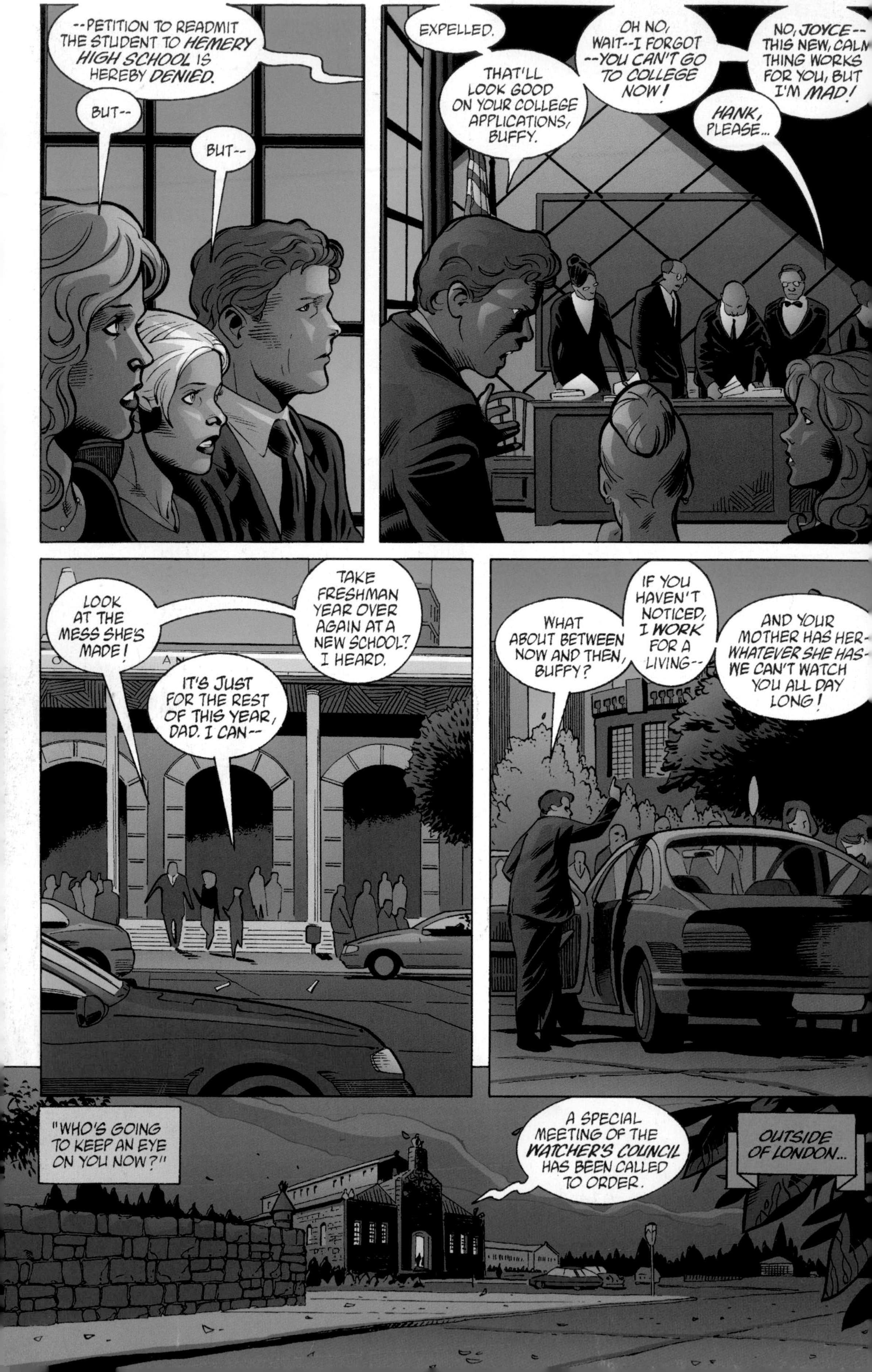
--PETITION TO READMIT THE STUDENT TO HEMERY HIGH SCHOOL IS HEREBY DENIED.
BUT--
BUT--
EXPELLED.
THAT'LL LOOK GOOD ON YOUR COLLEGE APPLICATIONS, BUFFY.
OH NO, WAIT--I FORGOT --YOU CAN'T GO TO COLLEGE NOW!
NO, JOYCE-- THIS NEW, CALM THING WORKS FOR YOU, BUT I'M MAD!
HANK, PLEASE...
LOOK AT THE MESS SHE'S MADE!
TAKE FRESHMAN YEAR OVER AGAIN AT A NEW SCHOOL? I HEARD.
IT'S JUST FOR THE REST OF THIS YEAR, DAD. I CAN--
WHAT ABOUT BETWEEN NOW AND THEN, BUFFY?
IF YOU HAVEN'T NOTICED, I WORK FOR A LIVING--
AND YOUR MOTHER HAS HER- WHATEVER SHE HAS- WE CAN'T WATCH YOU ALL DAY LONG!
"WHO'S GOING TO KEEP AN EYE ON YOU NOW?"
A SPECIAL MEETING OF THE WATCHER'S COUNCIL HAS BEEN CALLED TO ORDER.
OUTSIDE OF LONDON...

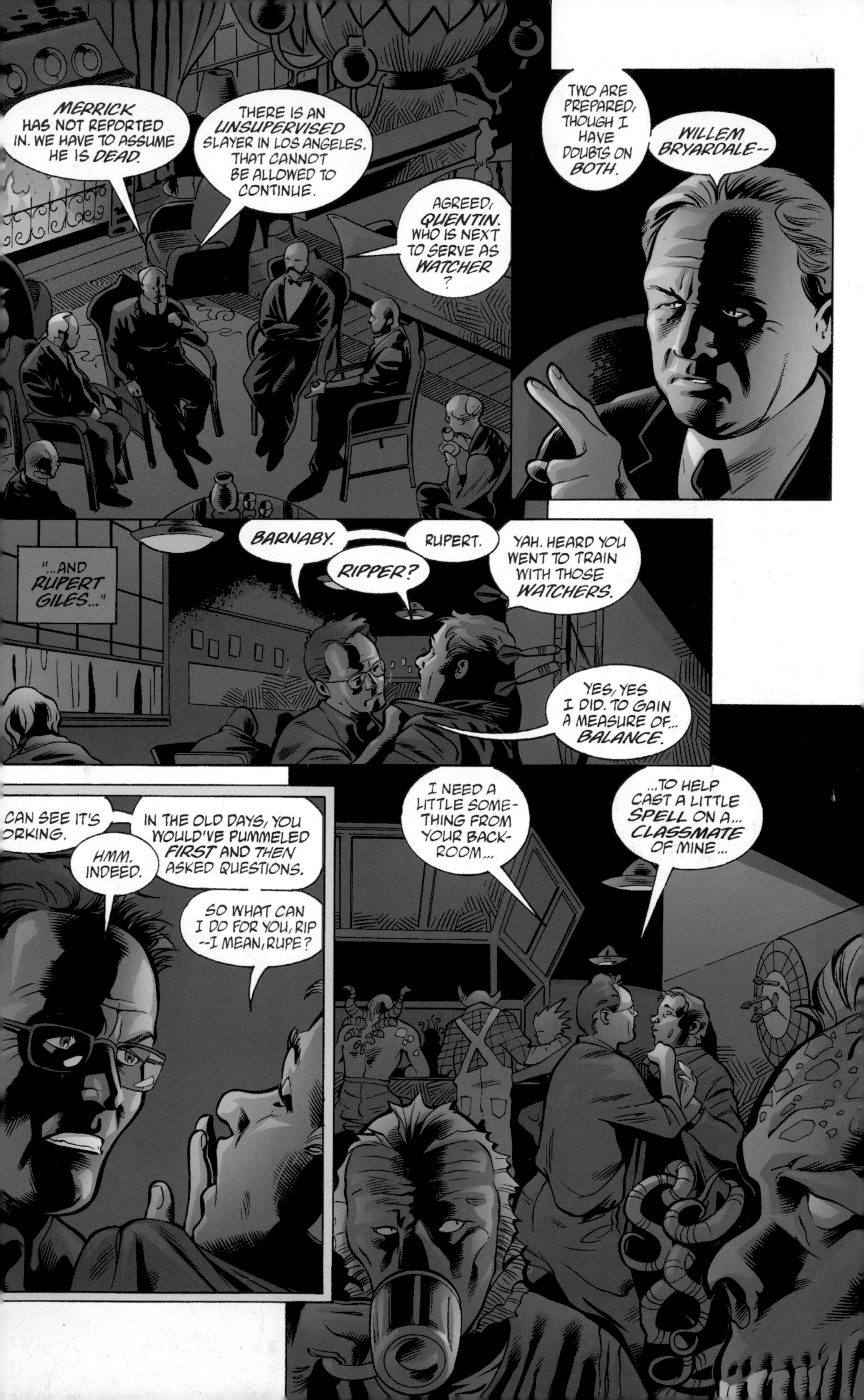
MERRICK HAS NOT REPORTED IN. WE HAVE TO ASSUME HE IS DEAD.
THERE IS AN UNSUPERVISED SLAYER IN LOS ANGELES. THAT CANNOT BE ALLOWED TO CONTINUE.
AGREED, QUENTIN. WHO IS NEXT TO SERVE AS WATCHER ?
TWO ARE PREPARED, THOUGH I HAVE DOUBTS ON BOTH.
WILLEM BRYARDALE--
"...AND RUPERT GILES..."
BARNABY.
RUPERT.
RIPPER?
YAH. HEARD YOU WENT TO TRAIN WITH THOSE WATCHERS.
YES, YES I DID. TO GAIN A MEASURE OF... BALANCE.
CAN SEE IT'S ORKING.
IN THE OLD DAYS, YOU WOULD'VE PUMMELED FIRST AND THEN ASKED QUESTIONS.
HMM. INDEED.
SO WHAT CAN I DO FOR YOU, RIP --I MEAN, RUPE?
I NEED A LITTLE SOME-THING FROM YOUR BACK-ROOM...
...TO HELP CAST A LITTLE SPELL ON A... CLASSMATE OF MINE...

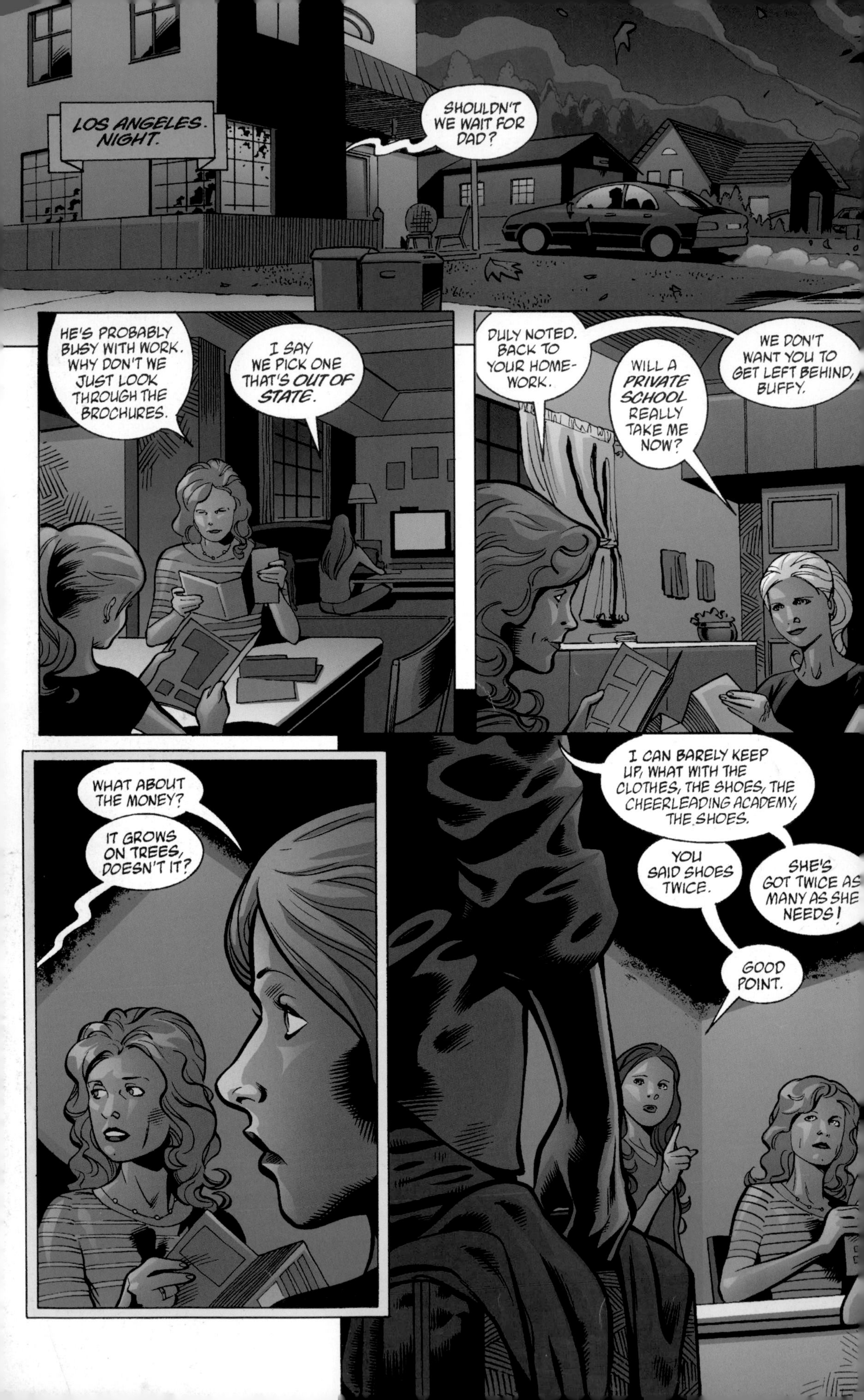
LOS ANGELES. NIGHT.
SHOULDN'T WE WAIT FOR DAD?
HE'S PROBABLY BUSY WITH WORK. WHY DON'T WE JUST LOOK THROUGH THE BROCHURES.
I SAY WE PICK ONE THAT'S OUT OF STATE.
DULY NOTED. BACK TO YOUR HOME-WORK.
WILL A PRIVATE SCHOOL REALLY TAKE ME NOW?
WE DON'T WANT YOU TO GET LEFT BEHIND, BUFFY.
WHAT ABOUT THE MONEY?
IT GROWS ON TREES, DOESN'T IT?
I CAN BARELY KEEP UP, WHAT WITH THE CLOTHES, THE SHOES, THE CHEERLEADING ACADEMY, THE SHOES.
YOU SAID SHOES TWICE.
SHE'S GOT TWICE AS MANY AS SHE NEEDS!
GOOD POINT.

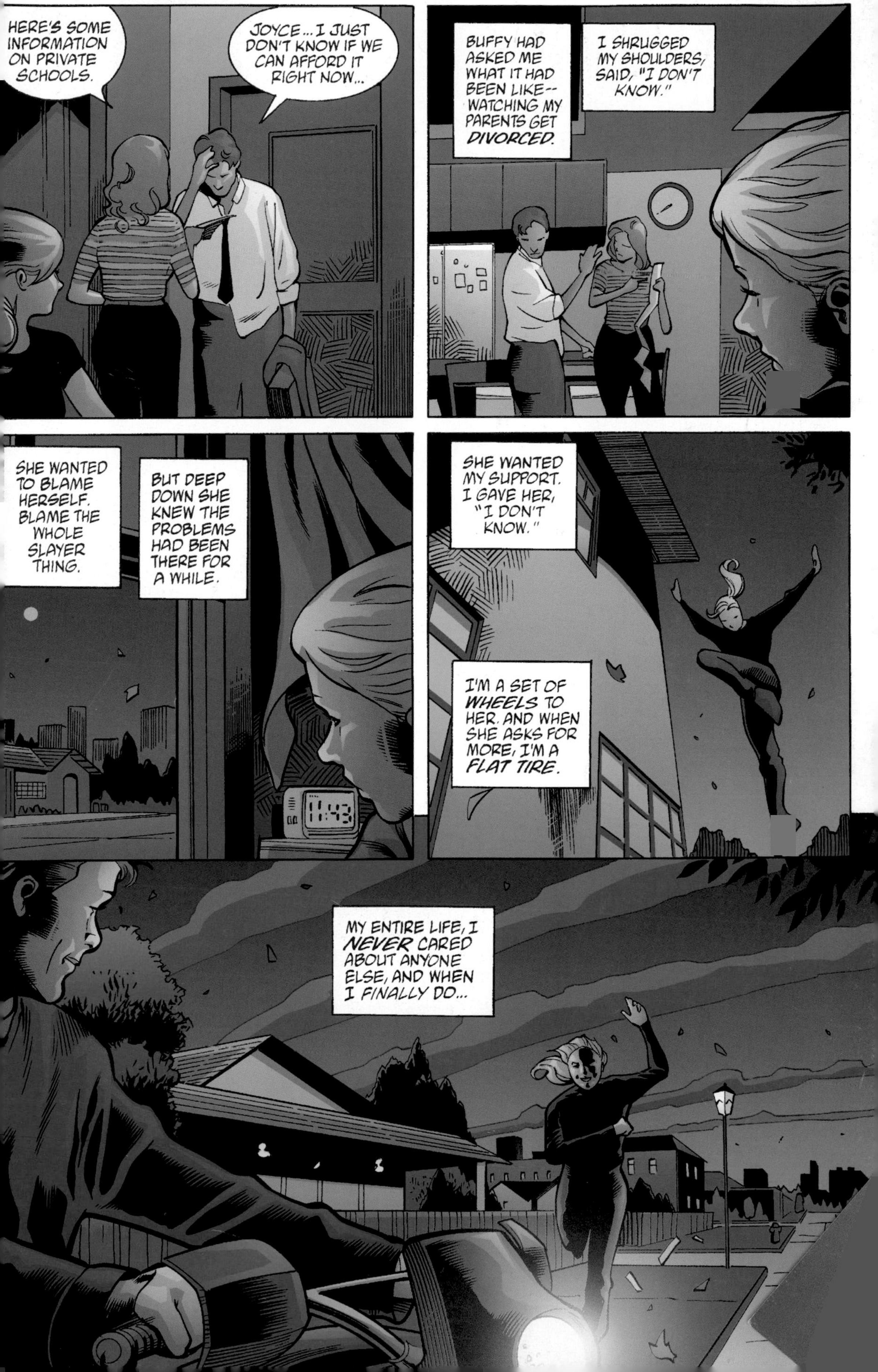
HERE'S SOME INFORMATION ON PRIVATE SCHOOLS.
JOYCE... I JUST DON'T KNOW IF WE CAN AFFORD IT RIGHT NOW...
BUFFY HAD ASKED ME WHAT IT HAD BEEN LIKE-- WATCHING MY PARENTS GET DIVORCED.
I SHRUGGED MY SHOULDERS, SAID, "I DON'T KNOW."
SHE WANTED TO BLAME HERSELF. BLAME THE WHOLE SLAYER THING.
BUT DEEP DOWN SHE KNEW THE PROBLEMS HAD BEEN THERE FOR A WHILE.
SHE WANTED MY SUPPORT. I GAVE HER, "I DON'T KNOW."
I'M A SET OF WHEELS TO HER. AND WHEN SHE ASKS FOR MORE, I'M A FLAT TIRE.
MY ENTIRE LIFE, I NEVER CARED ABOUT ANYONE ELSE, AND WHEN I FINALLY DO...

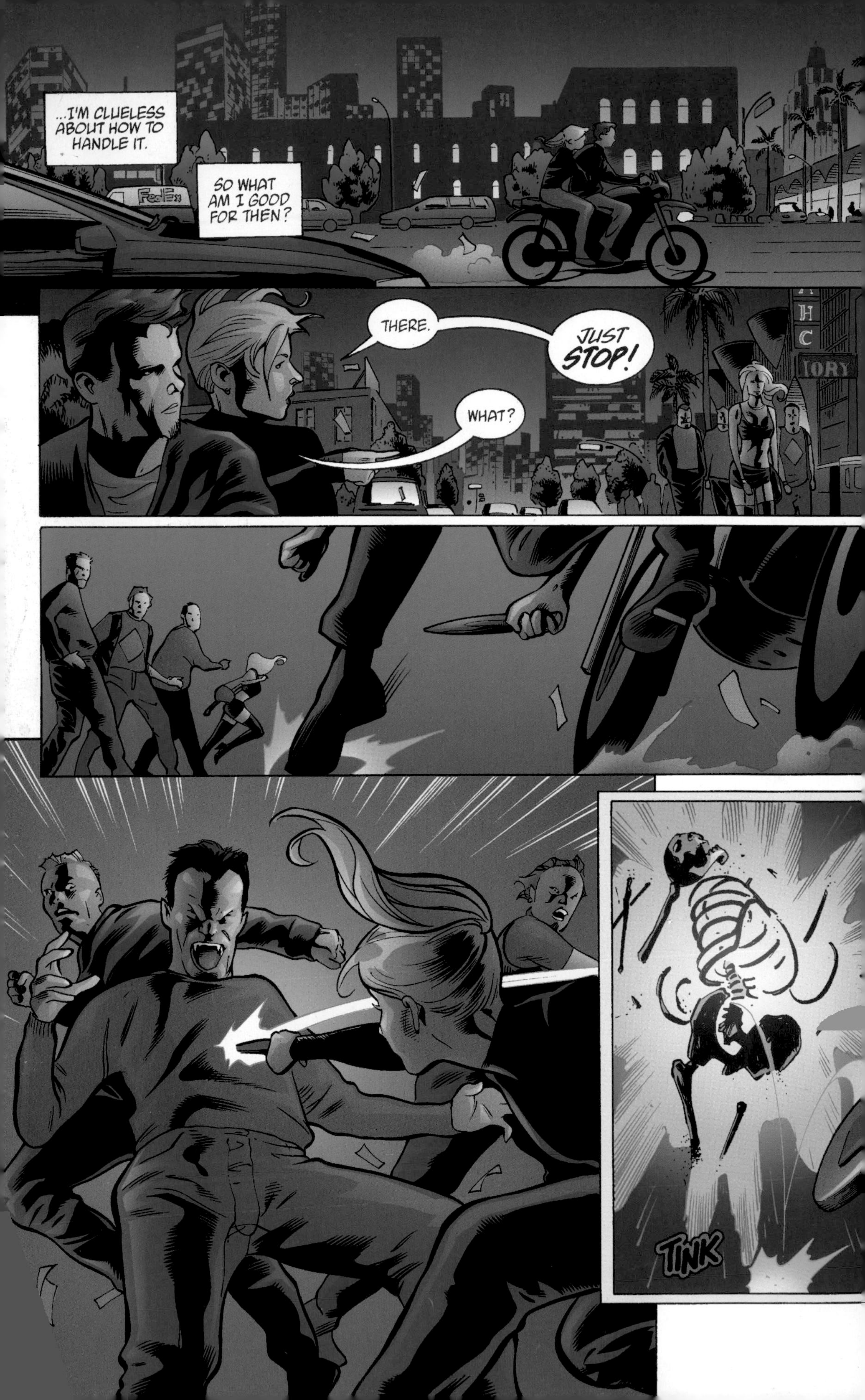
...I'M CLUELESS ABOUT HOW TO HANDLE IT.
SO WHAT AM I GOOD FOR THEN?
THERE.
JUST STOP!
WHAT?
TINK

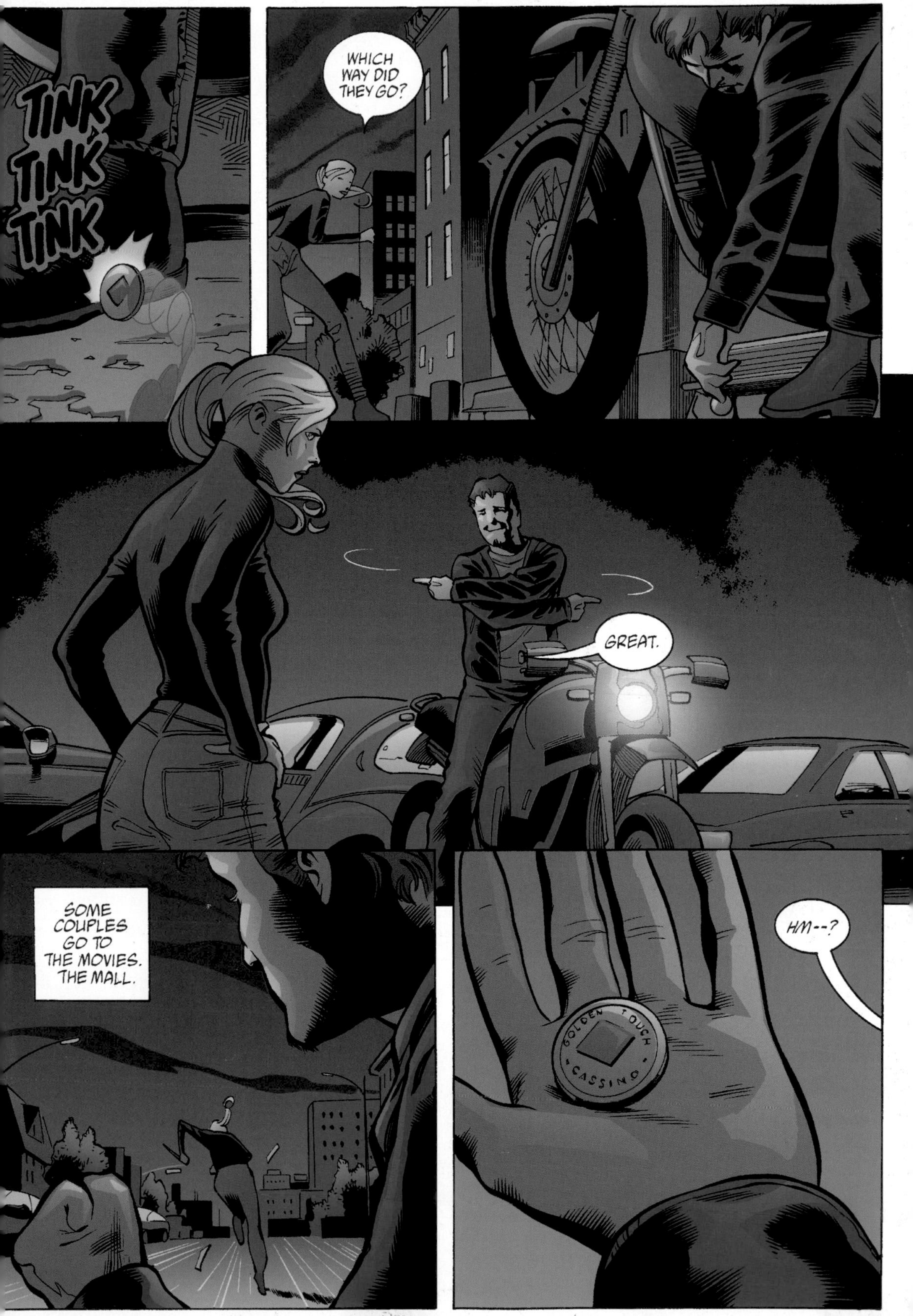

TINK TINK TINK
WHICH WAY DID THEY GO?
GREAT.
SOME COUPLES GO TO THE MOVIES. THE MALL.
HM--?
GOLDEN TOUCH CASSINO

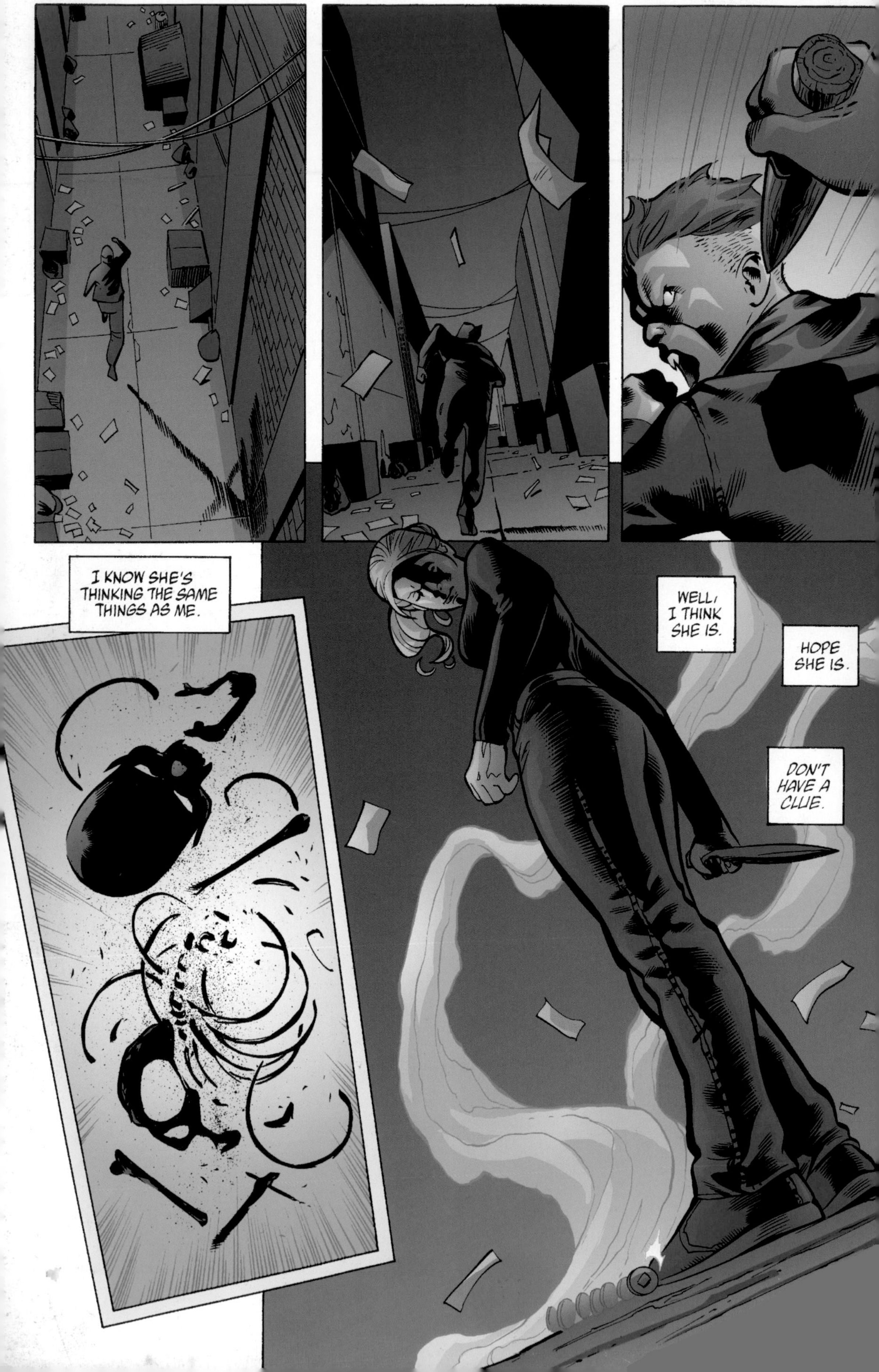
I KNOW SHE'S THINKING THE SAME THINGS AS ME.
WELL, I THINK SHE IS.
HOPE SHE IS.
DON'T HAVE A CLUE.

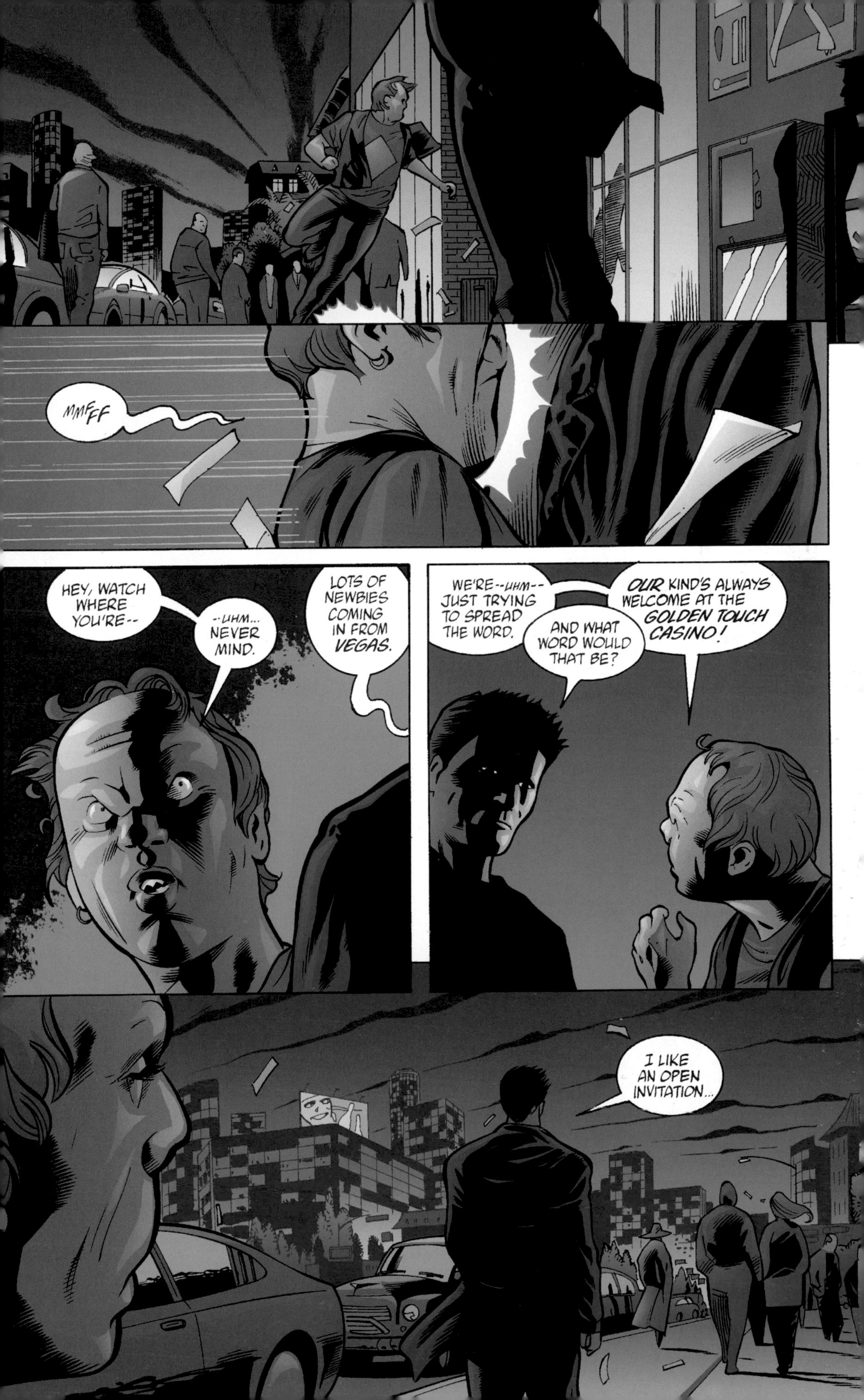
MMFFF
HEY, WATCH WHERE YOU'RE--
--UHM... NEVER MIND.
LOTS OF NEWBIES COMING IN FROM VEGAS.
WE'RE--UHM--JUST TRYING TO SPREAD THE WORD.
AND WHAT WORD WOULD THAT BE?
OUR KIND'S ALWAYS WELCOME AT THE GOLDEN TOUCH CASINO!
I LIKE AN OPEN INVITATION...

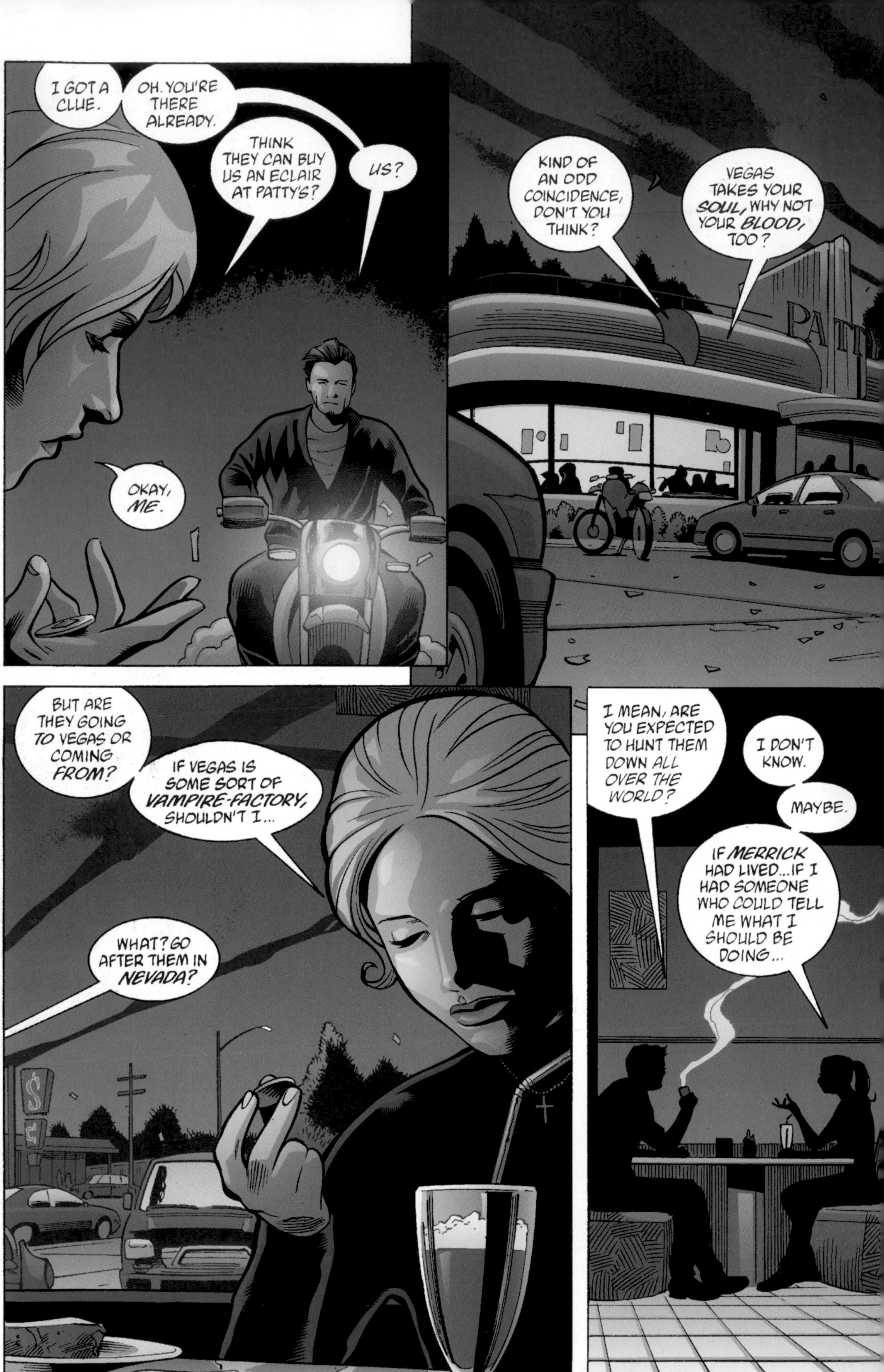
I GOT A CLUE.
OH. YOU'RE THERE ALREADY.
THINK THEY CAN BUY US AN ECLAIR AT PATTY'S?
US?
OKAY, *ME*.
KIND OF AN ODD COINCIDENCE, DON'T YOU THINK?
VEGAS TAKES YOUR *SOUL*, WHY NOT YOUR *BLOOD*, TOO?
PATTY
BUT ARE THEY GOING TO VEGAS OR COMING *FROM*?
IF VEGAS IS SOME SORT OF *VAMPIRE-FACTORY*, SHOULDN'T I...
WHAT? GO AFTER THEM IN *NEVADA*?
I MEAN, ARE YOU EXPECTED TO HUNT THEM DOWN ALL OVER THE WORLD?
I DON'T KNOW.
MAYBE.
IF *MERRICK* HAD LIVED...IF I HAD SOMEONE WHO COULD TELL ME WHAT I SHOULD BE DOING...

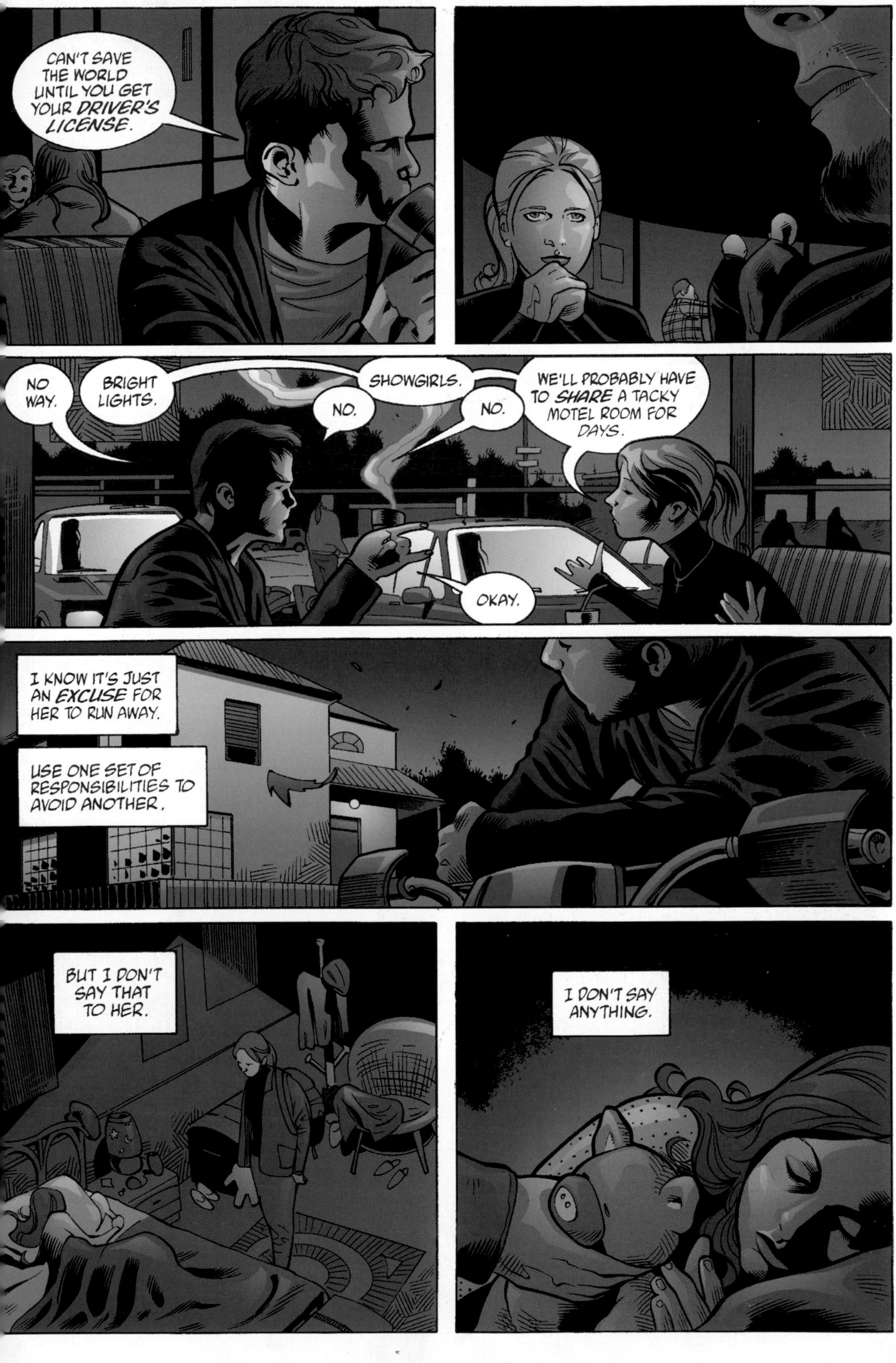
CAN'T SAVE THE WORLD UNTIL YOU GET YOUR DRIVER'S LICENSE.
NO WAY.
BRIGHT LIGHTS.
NO.
SHOWGIRLS.
NO.
WE'LL PROBABLY HAVE TO SHARE A TACKY MOTEL ROOM FOR DAYS.
OKAY.
I KNOW IT'S JUST AN EXCUSE FOR HER TO RUN AWAY.
USE ONE SET OF RESPONSIBILITIES TO AVOID ANOTHER.
BUT I DON'T SAY THAT TO HER.
I DON'T SAY ANYTHING.

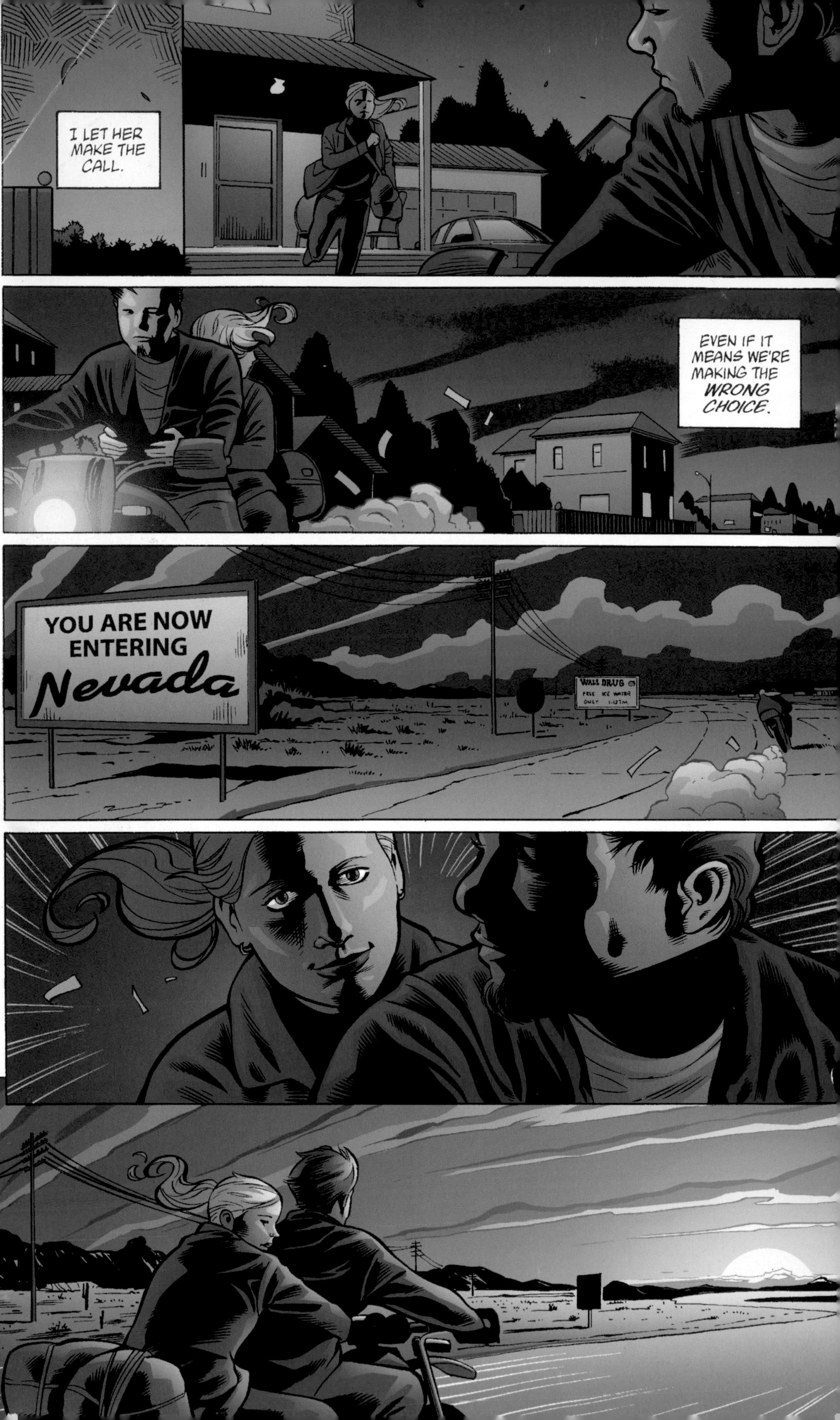
I LET HER MAKE THE CALL.
EVEN IF IT MEANS WE'RE MAKING THE WRONG CHOICE.
YOU ARE NOW ENTERING Nevada
WALL DRUG
FREE ICE WATER
ONLY 1,127M.

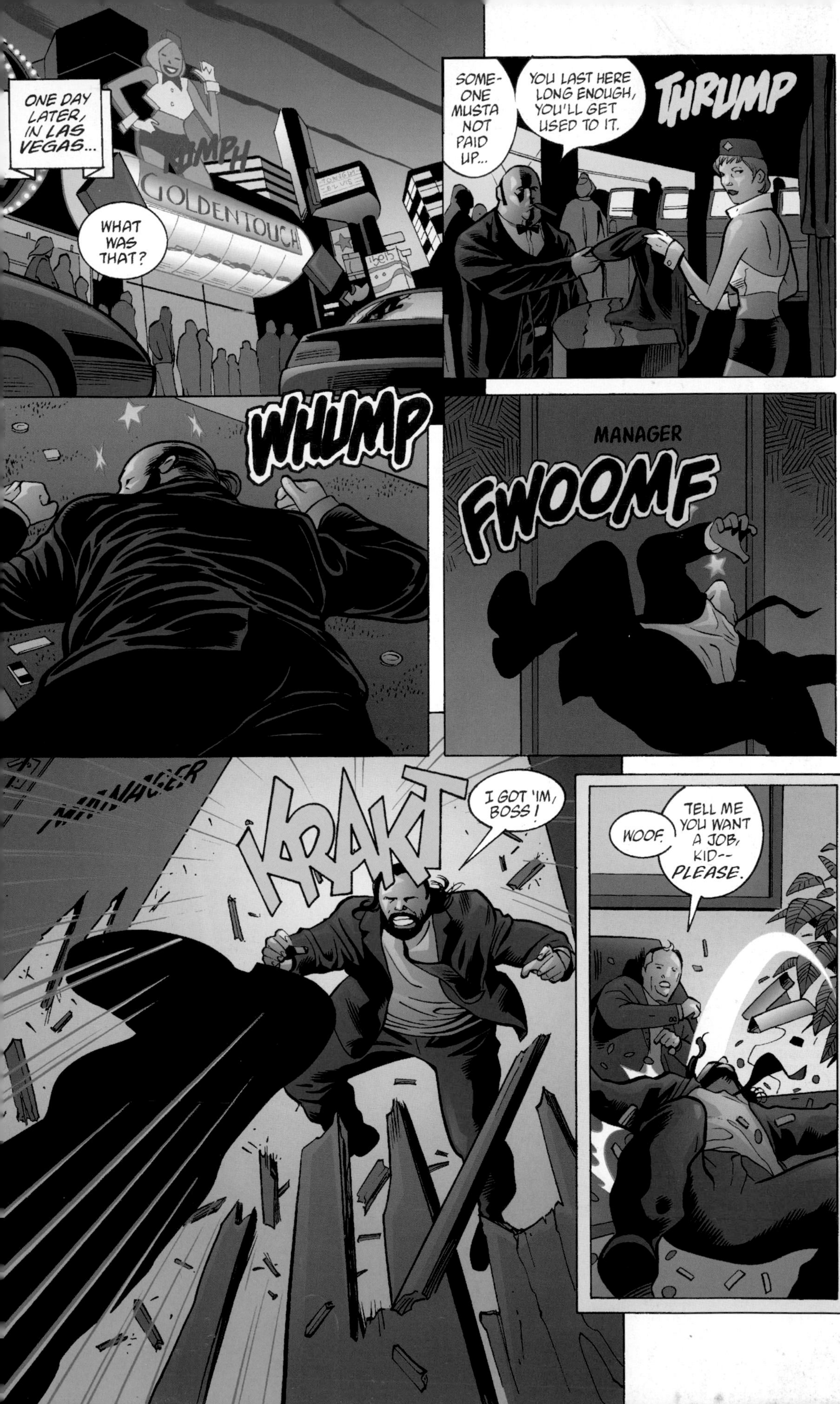
ONE DAY LATER, IN LAS VEGAS...
RUMPH
GOLDENTOUCH
WHAT WAS THAT?
SOME-ONE MUSTA NOT PAID UP...
YOU LAST HERE LONG ENOUGH, YOU'LL GET USED TO IT.
THRUMP
WHUMP
MANAGER
FWOOMF
MANAGER
KRAKT
I GOT 'IM, BOSS!
WOOF.
TELL ME YOU WANT A JOB, KID-- *PLEASE*.

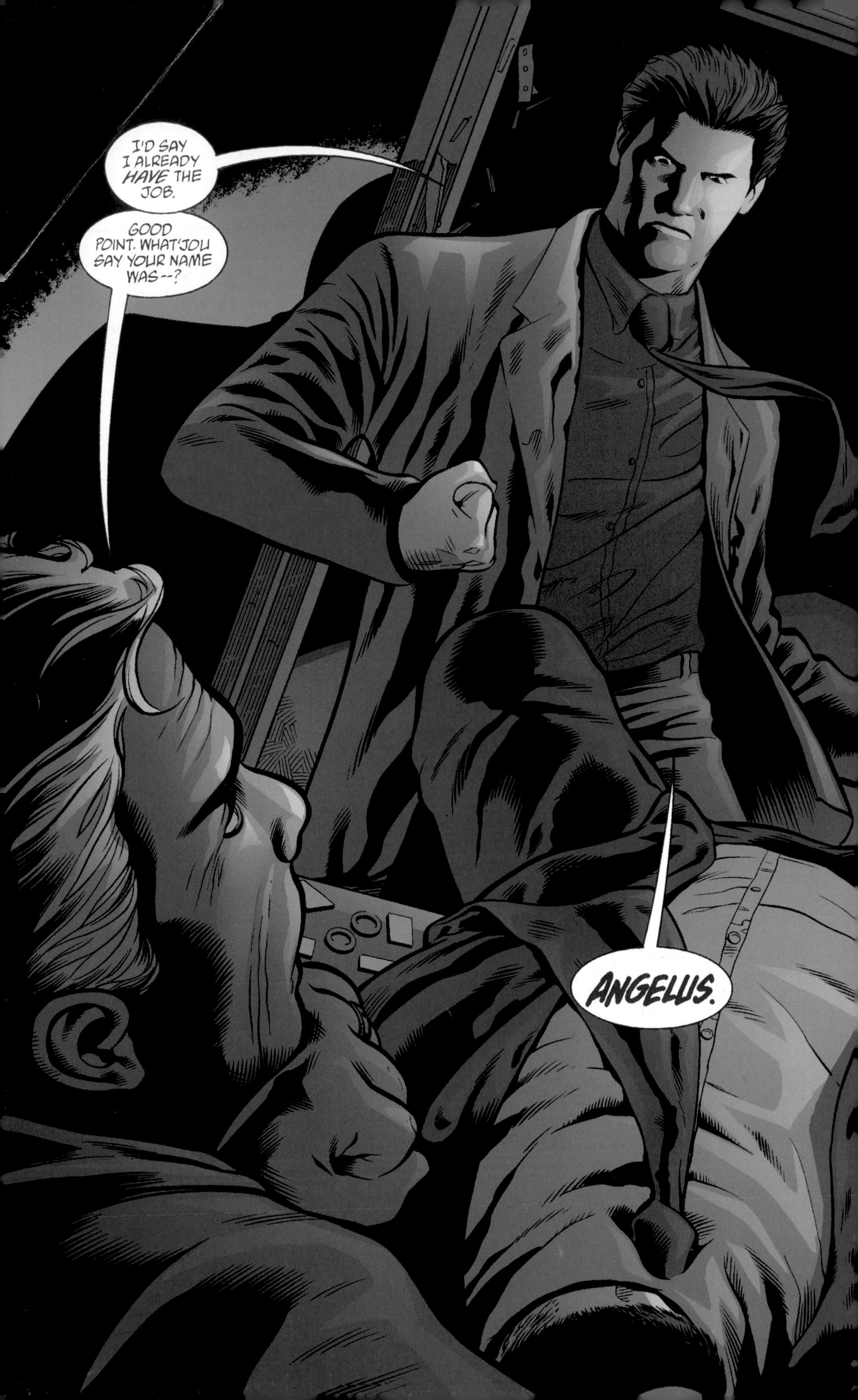
I'D SAY I ALREADY *HAVE* THE JOB.
GOOD POINT. WHAT'JOU SAY YOUR NAME WAS--?
ANGELUS.

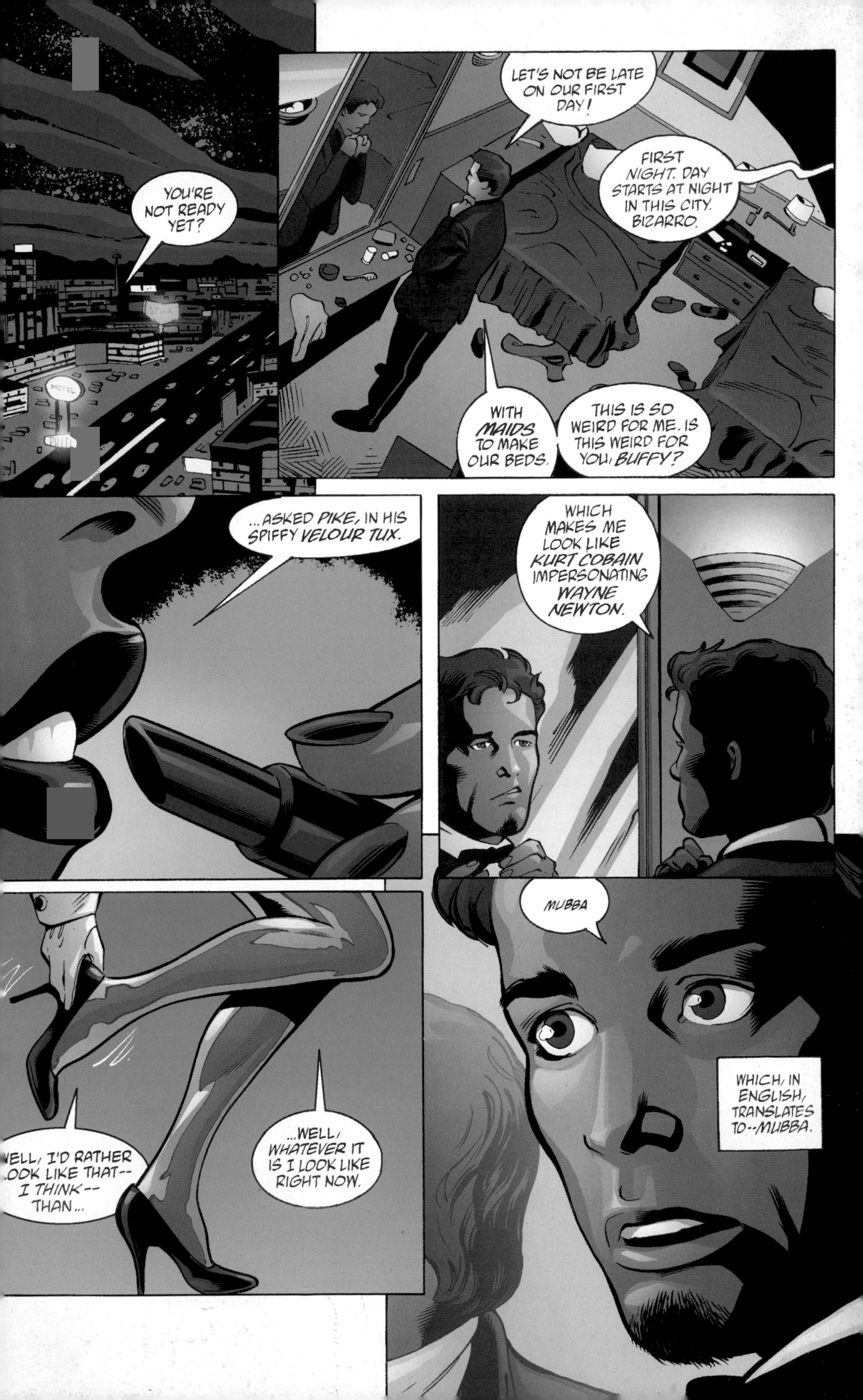
YOU'RE NOT READY YET?
MOTEL
LET'S NOT BE LATE ON OUR FIRST DAY!
FIRST NIGHT. DAY STARTS AT NIGHT IN THIS CITY. BIZARRO.
WITH MAIDS TO MAKE OUR BEDS.
THIS IS SO WEIRD FOR ME. IS THIS WEIRD FOR YOU, BUFFY?
...ASKED PIKE, IN HIS SPIFFY VELOUR TUX.
WHICH MAKES ME LOOK LIKE KURT COBAIN IMPERSONATING WAYNE NEWTON.
ELL, I'D RATHER OOK LIKE THAT-- I THINK-- THAN...
...WELL, WHATEVER IT IS I LOOK LIKE RIGHT NOW.
MUBBA
WHICH, IN ENGLISH, TRANSLATES TO--MUBBA.

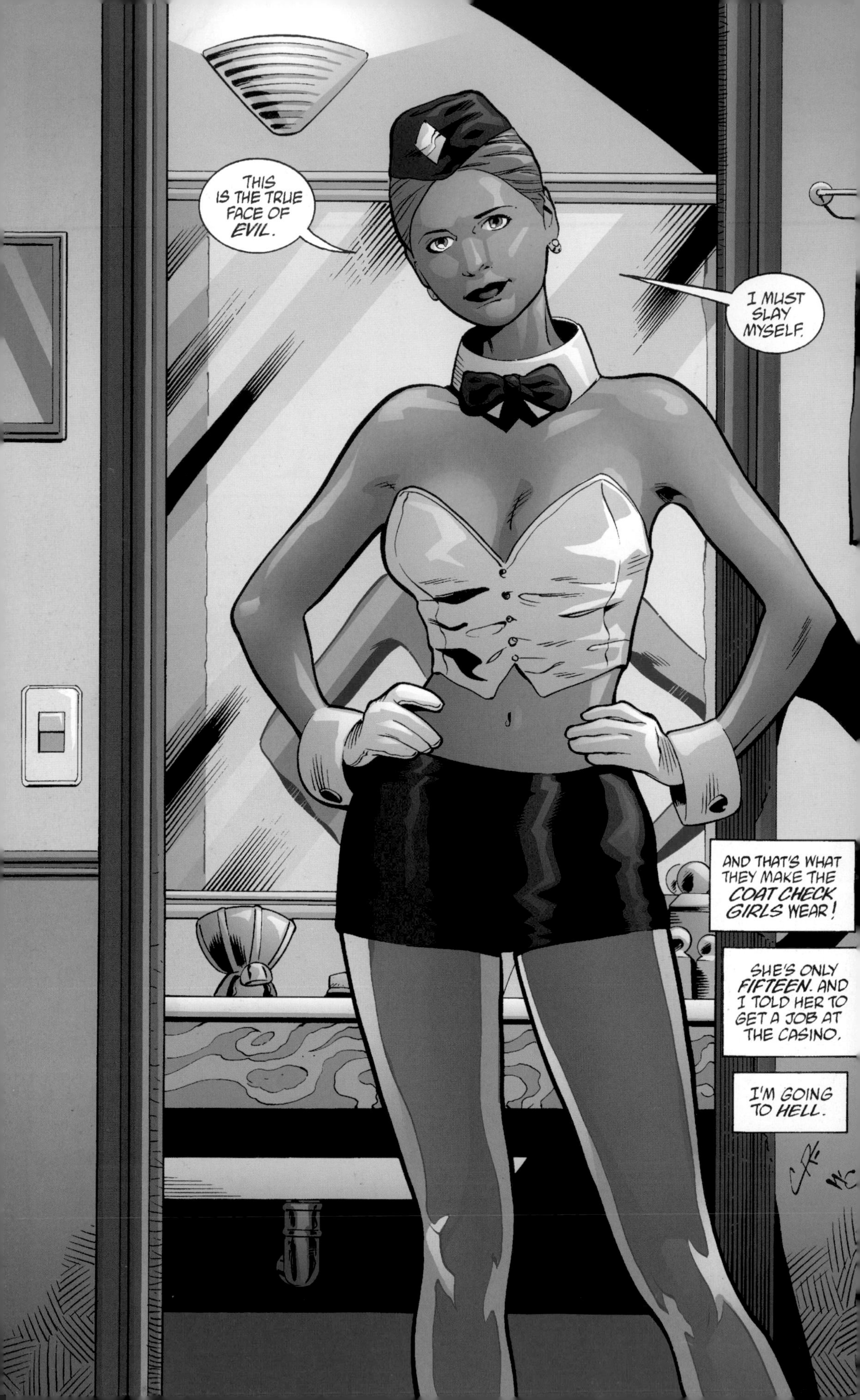
THIS IS THE TRUE FACE OF EVIL.
I MUST SLAY MYSELF.
AND THAT'S WHAT THEY MAKE THE COAT CHECK GIRLS WEAR!
SHE'S ONLY FIFTEEN. AND I TOLD HER TO GET A JOB AT THE CASINO.
I'M GOING TO HELL.

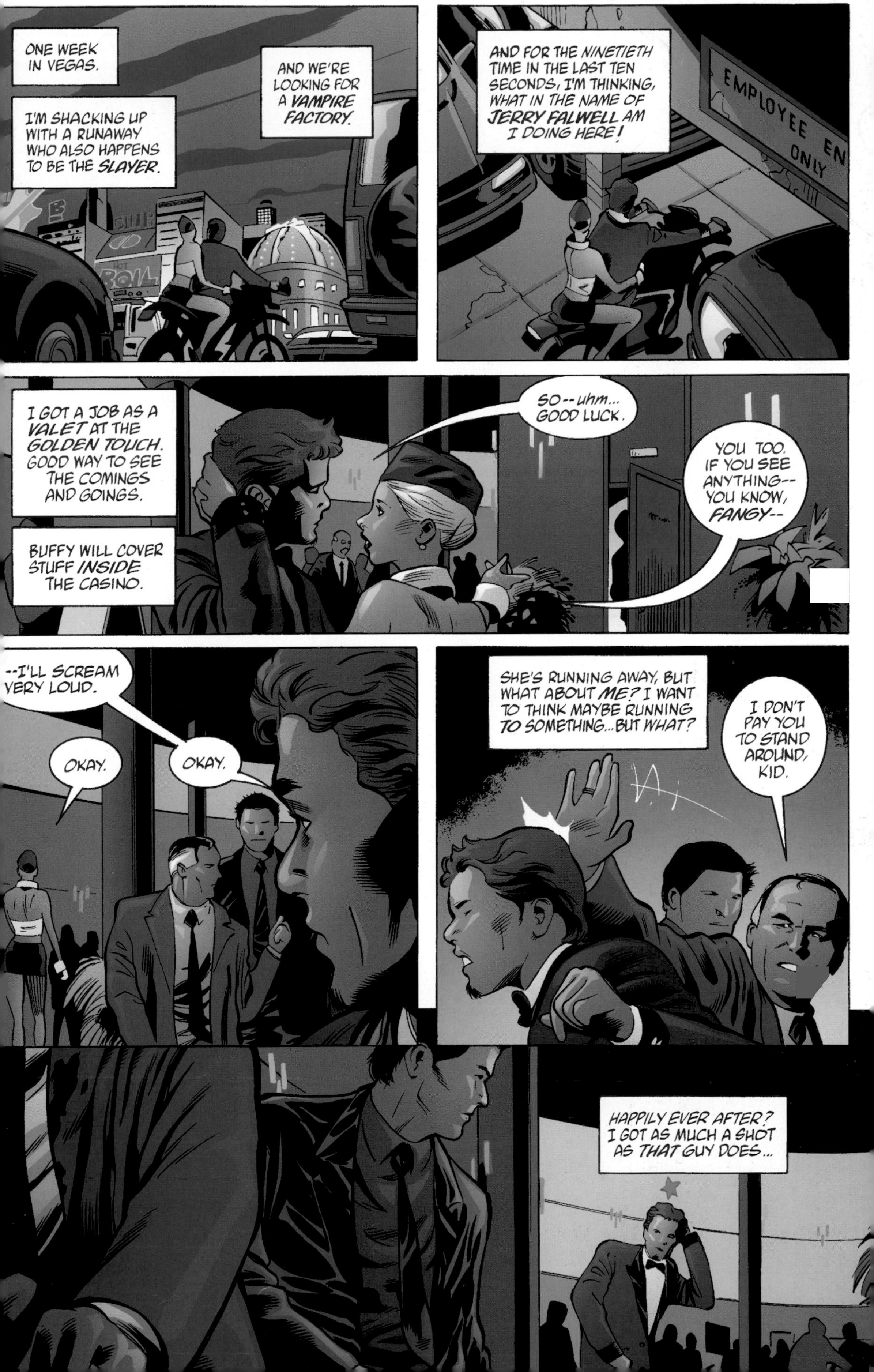

ONE WEEK IN VEGAS.
I'M SHACKING UP WITH A RUNAWAY WHO ALSO HAPPENS TO BE THE SLAYER.
AND WE'RE LOOKING FOR A VAMPIRE FACTORY.
AND FOR THE NINETIETH TIME IN THE LAST TEN SECONDS, I'M THINKING, WHAT IN THE NAME OF JERRY FALWELL AM I DOING HERE!
EMPLOYEE EN ONLY
I GOT A JOB AS A VALET AT THE GOLDEN TOUCH. GOOD WAY TO SEE THE COMINGS AND GOINGS.
BUFFY WILL COVER STUFF INSIDE THE CASINO.
SO--uhm... GOOD LUCK.
YOU TOO. IF YOU SEE ANYTHING--YOU KNOW, FANGY--
--I'LL SCREAM VERY LOUD.
OKAY.
OKAY.
SHE'S RUNNING AWAY, BUT WHAT ABOUT ME? I WANT TO THINK MAYBE RUNNING TO SOMETHING...BUT WHAT?
I DON'T PAY YOU TO STAND AROUND, KID.
HAPPILY EVER AFTER? I GOT AS MUCH A SHOT AS THAT GUY DOES...

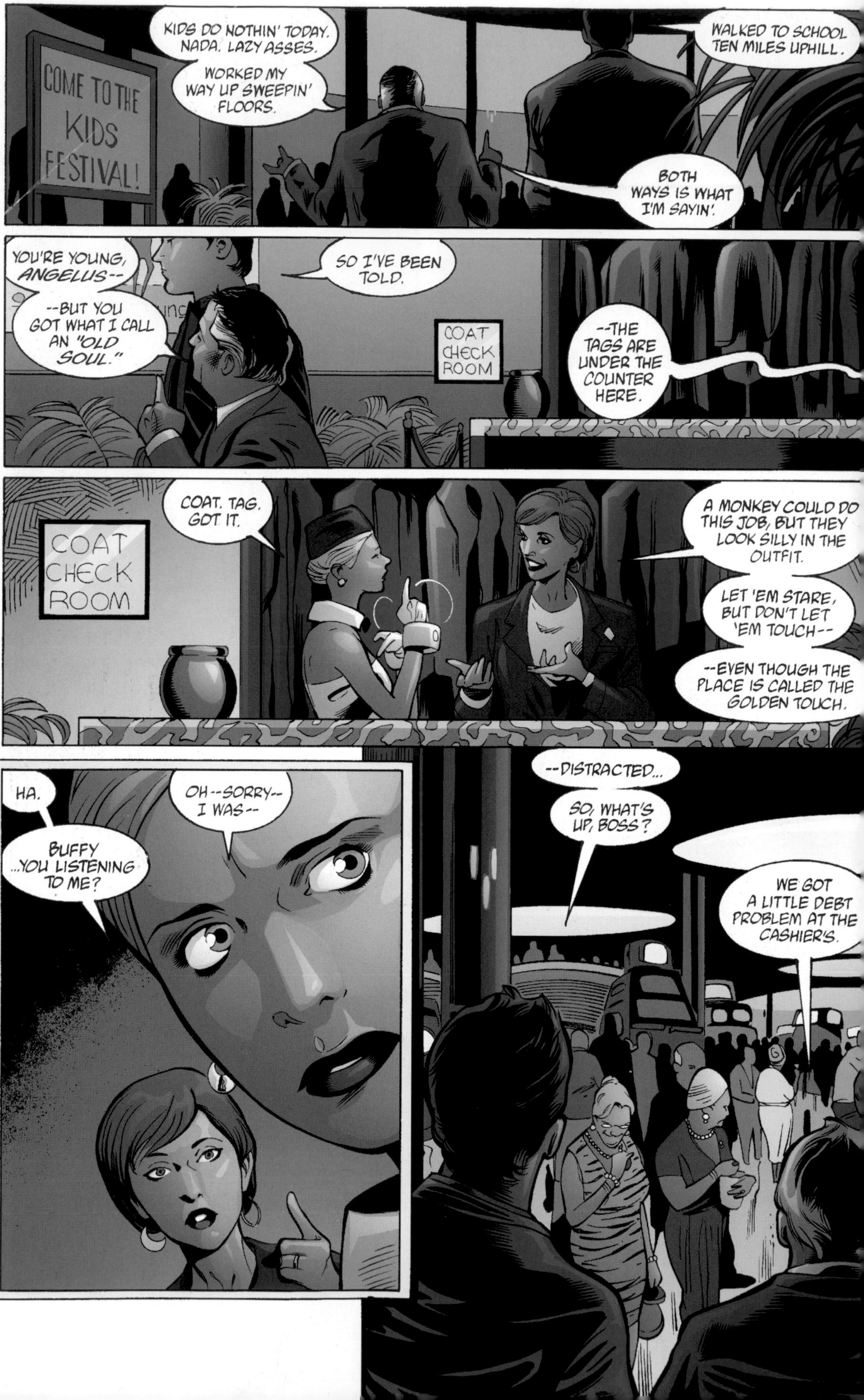
COME TO THE KIDS FESTIVAL!
KIDS DO NOTHIN' TODAY. NADA. LAZY ASSES.
WORKED MY WAY UP SWEEPIN' FLOORS.
WALKED TO SCHOOL TEN MILES UPHILL.
BOTH WAYS IS WHAT I'M SAYIN'.
YOU'RE YOUNG, ANGELUS--
--BUT YOU GOT WHAT I CALL AN "OLD SOUL."
SO I'VE BEEN TOLD.
COAT CHECK ROOM
--THE TAGS ARE UNDER THE COUNTER HERE.
COAT CHECK ROOM
COAT. TAG. GOT IT.
A MONKEY COULD DO THIS JOB, BUT THEY LOOK SILLY IN THE OUTFIT.
LET 'EM STARE, BUT DON'T LET 'EM TOUCH--
--EVEN THOUGH THE PLACE IS CALLED THE GOLDEN TOUCH.
HA.
BUFFY ...YOU LISTENING TO ME?
OH--SORRY-- I WAS--
--DISTRACTED...
SO, WHAT'S UP, BOSS?
WE GOT A LITTLE DEBT PROBLEM AT THE CASHIER'S.

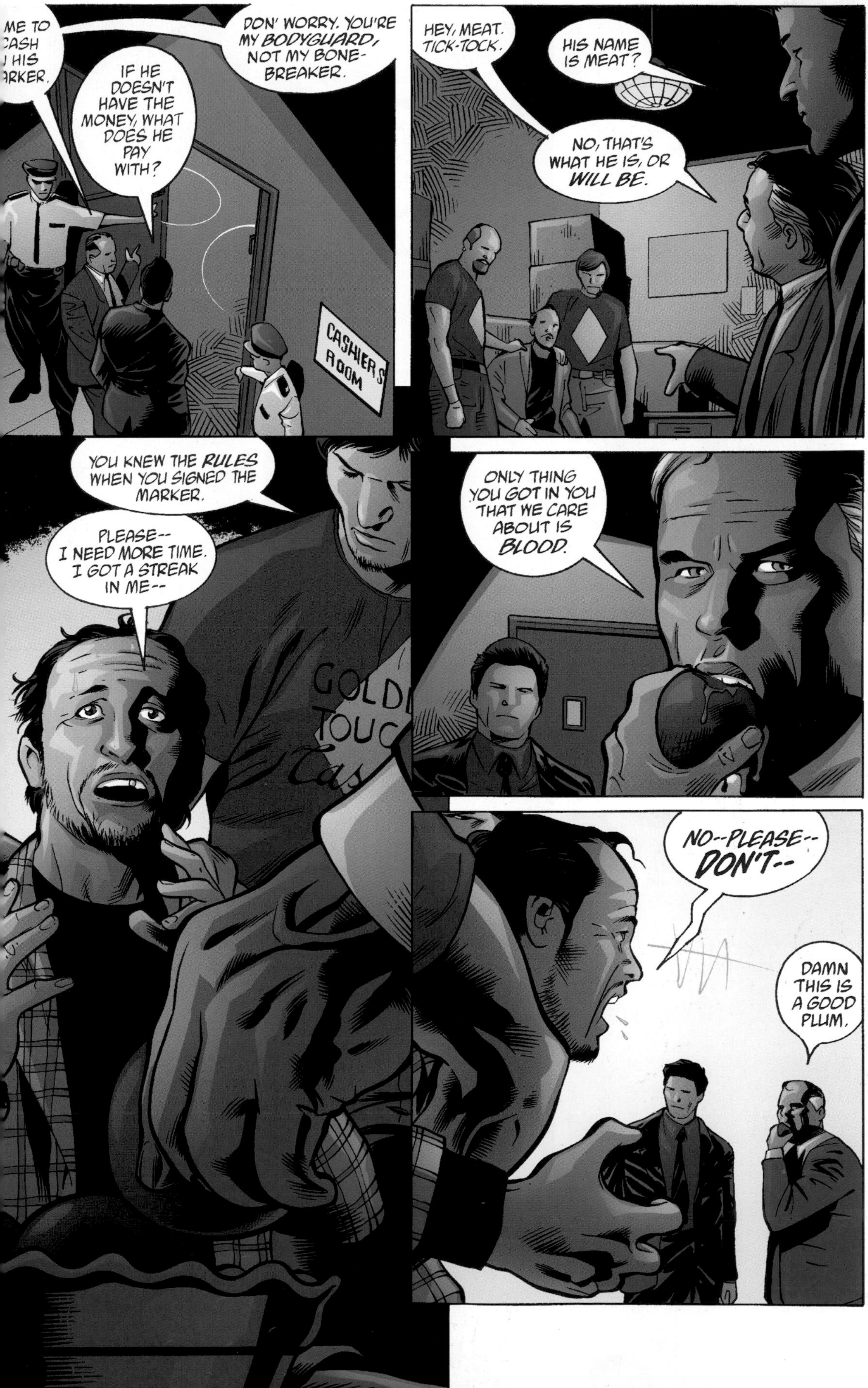
ME TO CASH HIS ARKER.
IF HE DOESN'T HAVE THE MONEY, WHAT DOES HE PAY WITH?
DON' WORRY. YOU'RE MY *BODYGUARD*, NOT MY BONE-BREAKER.
CASHIER'S ROOM
HEY, MEAT. TICK-TOCK.
HIS NAME IS MEAT?
NO, THAT'S WHAT HE IS, OR ***WILL BE***.
YOU KNEW THE *RULES* WHEN YOU SIGNED THE MARKER.
PLEASE-- I NEED MORE TIME. I GOT A STREAK IN ME--
ONLY THING YOU GOT IN YOU THAT WE CARE ABOUT IS *BLOOD*.
NO--PLEASE-- ***DON'T--***
DAMN THIS IS A GOOD PLUM.

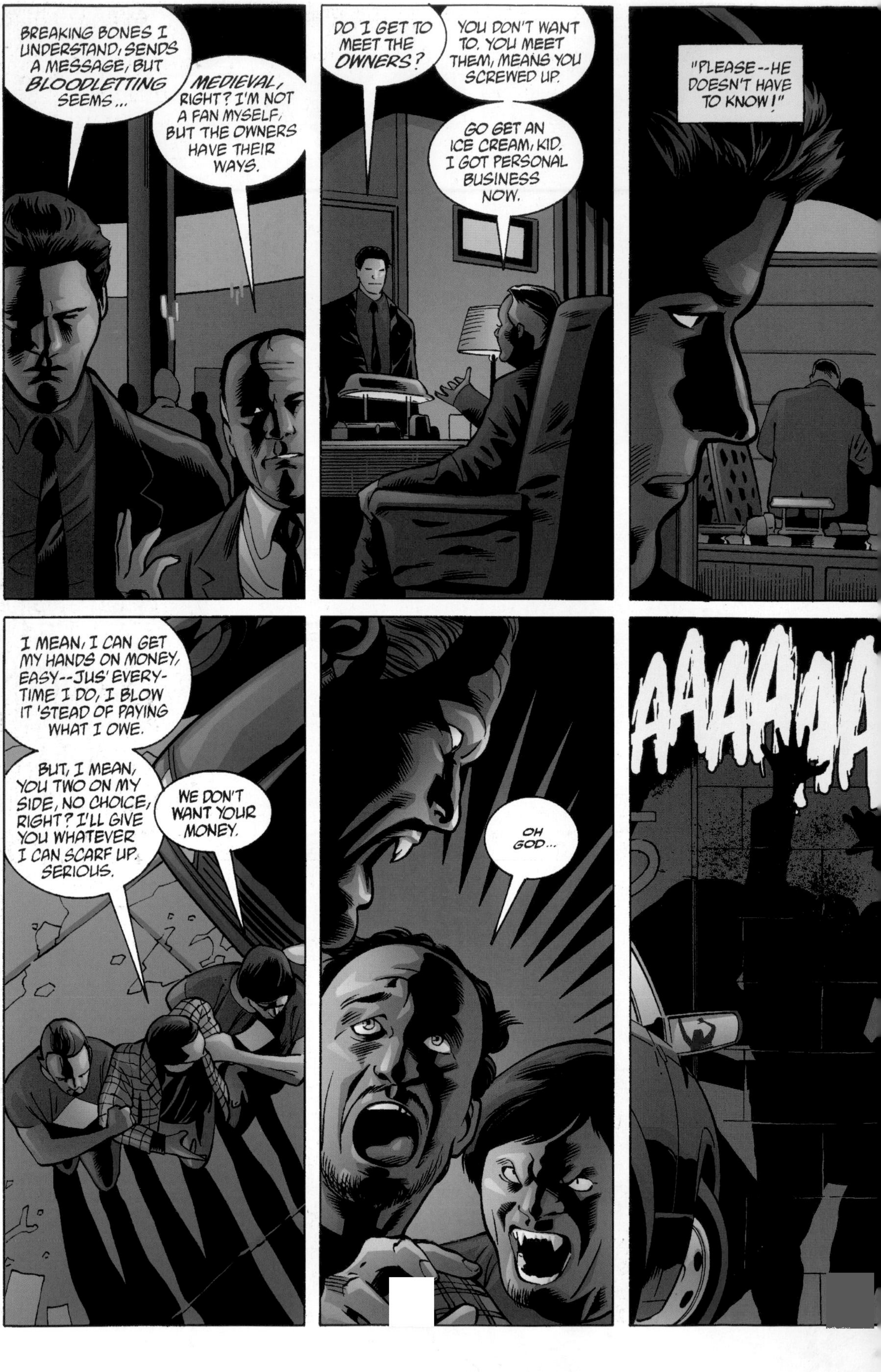
BREAKING BONES I UNDERSTAND, SENDS A MESSAGE, BUT BLOODLETTING SEEMS...
MEDIEVAL, RIGHT? I'M NOT A FAN MYSELF, BUT THE OWNERS HAVE THEIR WAYS.
DO I GET TO MEET THE OWNERS?
YOU DON'T WANT TO. YOU MEET THEM, MEANS YOU SCREWED UP.
GO GET AN ICE CREAM, KID. I GOT PERSONAL BUSINESS NOW.
"PLEASE--HE DOESN'T HAVE TO KNOW!"
I MEAN, I CAN GET MY HANDS ON MONEY, EASY--JUS' EVERY-TIME I DO, I BLOW IT 'STEAD OF PAYING WHAT I OWE.
BUT, I MEAN, YOU TWO ON MY SIDE, NO CHOICE, RIGHT? I'LL GIVE YOU WHATEVER I CAN SCARF UP. SERIOUS.
WE DON'T WANT YOUR MONEY.
OH GOD...
AAAAAA

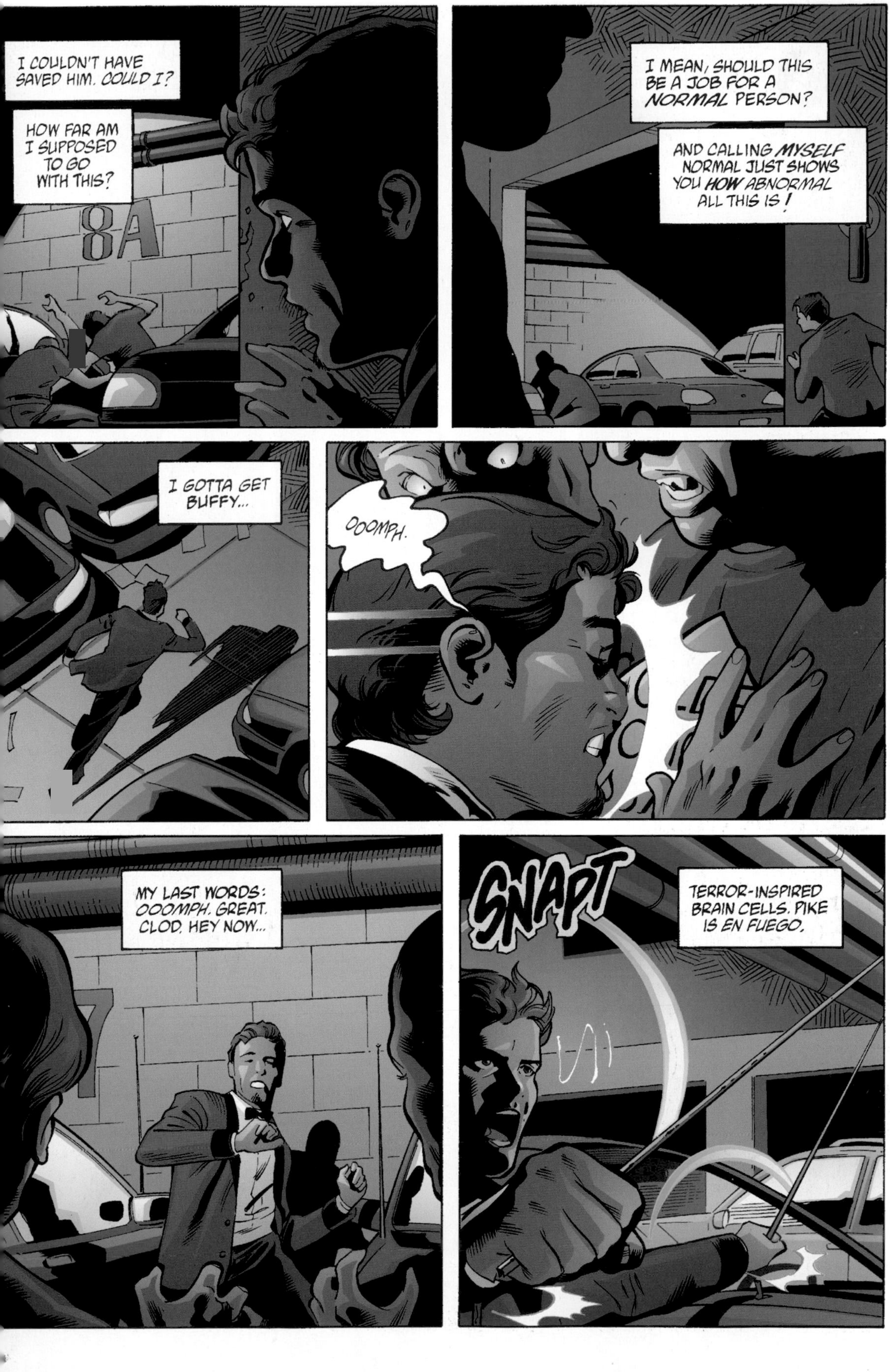
I COULDN'T HAVE SAVED HIM. COULD I?
HOW FAR AM I SUPPOSED TO GO WITH THIS?
8A
I MEAN, SHOULD THIS BE A JOB FOR A NORMAL PERSON?
AND CALLING MYSELF NORMAL JUST SHOWS YOU HOW ABNORMAL ALL THIS IS!
I GOTTA GET BUFFY...
OOOMPH.
MY LAST WORDS: OOOMPH. GREAT. CLOD. HEY NOW...
SNAPT
TERROR-INSPIRED BRAIN CELLS. PIKE IS EN FUEGO.

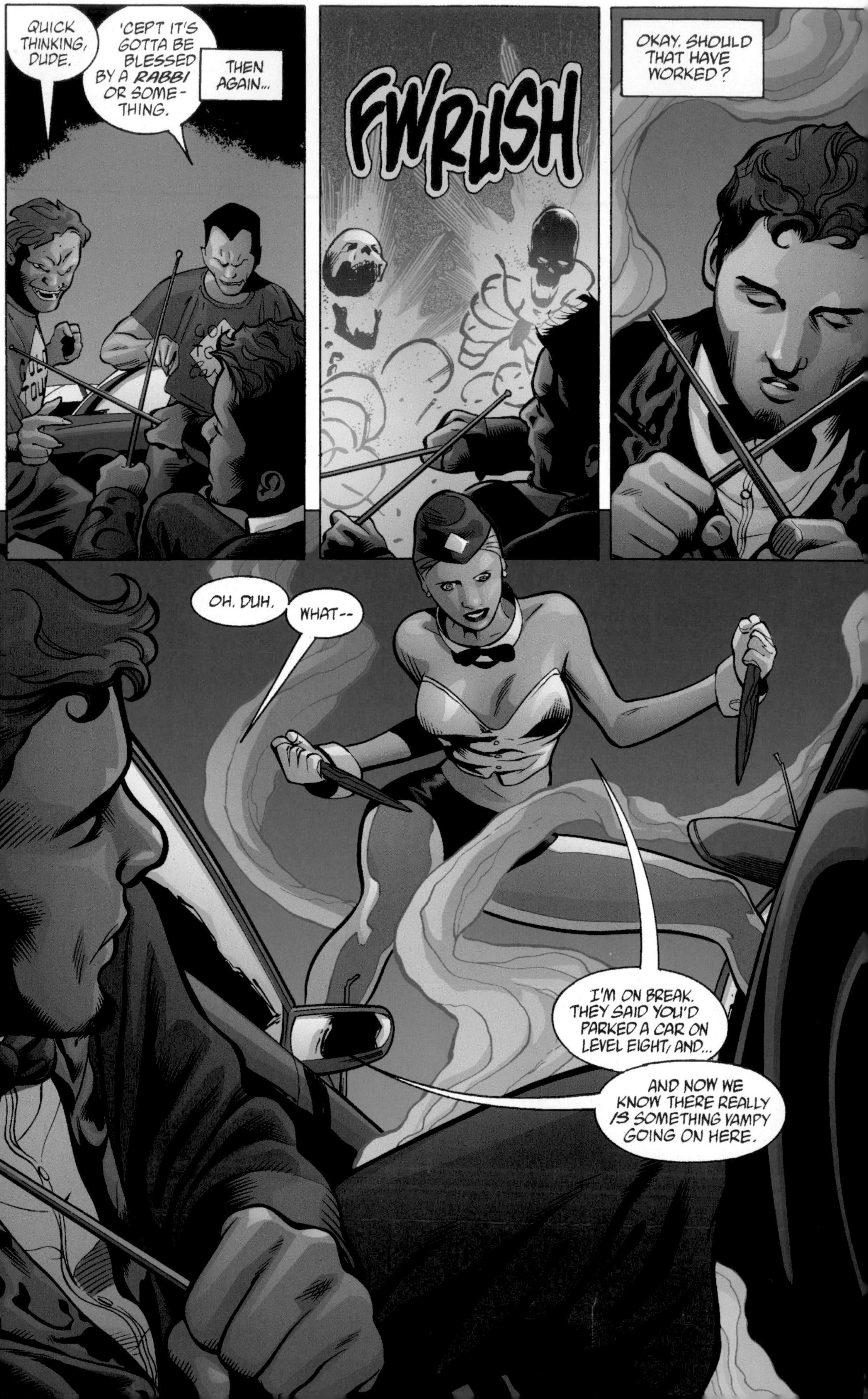
QUICK THINKING, DUDE.
'CEPT IT'S GOTTA BE BLESSED BY A RABBI OR SOME-THING.
THEN AGAIN...
FWRUSH
OKAY. SHOULD THAT HAVE WORKED?
OH. DUH.
WHAT--
I'M ON BREAK. THEY SAID YOU'D PARKED A CAR ON LEVEL EIGHT, AND...
AND NOW WE KNOW THERE REALLY IS SOMETHING VAMPY GOING ON HERE.

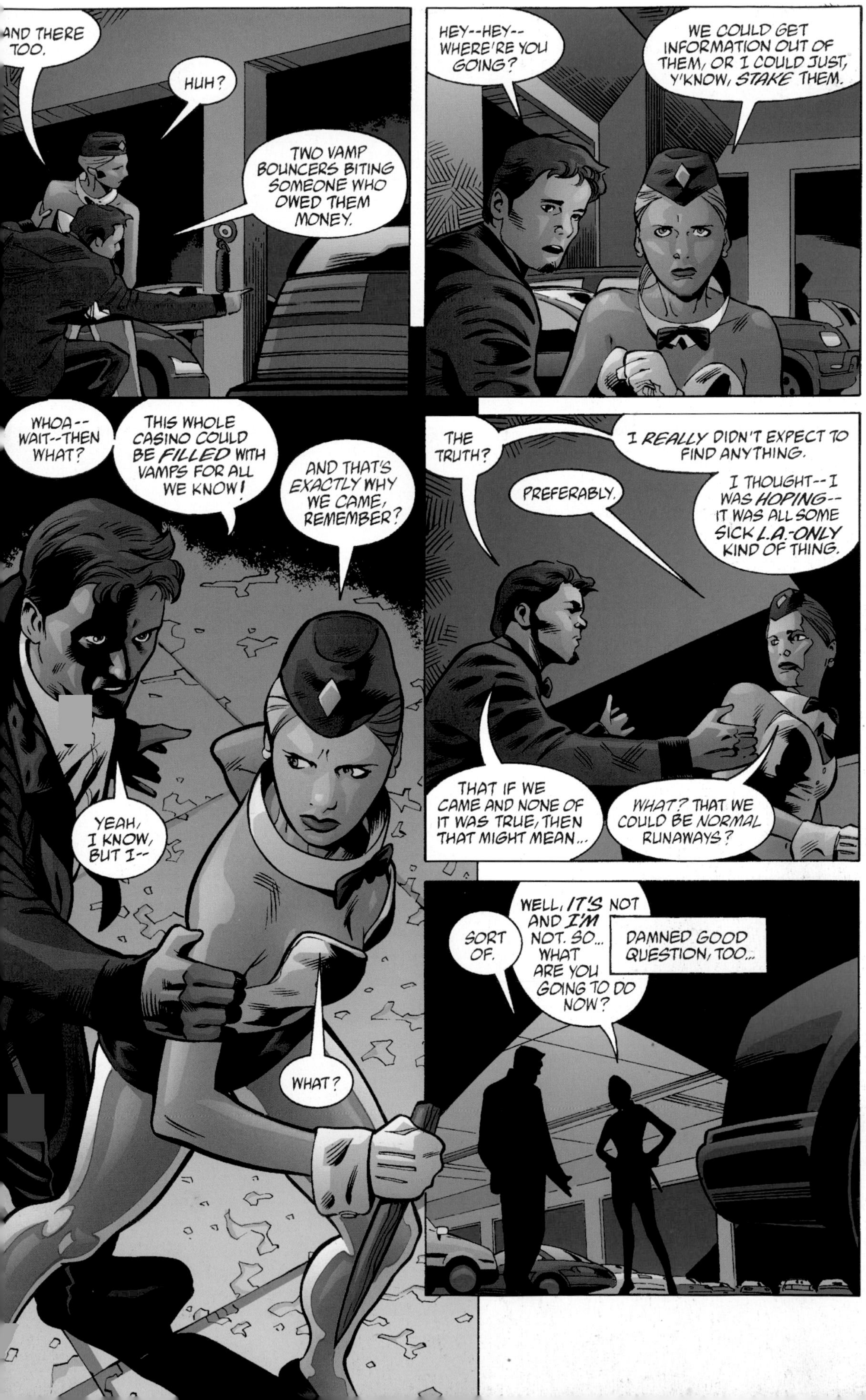
AND THERE TOO.
HUH?
TWO VAMP BOUNCERS BITING SOMEONE WHO OWED THEM MONEY.
HEY--HEY-- WHERE'RE YOU GOING?
WE COULD GET INFORMATION OUT OF THEM, OR I COULD JUST, Y'KNOW, *STAKE* THEM.
WHOA-- WAIT--THEN WHAT?
THIS WHOLE CASINO COULD BE *FILLED* WITH VAMPS FOR ALL WE KNOW!
AND THAT'S EXACTLY WHY WE CAME, REMEMBER?
YEAH, I KNOW, BUT I--
WHAT?
THE TRUTH?
I *REALLY* DIDN'T EXPECT TO FIND ANYTHING.
PREFERABLY.
I THOUGHT-- I WAS *HOPING*-- IT WAS ALL SOME SICK *L.A.-ONLY* KIND OF THING.
THAT IF WE CAME AND NONE OF IT WAS TRUE, THEN THAT MIGHT MEAN...
WHAT? THAT WE COULD BE *NORMAL* RUNAWAYS?
SORT OF.
WELL, *IT'S* NOT AND *I'M* NOT. SO... WHAT ARE YOU GOING TO DO NOW?
DAMNED GOOD QUESTION, TOO...

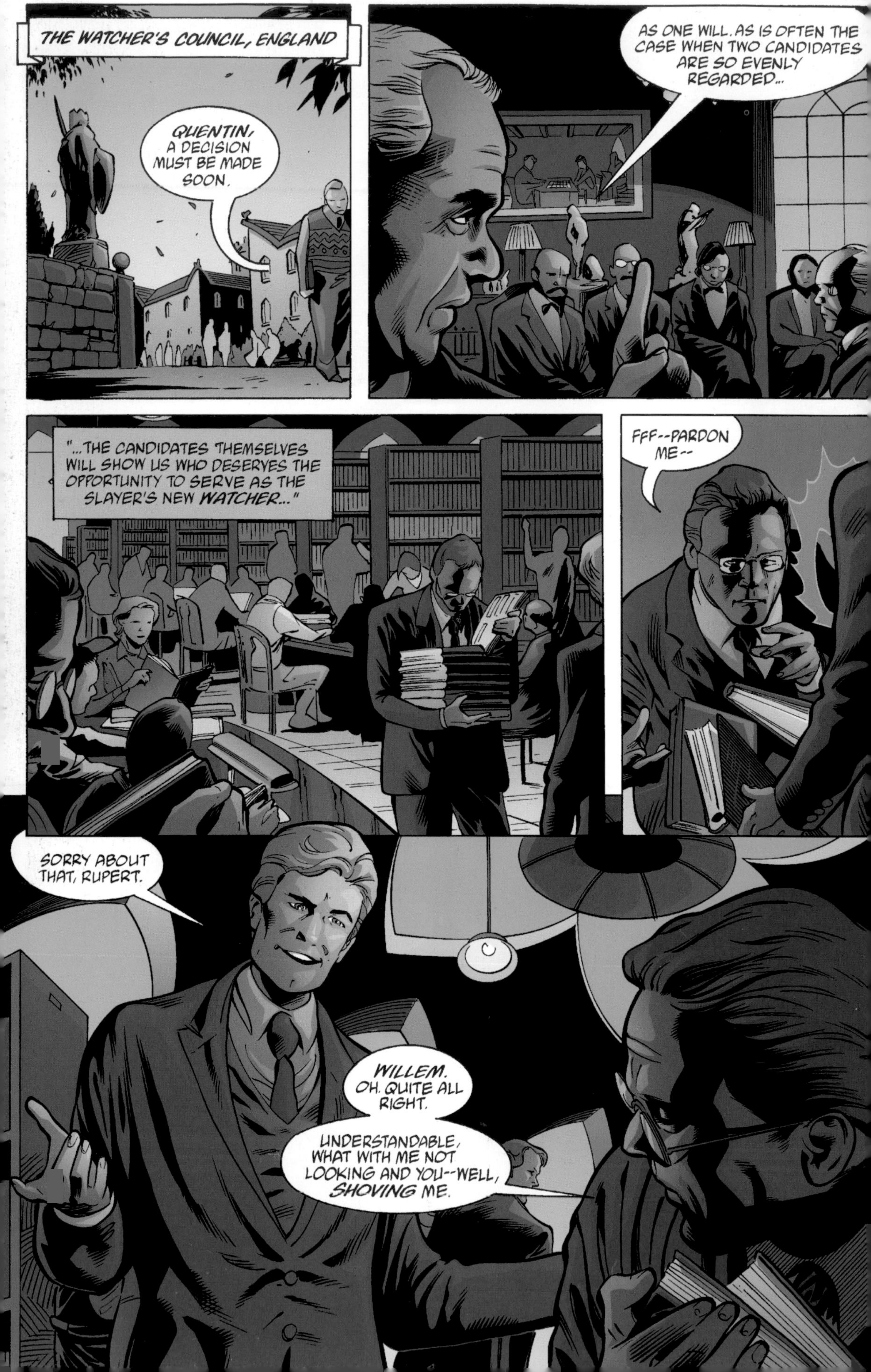
THE WATCHER'S COUNCIL, ENGLAND
QUENTIN, A DECISION MUST BE MADE SOON.
AS ONE WILL. AS IS OFTEN THE CASE WHEN TWO CANDIDATES ARE SO EVENLY REGARDED...
"...THE CANDIDATES THEMSELVES WILL SHOW US WHO DESERVES THE OPPORTUNITY TO SERVE AS THE SLAYER'S NEW WATCHER..."
FFF--PARDON ME--
SORRY ABOUT THAT, RUPERT.
WILLEM. OH. QUITE ALL RIGHT.
UNDERSTANDABLE, WHAT WITH ME NOT LOOKING AND YOU--WELL, SHOVING ME.

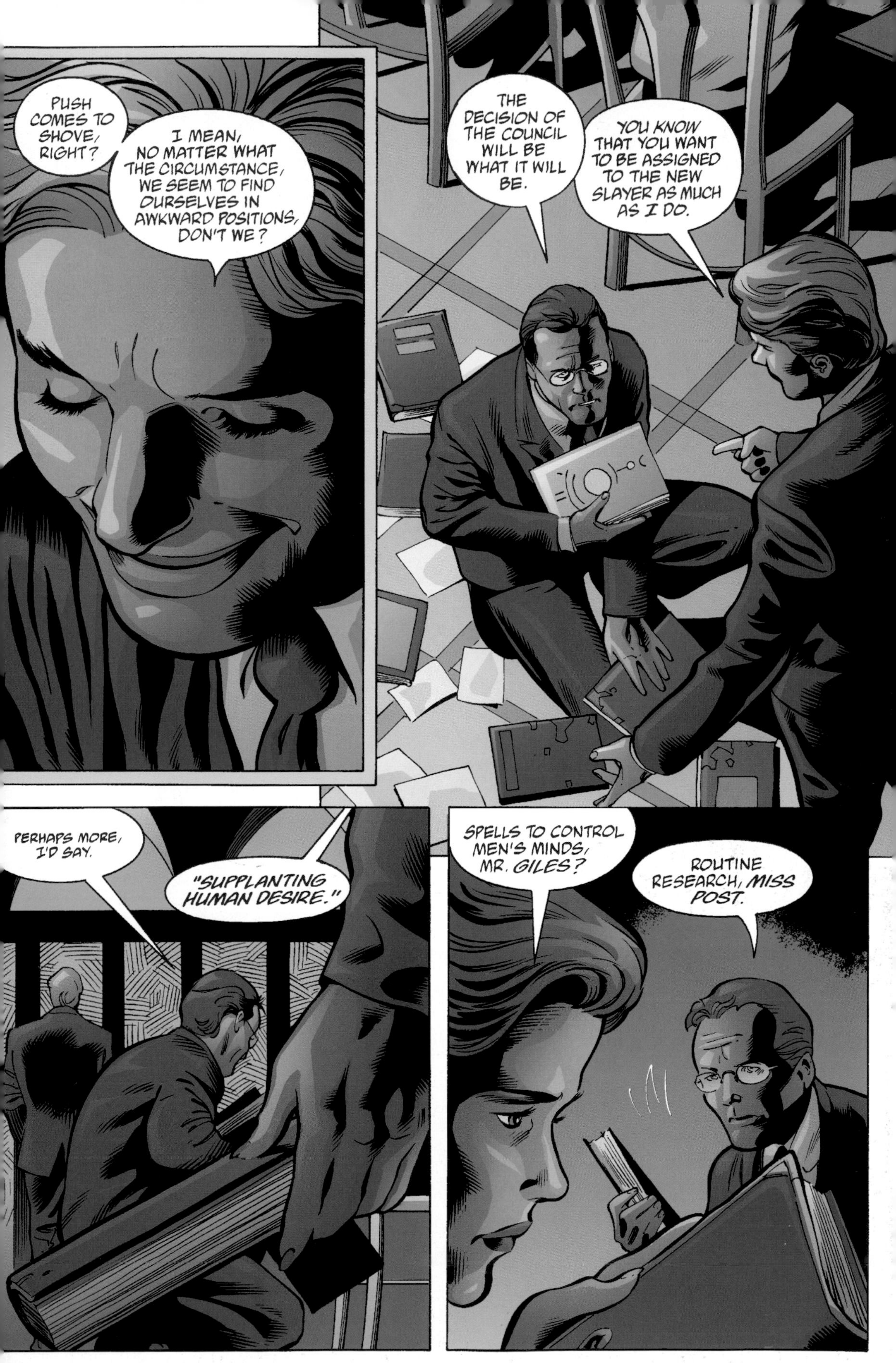
PUSH COMES TO SHOVE, RIGHT?
I MEAN, NO MATTER WHAT THE CIRCUMSTANCE, WE SEEM TO FIND OURSELVES IN AWKWARD POSITIONS, DON'T WE?
THE DECISION OF THE COUNCIL WILL BE WHAT IT WILL BE.
YOU KNOW THAT YOU WANT TO BE ASSIGNED TO THE NEW SLAYER AS MUCH AS I DO.
PERHAPS MORE, I'D SAY.
"SUPPLANTING HUMAN DESIRE."
SPELLS TO CONTROL MEN'S MINDS, MR. GILES?
ROUTINE RESEARCH, MISS POST.

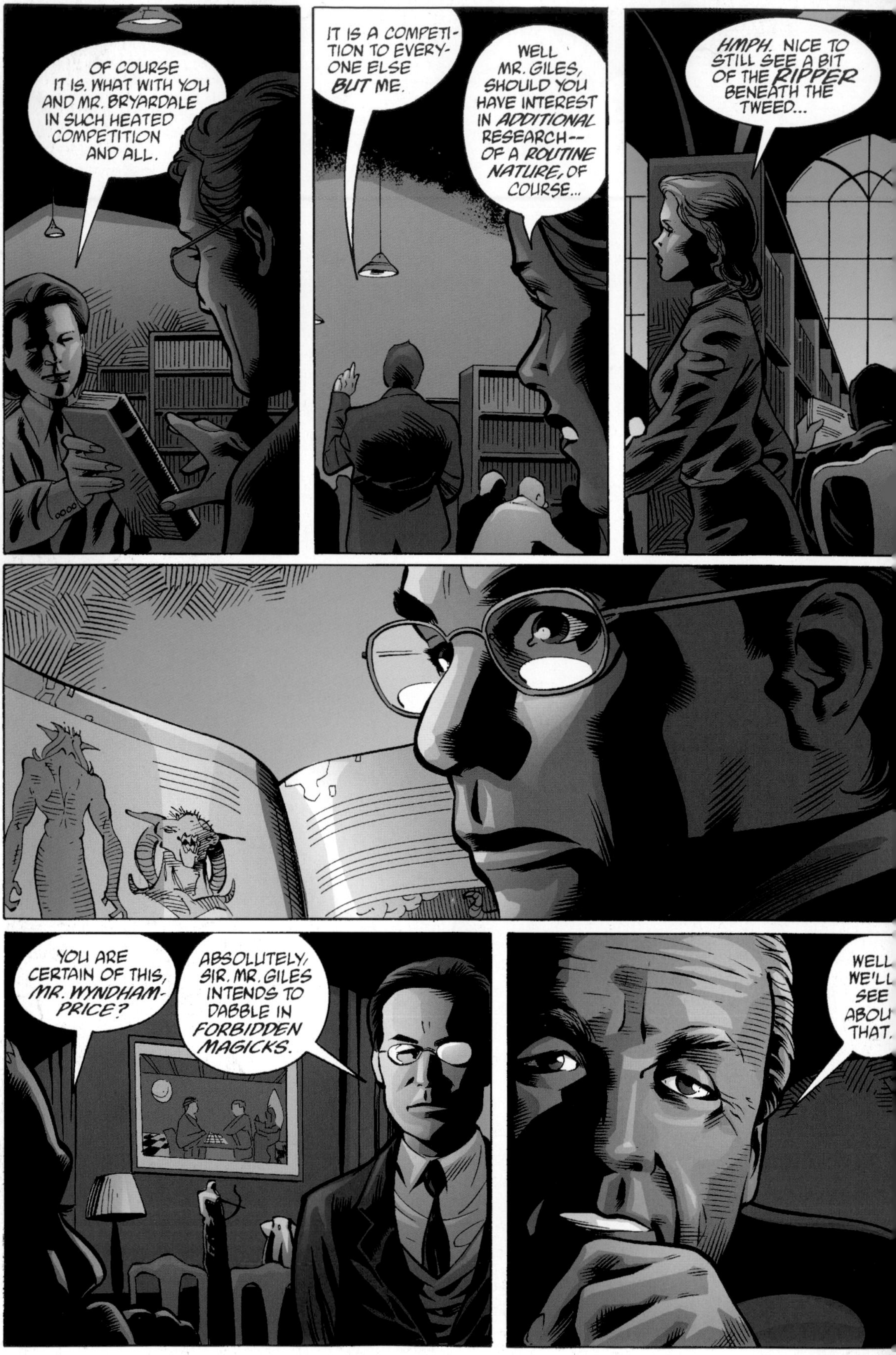
OF COURSE IT IS. WHAT WITH YOU AND MR. BRYARDALE IN SUCH HEATED COMPETITION AND ALL.
IT IS A COMPETITION TO EVERYONE ELSE BUT ME.
WELL MR. GILES, SHOULD YOU HAVE INTEREST IN ADDITIONAL RESEARCH-- OF A ROUTINE NATURE, OF COURSE...
HMPH. NICE TO STILL SEE A BIT OF THE RIPPER BENEATH THE TWEED...
YOU ARE CERTAIN OF THIS, MR. WYNDHAM-PRICE?
ABSOLUTELY, SIR. MR. GILES INTENDS TO DABBLE IN FORBIDDEN MAGICKS.
WELL WE'LL SEE ABOU THAT.

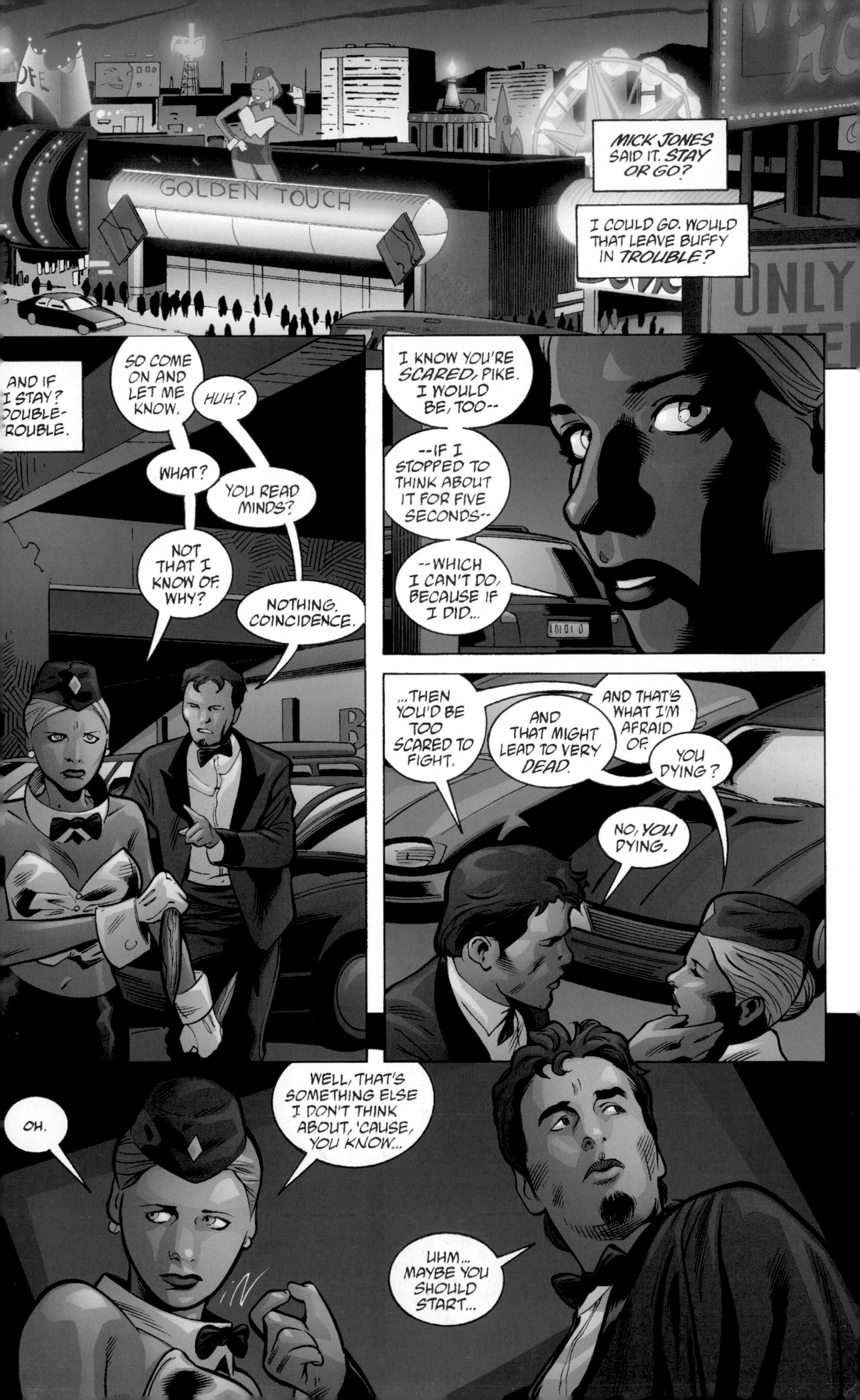
GOLDEN TOUCH
MICK JONES SAID IT. STAY OR GO?
I COULD GO. WOULD THAT LEAVE BUFFY IN TROUBLE?
ONLY
AND IF I STAY? DOUBLE-TROUBLE.
SO COME ON AND LET ME KNOW.
HUH?
WHAT?
YOU READ MINDS?
NOT THAT I KNOW OF. WHY?
NOTHING. COINCIDENCE.
I KNOW YOU'RE SCARED, PIKE. I WOULD BE, TOO--
--IF I STOPPED TO THINK ABOUT IT FOR FIVE SECONDS--
--WHICH I CAN'T DO, BECAUSE IF I DID...
...THEN YOU'D BE TOO SCARED TO FIGHT.
AND THAT MIGHT LEAD TO VERY DEAD.
AND THAT'S WHAT I'M AFRAID OF.
YOU DYING?
NO, YOU DYING.
OH.
WELL, THAT'S SOMETHING ELSE I DON'T THINK ABOUT, 'CAUSE, YOU KNOW...
UHM... MAYBE YOU SHOULD START...

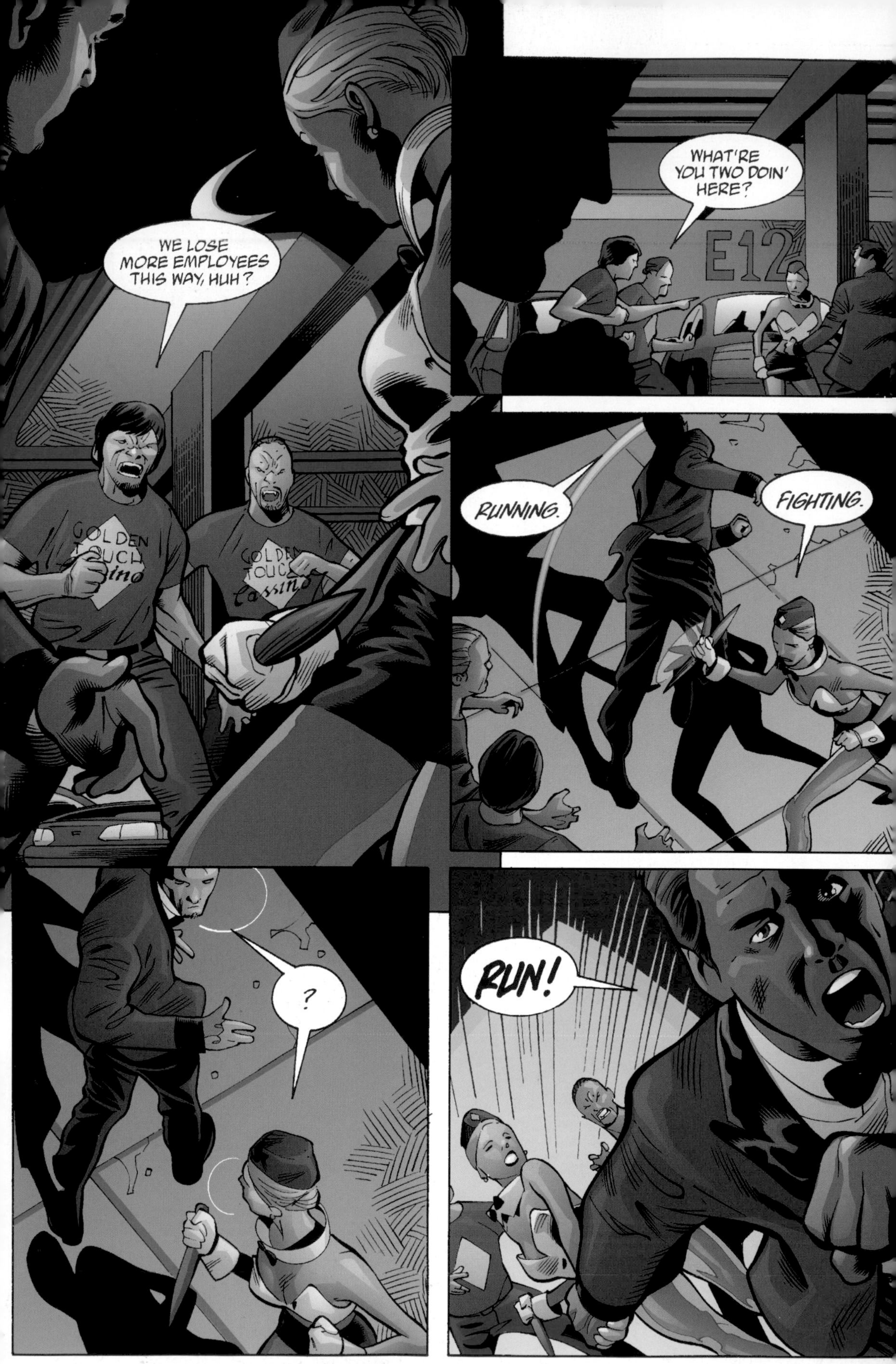
WE LOSE MORE EMPLOYEES THIS WAY, HUH?
WHAT'RE YOU TWO DOIN' HERE?
E12
GOLDEN TOUCH Casino
GOLDEN TOUCH Cassino
RUNNING.
FIGHTING.
?
RUN!

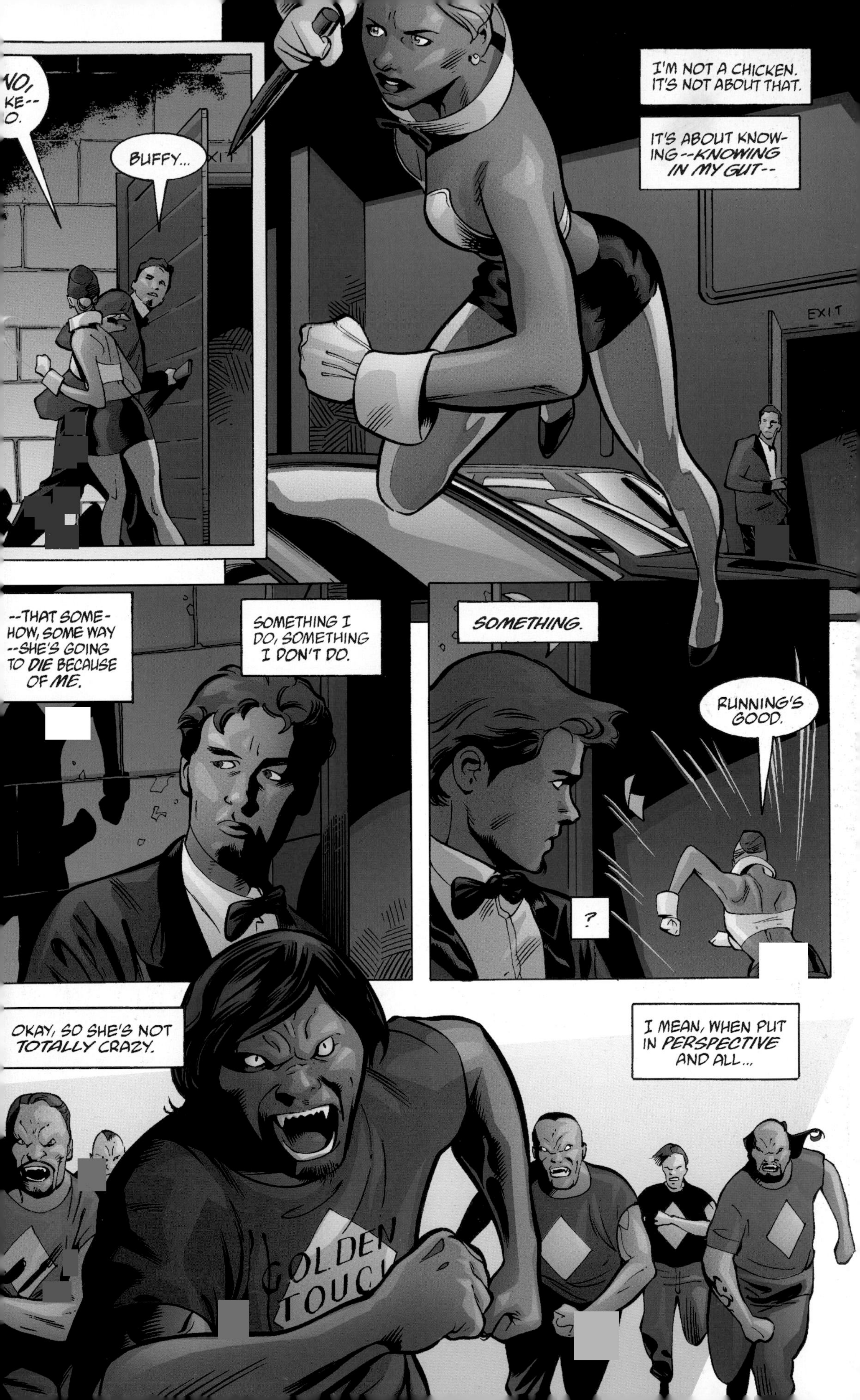

BUFFY...
I'M NOT A CHICKEN. IT'S NOT ABOUT THAT.
IT'S ABOUT KNOWING--KNOWING IN MY GUT--
EXIT
--THAT SOMEHOW, SOME WAY--SHE'S GOING TO DIE BECAUSE OF ME.
SOMETHING I DO, SOMETHING I DON'T DO.
SOMETHING.
RUNNING'S GOOD.
?
OKAY, SO SHE'S NOT TOTALLY CRAZY.
I MEAN, WHEN PUT IN PERSPECTIVE AND ALL...

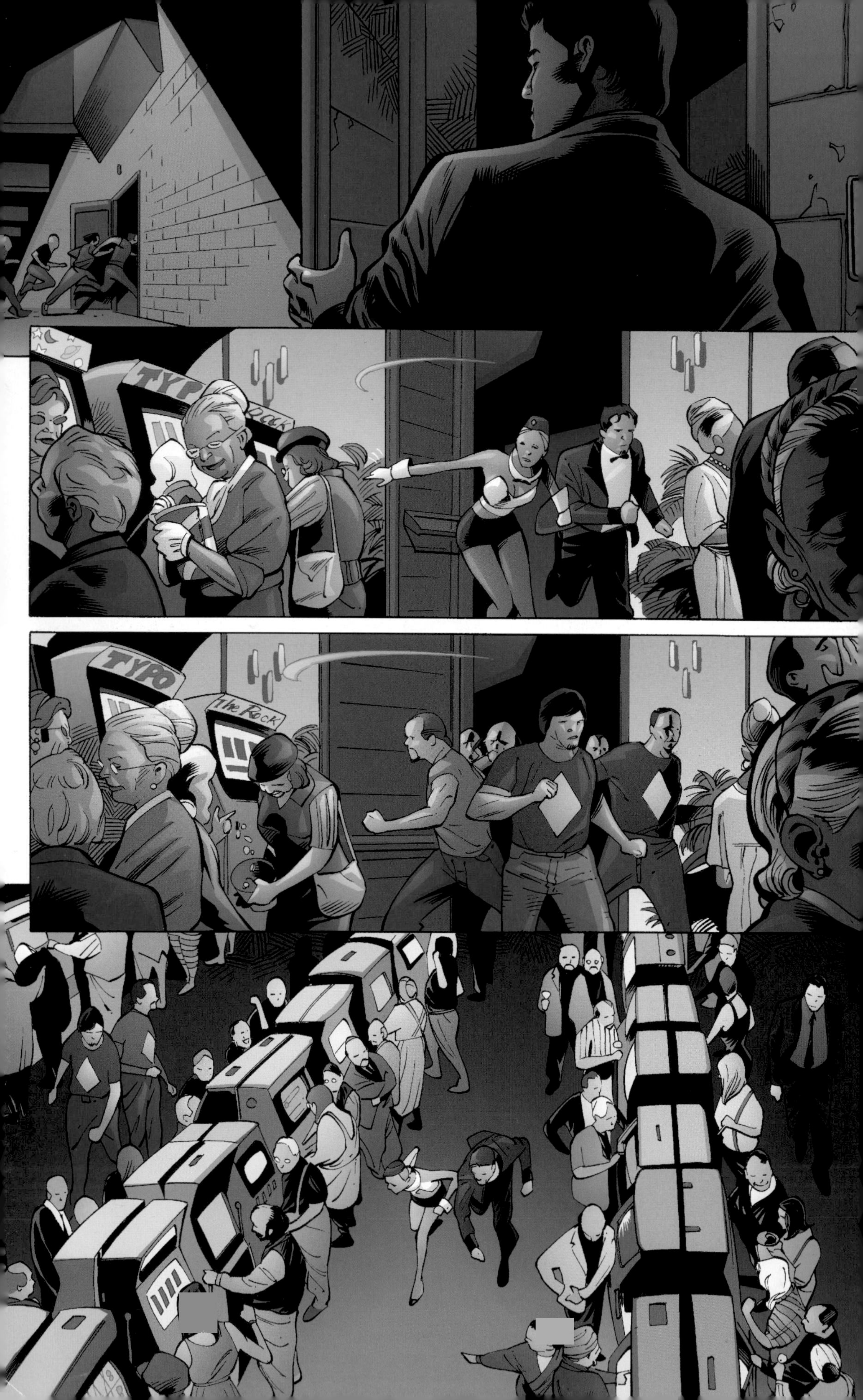
TYPO
The Rock

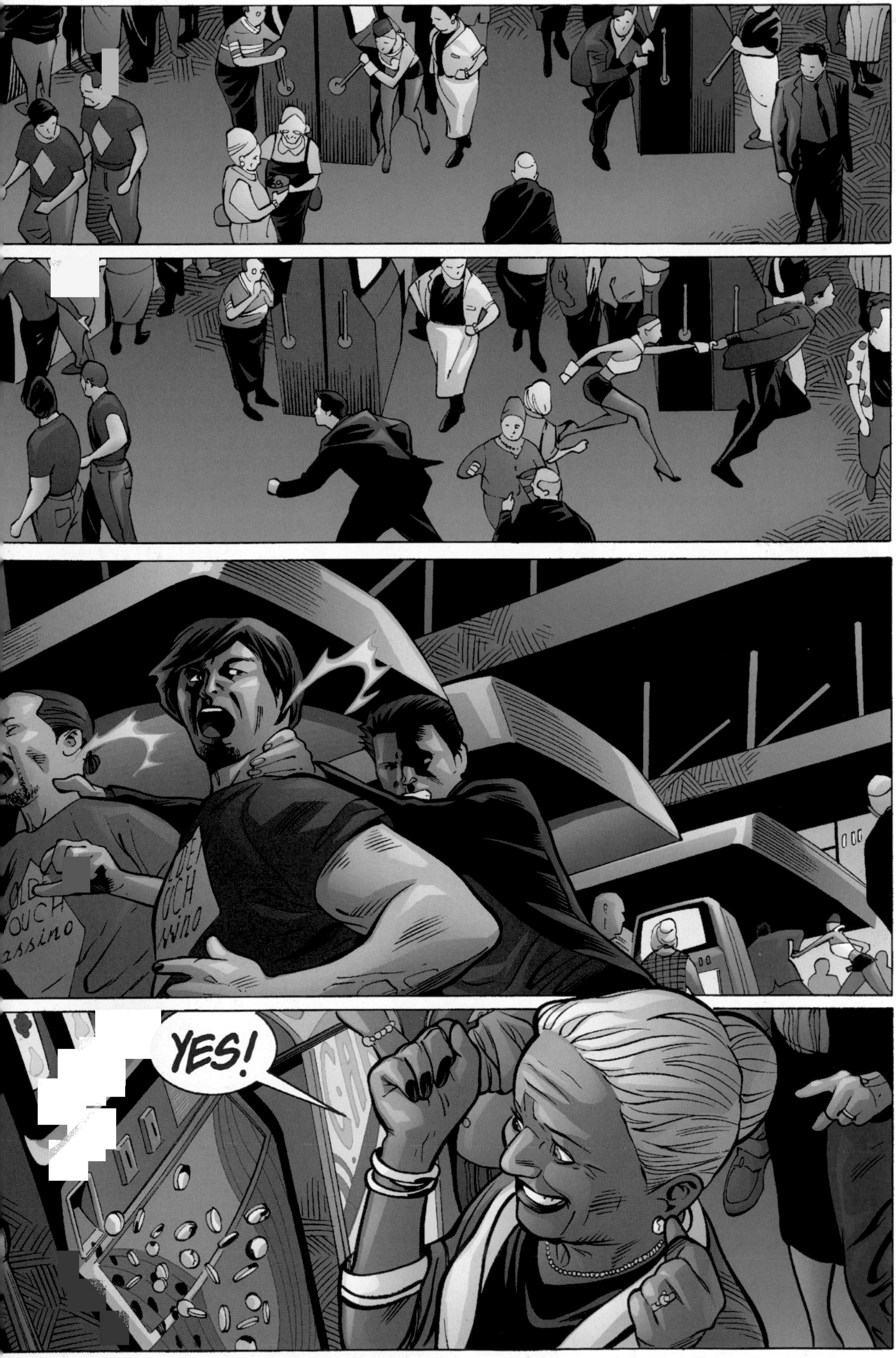
YES!

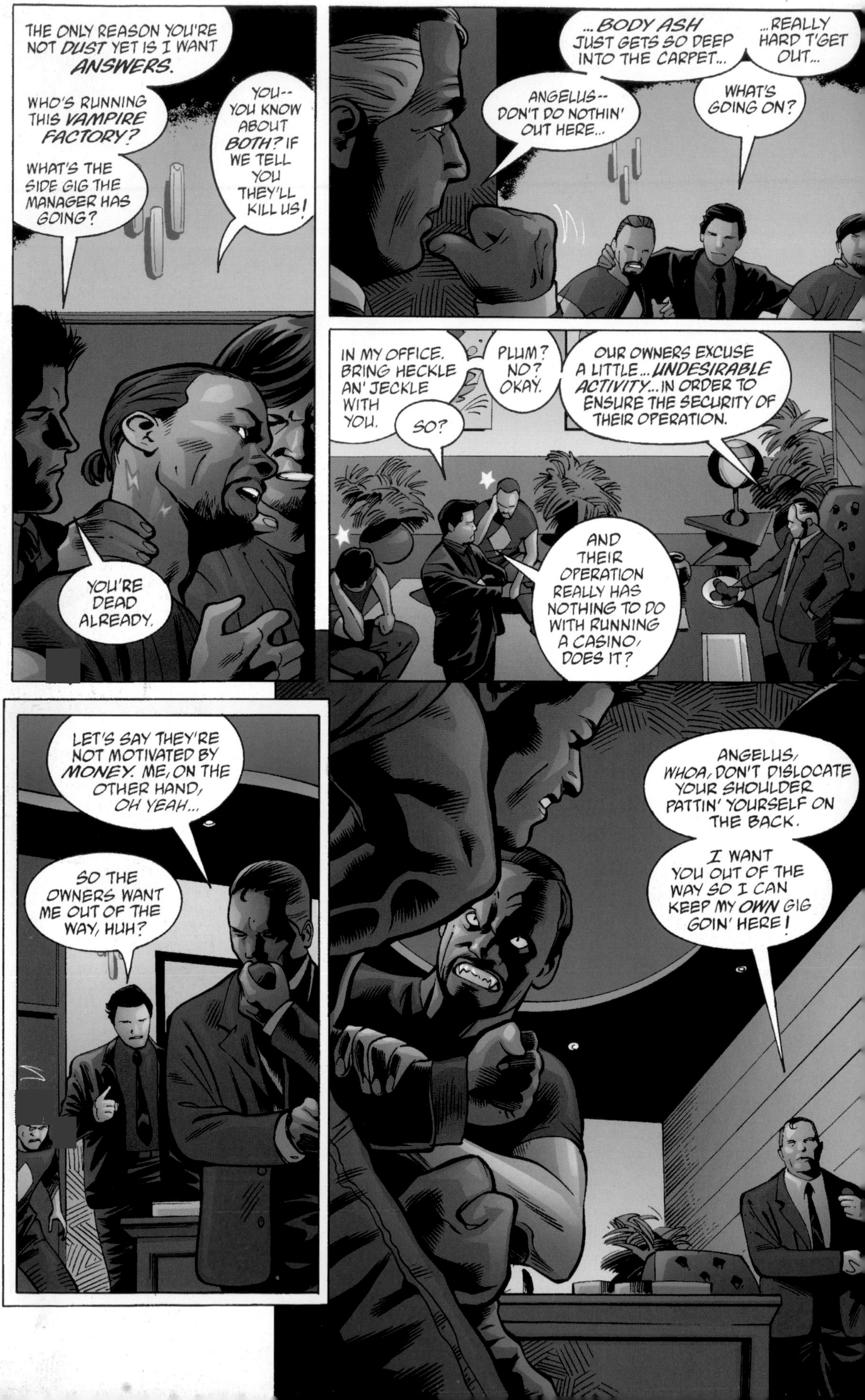
THE ONLY REASON YOU'RE NOT DUST YET IS I WANT ANSWERS.
WHO'S RUNNING THIS VAMPIRE FACTORY?
WHAT'S THE SIDE GIG THE MANAGER HAS GOING?
YOU-- YOU KNOW ABOUT BOTH? IF WE TELL YOU THEY'LL KILL US!
YOU'RE DEAD ALREADY.
...BODY ASH JUST GETS SO DEEP INTO THE CARPET...
...REALLY HARD T'GET OUT...
ANGELUS-- DON'T DO NOTHIN' OUT HERE...
WHAT'S GOING ON?
IN MY OFFICE. BRING HECKLE AN' JECKLE WITH YOU.
PLUM? NO? OKAY.
SO?
OUR OWNERS EXCUSE A LITTLE... UNDESIRABLE ACTIVITY... IN ORDER TO ENSURE THE SECURITY OF THEIR OPERATION.
AND THEIR OPERATION REALLY HAS NOTHING TO DO WITH RUNNING A CASINO, DOES IT?
LET'S SAY THEY'RE NOT MOTIVATED BY MONEY. ME, ON THE OTHER HAND, OH YEAH...
SO THE OWNERS WANT ME OUT OF THE WAY, HUH?
ANGELUS, WHOA, DON'T DISLOCATE YOUR SHOULDER PATTIN' YOURSELF ON THE BACK.
I WANT YOU OUT OF THE WAY SO I CAN KEEP MY OWN GIG GOIN' HERE!

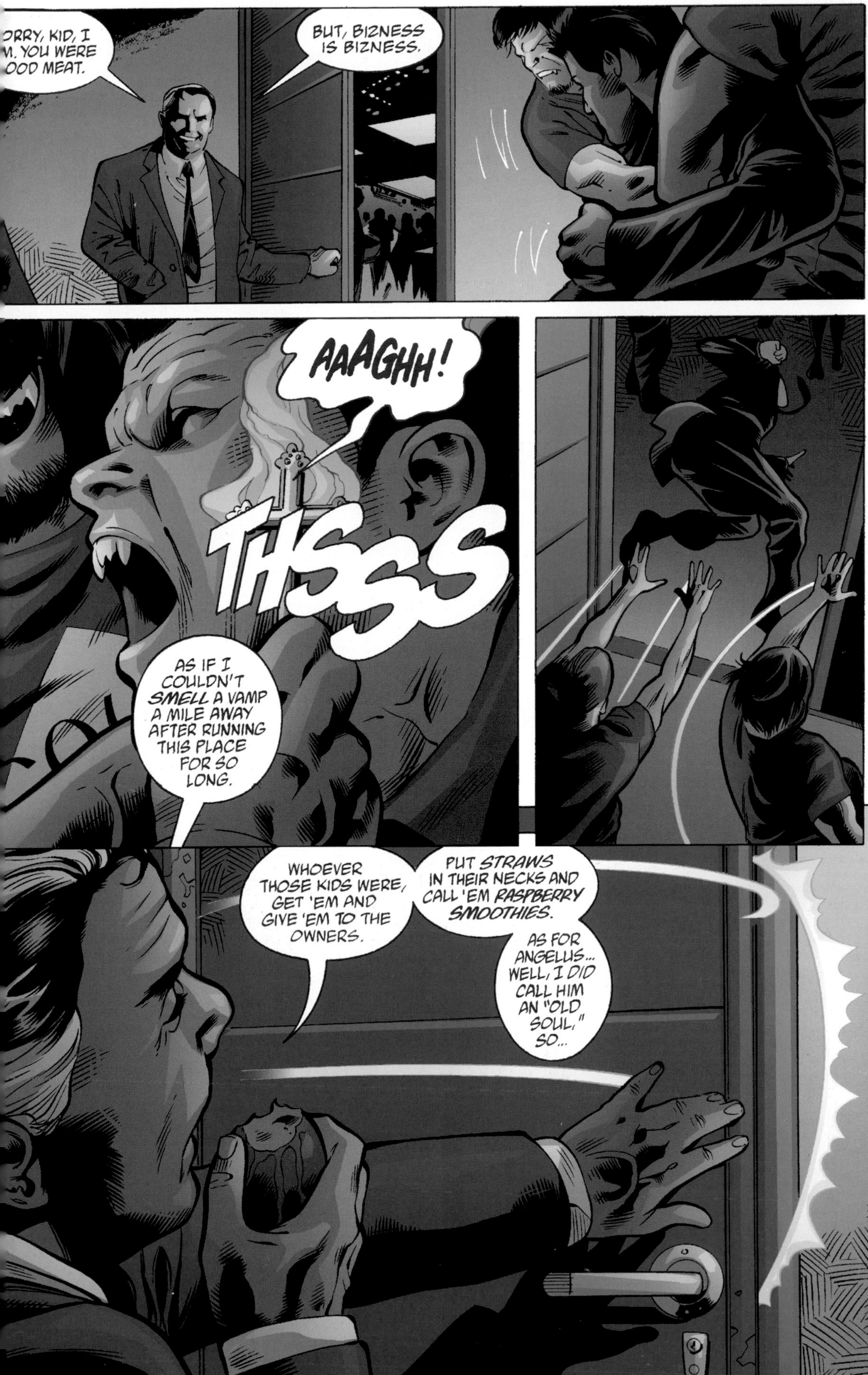

ORRY, KID, I
M. YOU WERE
OOD MEAT.
BUT, BIZNESS IS BIZNESS.
AAAGHH!
THSSS
AS IF I COULDN'T SMELL A VAMP A MILE AWAY AFTER RUNNING THIS PLACE FOR SO LONG.
WHOEVER THOSE KIDS WERE, GET 'EM AND GIVE 'EM TO THE OWNERS.
PUT STRAWS IN THEIR NECKS AND CALL 'EM RASPBERRY SMOOTHIES.
AS FOR ANGELUS... WELL, I DID CALL HIM AN "OLD SOUL," SO...

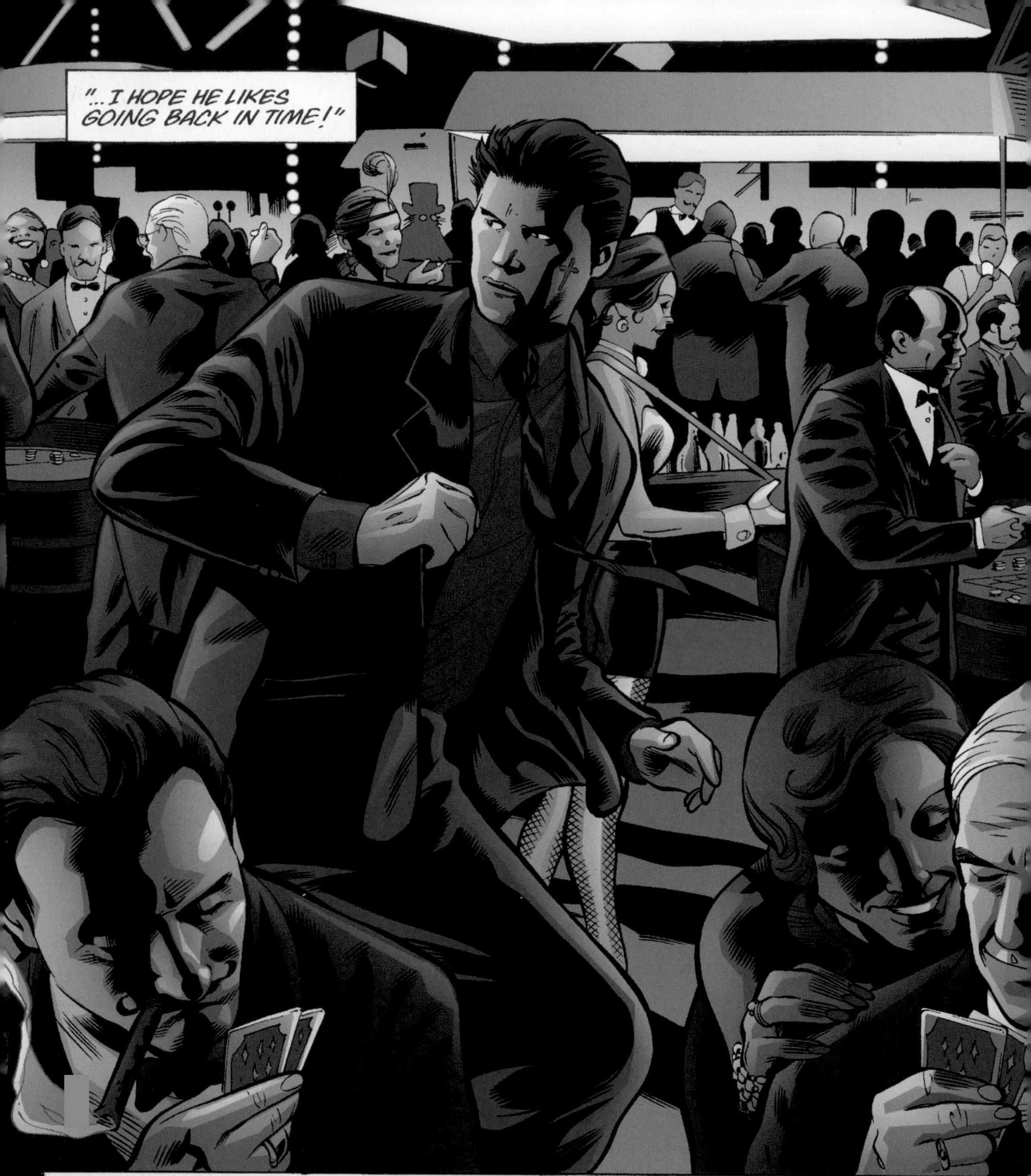
"...I HOPE HE LIKES GOING BACK IN TIME!"

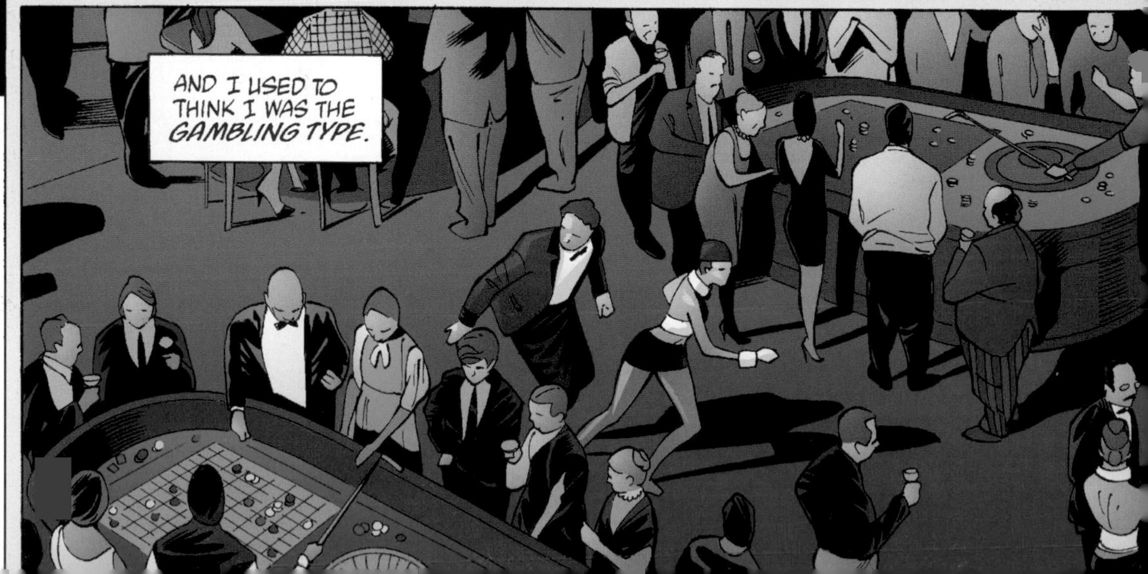
AND I USED TO THINK I WAS THE GAMBLING TYPE.

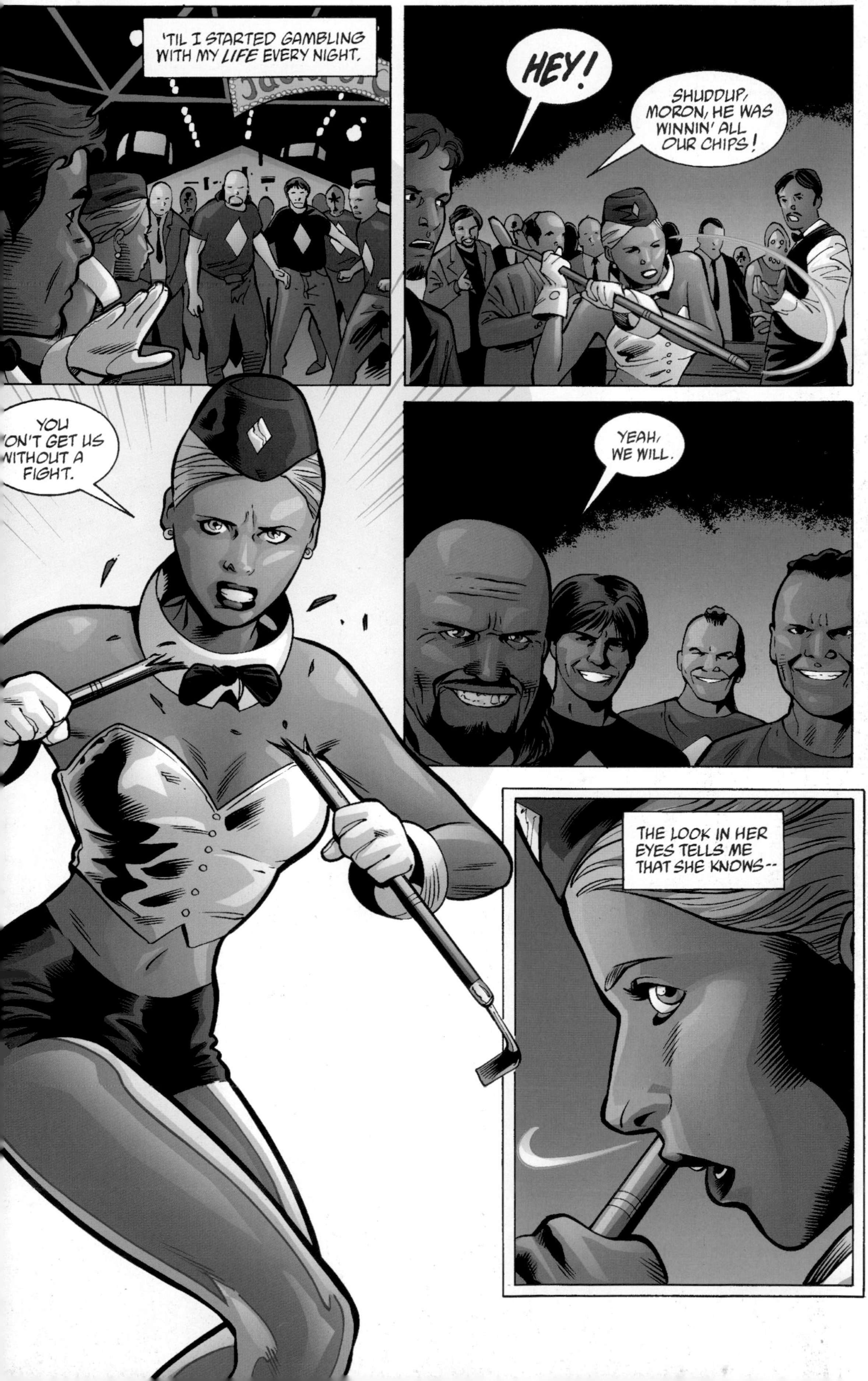
'TIL I STARTED GAMBLING WITH MY *LIFE* EVERY NIGHT.
HEY!
SHUDDUP, MORON, HE WAS WINNIN' ALL OUR CHIPS!
YOU WON'T GET US WITHOUT A FIGHT.
YEAH, WE WILL.
THE LOOK IN HER EYES TELLS ME THAT SHE KNOWS--

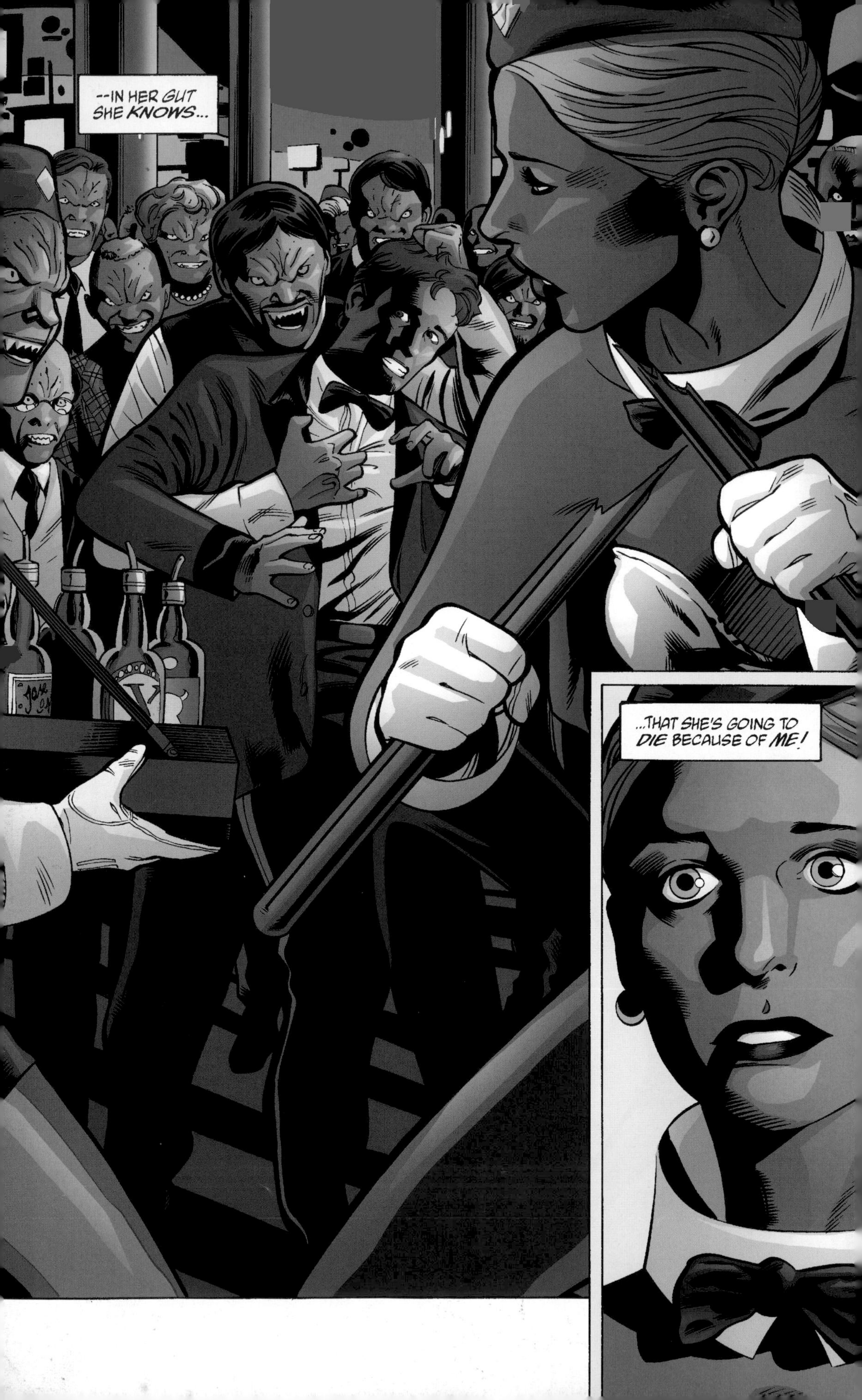
--IN HER GUT SHE KNOWS...
...THAT SHE'S GOING TO DIE BECAUSE OF ME!

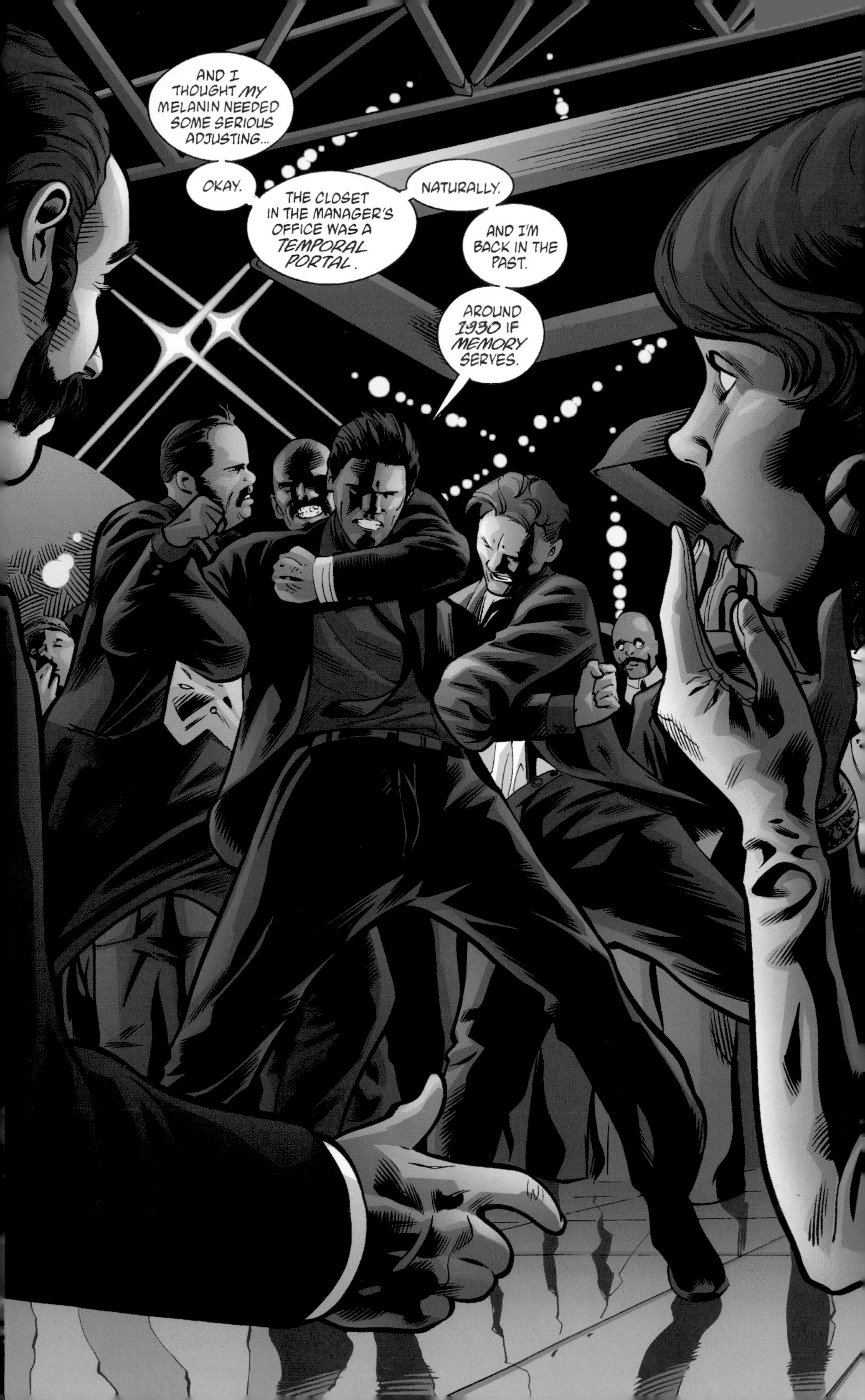
AND I THOUGHT MY MELANIN NEEDED SOME SERIOUS ADJUSTING...
OKAY.
THE CLOSET IN THE MANAGER'S OFFICE WAS A TEMPORAL PORTAL.
NATURALLY.
AND I'M BACK IN THE PAST.
AROUND 1930 IF MEMORY SERVES.

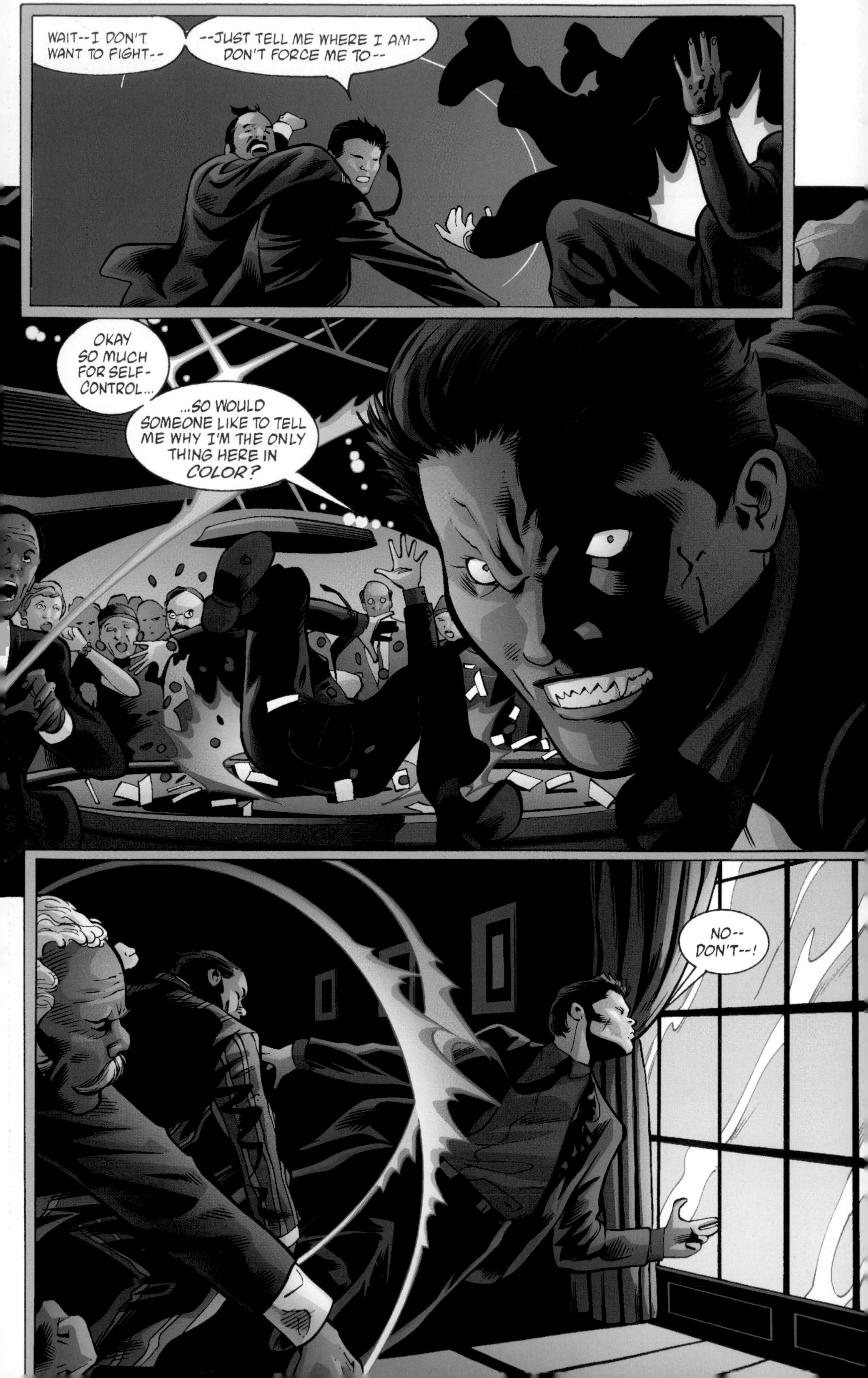
WAIT--I DON'T WANT TO FIGHT--
--JUST TELL ME WHERE I AM-- DON'T FORCE ME TO--
OKAY SO MUCH FOR SELF-CONTROL...
...SO WOULD SOMEONE LIKE TO TELL ME WHY I'M THE ONLY THING HERE IN COLOR?
NO-- DON'T--!

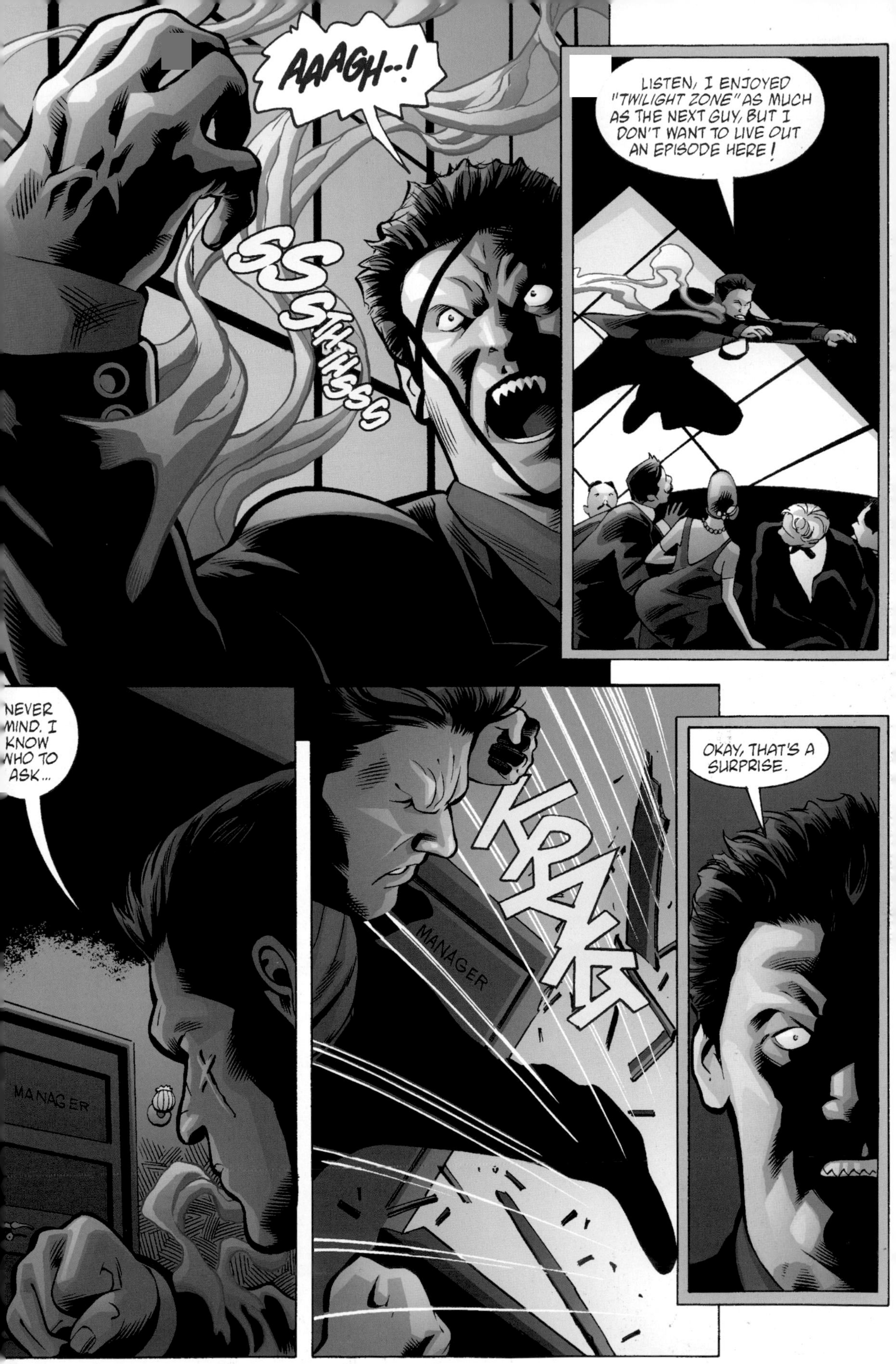
AAAGH--!
SSSHHHSSS
LISTEN, I ENJOYED "TWILIGHT ZONE" AS MUCH AS THE NEXT GUY, BUT I DON'T WANT TO LIVE OUT AN EPISODE HERE!
NEVER MIND. I KNOW NHO TO ASK...
MANAGER
MANAGER
KRAK
OKAY, THAT'S A SURPRISE.

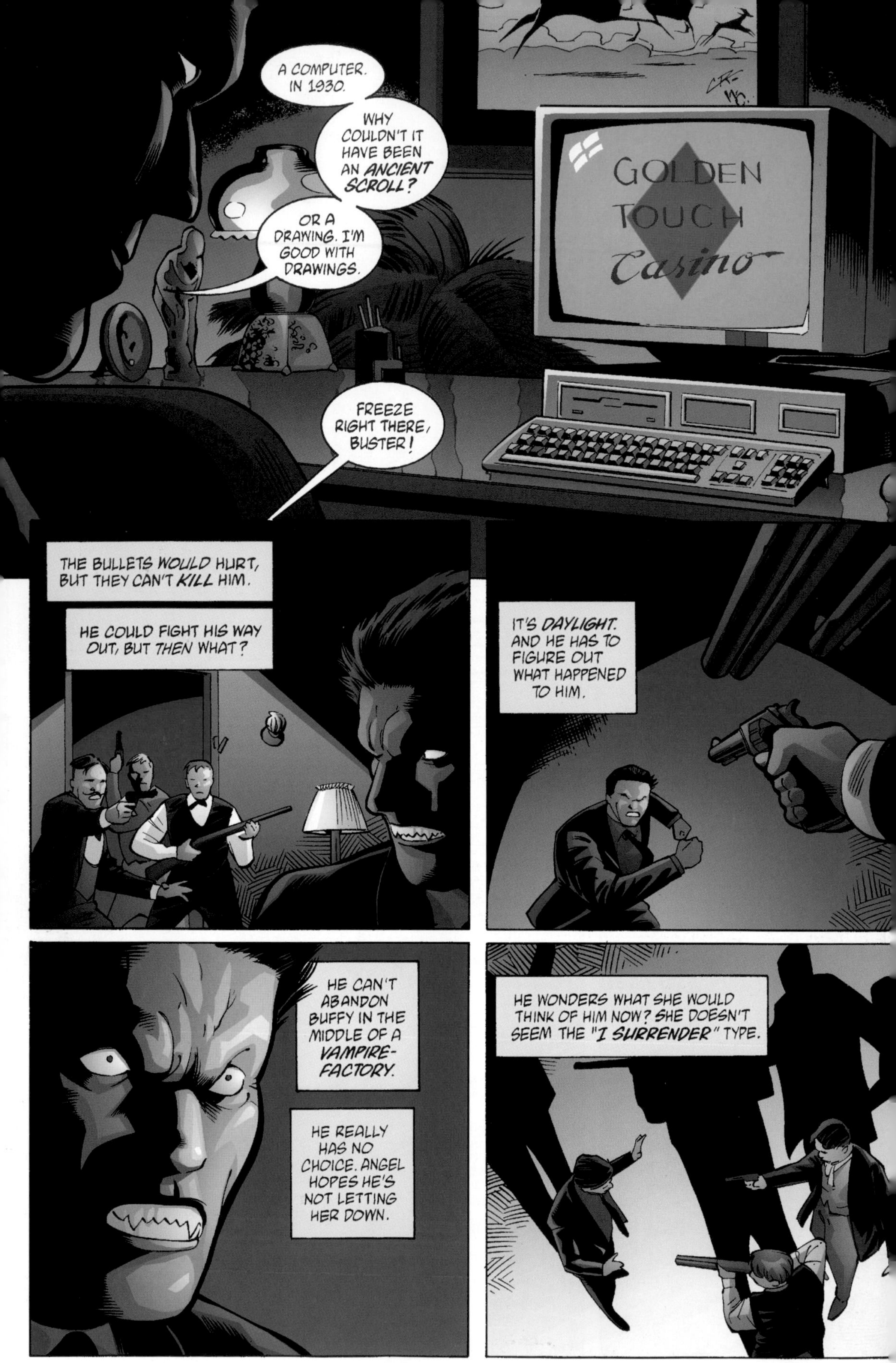

A COMPUTER. IN 1930.
WHY COULDN'T IT HAVE BEEN AN ANCIENT SCROLL?
OR A DRAWING. I'M GOOD WITH DRAWINGS.
GOLDEN TOUCH Casino
FREEZE RIGHT THERE, BUSTER!
THE BULLETS WOULD HURT, BUT THEY CAN'T KILL HIM.
HE COULD FIGHT HIS WAY OUT, BUT THEN WHAT?
IT'S DAYLIGHT. AND HE HAS TO FIGURE OUT WHAT HAPPENED TO HIM.
HE CAN'T ABANDON BUFFY IN THE MIDDLE OF A VAMPIRE-FACTORY.
HE REALLY HAS NO CHOICE. ANGEL HOPES HE'S NOT LETTING HER DOWN.
HE WONDERS WHAT SHE WOULD THINK OF HIM NOW? SHE DOESN'T SEEM THE "I SURRENDER" TYPE.

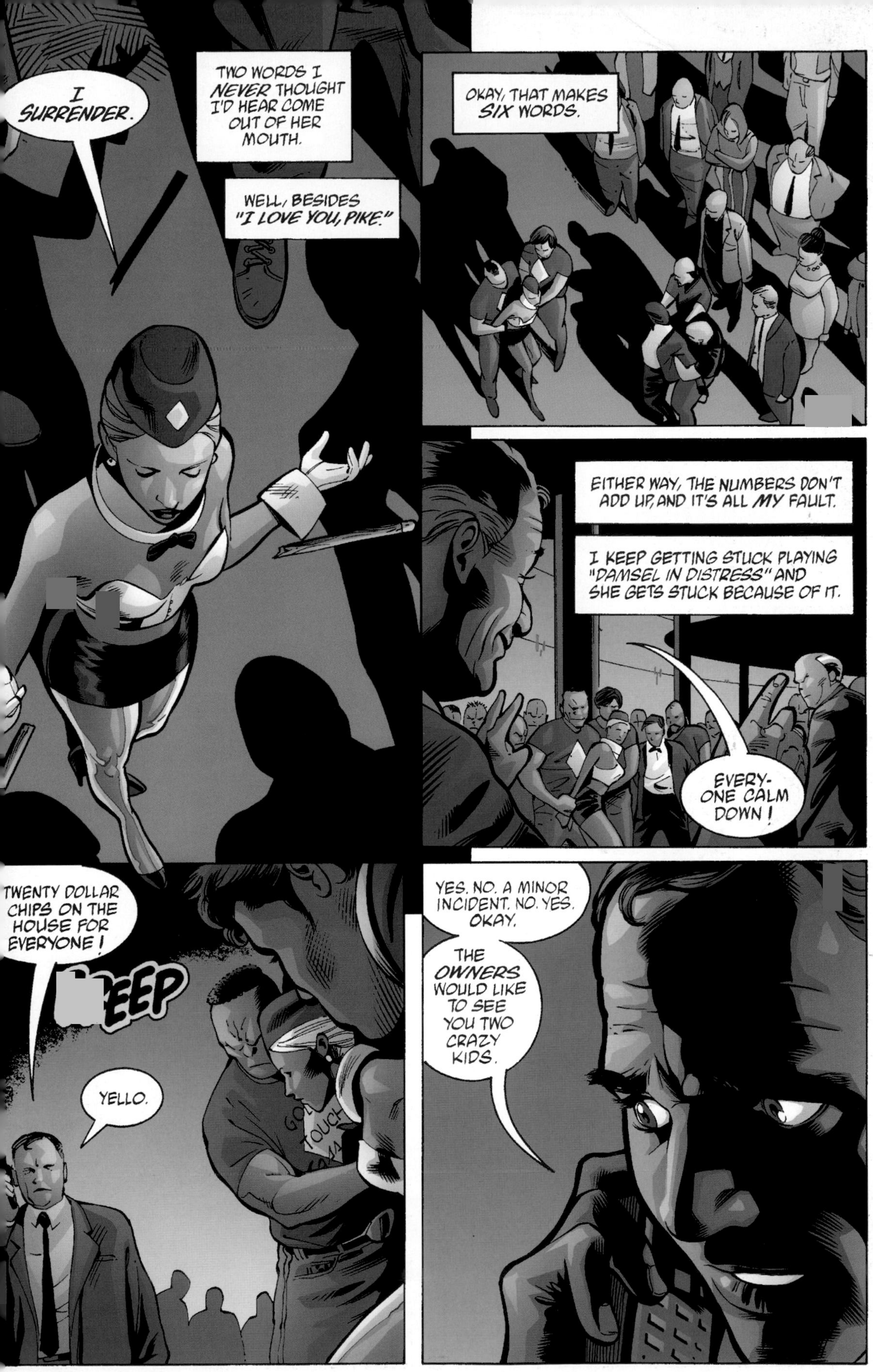
I SURRENDER.
TWO WORDS I NEVER THOUGHT I'D HEAR COME OUT OF HER MOUTH.
WELL, BESIDES "I LOVE YOU, PIKE."
OKAY, THAT MAKES SIX WORDS.
EITHER WAY, THE NUMBERS DON'T ADD UP, AND IT'S ALL MY FAULT.
I KEEP GETTING STUCK PLAYING "DAMSEL IN DISTRESS" AND SHE GETS STUCK BECAUSE OF IT.
EVERY-ONE CALM DOWN!
TWENTY DOLLAR CHIPS ON THE HOUSE FOR EVERYONE!
EEP
YELLO.
YES. NO. A MINOR INCIDENT. NO. YES. OKAY.
THE OWNERS WOULD LIKE TO SEE YOU TWO CRAZY KIDS.

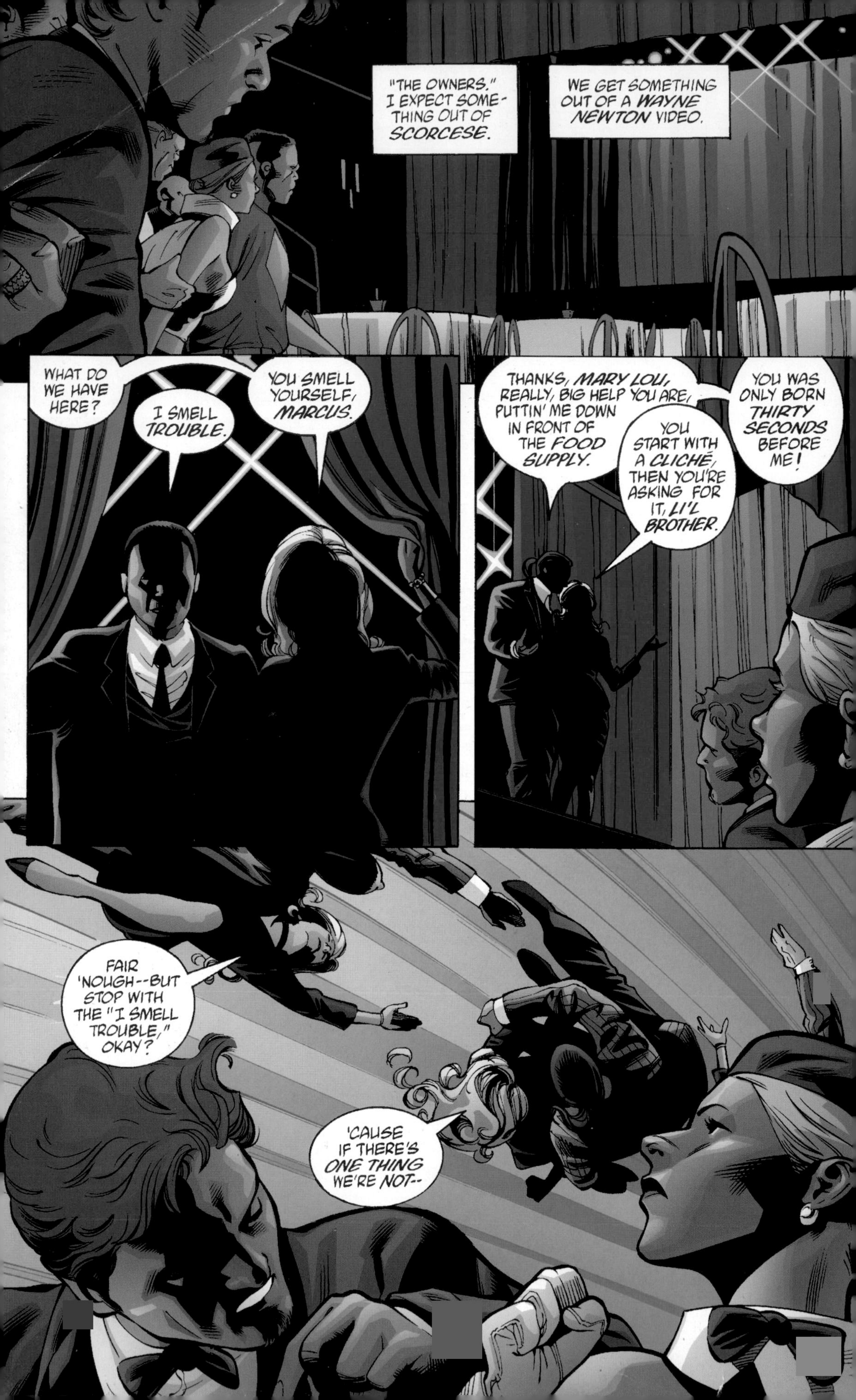
"THE OWNERS." I EXPECT SOME-THING OUT OF SCORCESE.
WE GET SOMETHING OUT OF A WAYNE NEWTON VIDEO.
WHAT DO WE HAVE HERE?
I SMELL TROUBLE.
YOU SMELL YOURSELF, MARCUS.
THANKS, MARY LOU, REALLY, BIG HELP YOU ARE, PUTTIN' ME DOWN IN FRONT OF THE FOOD SUPPLY.
YOU WAS ONLY BORN THIRTY SECONDS BEFORE ME!
YOU START WITH A CLICHÉ, THEN YOU'RE ASKING FOR IT, LI'L BROTHER.
FAIR 'NOUGH--BUT STOP WITH THE "I SMELL TROUBLE," OKAY?
'CAUSE IF THERE'S ONE THING WE'RE NOT--

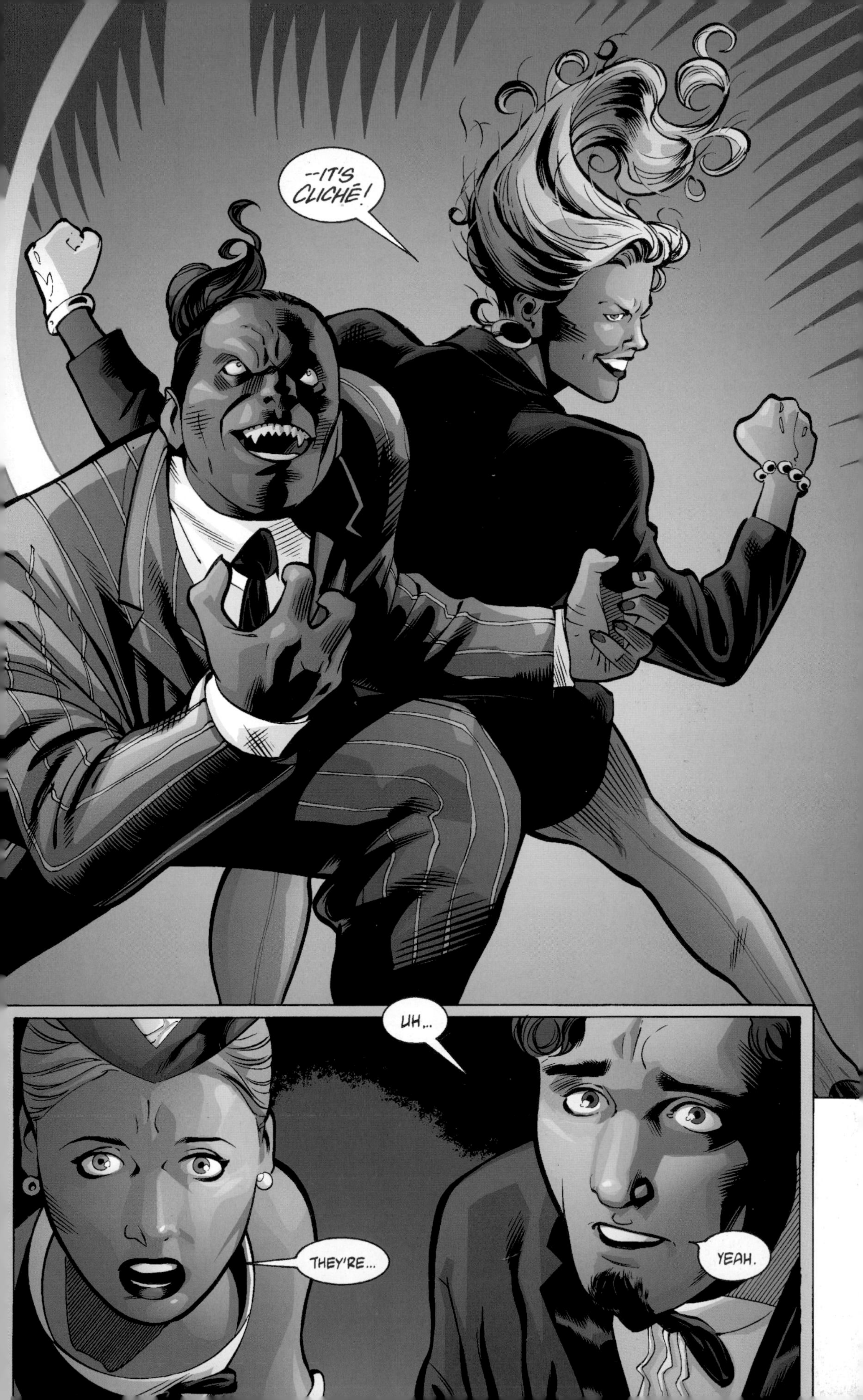
--IT'S CLICHÉ!
UH...
THEY'RE...
YEAH.

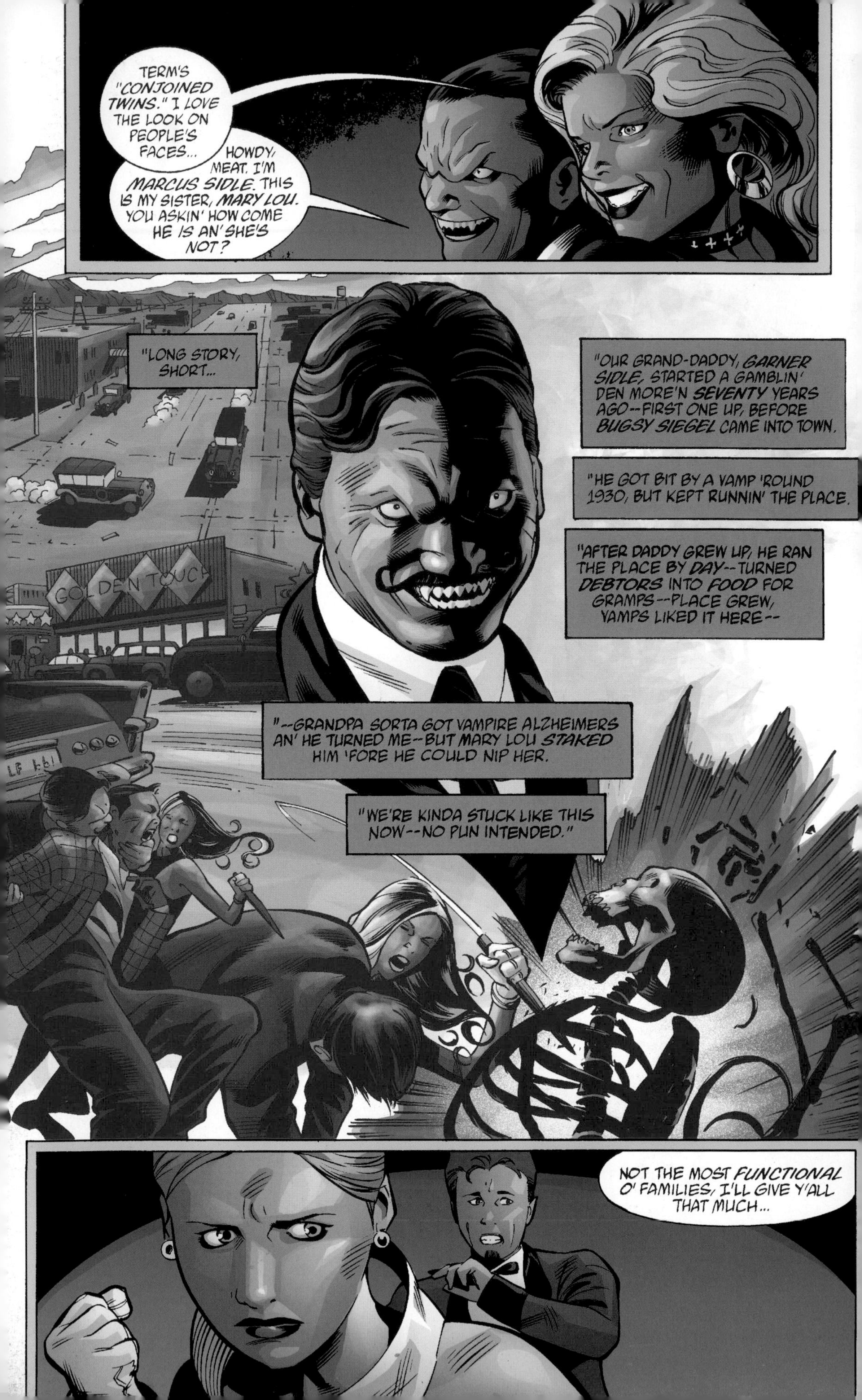

TERM'S "CONJOINED TWINS." I LOVE THE LOOK ON PEOPLE'S FACES...
HOWDY, MEAT. I'M MARCUS SIDLE. THIS IS MY SISTER, MARY LOU. YOU ASKIN' HOW COME HE IS AN' SHE'S NOT?
"LONG STORY, SHORT...
"OUR GRAND-DADDY, GARNER SIDLE, STARTED A GAMBLIN' DEN MORE'N SEVENTY YEARS AGO--FIRST ONE UP, BEFORE BUGSY SIEGEL CAME INTO TOWN.
"HE GOT BIT BY A VAMP 'ROUND 1930, BUT KEPT RUNNIN' THE PLACE.
"AFTER DADDY GREW UP, HE RAN THE PLACE BY DAY--TURNED DEBTORS INTO FOOD FOR GRAMPS--PLACE GREW, VAMPS LIKED IT HERE--
GOLDEN TOUCH
"--GRANDPA SORTA GOT VAMPIRE ALZHEIMERS AN' HE TURNED ME--BUT MARY LOU STAKED HIM 'FORE HE COULD NIP HER.
"WE'RE KINDA STUCK LIKE THIS NOW--NO PUN INTENDED."
NOT THE MOST FUNCTIONAL O' FAMILIES, I'LL GIVE Y'ALL THAT MUCH...

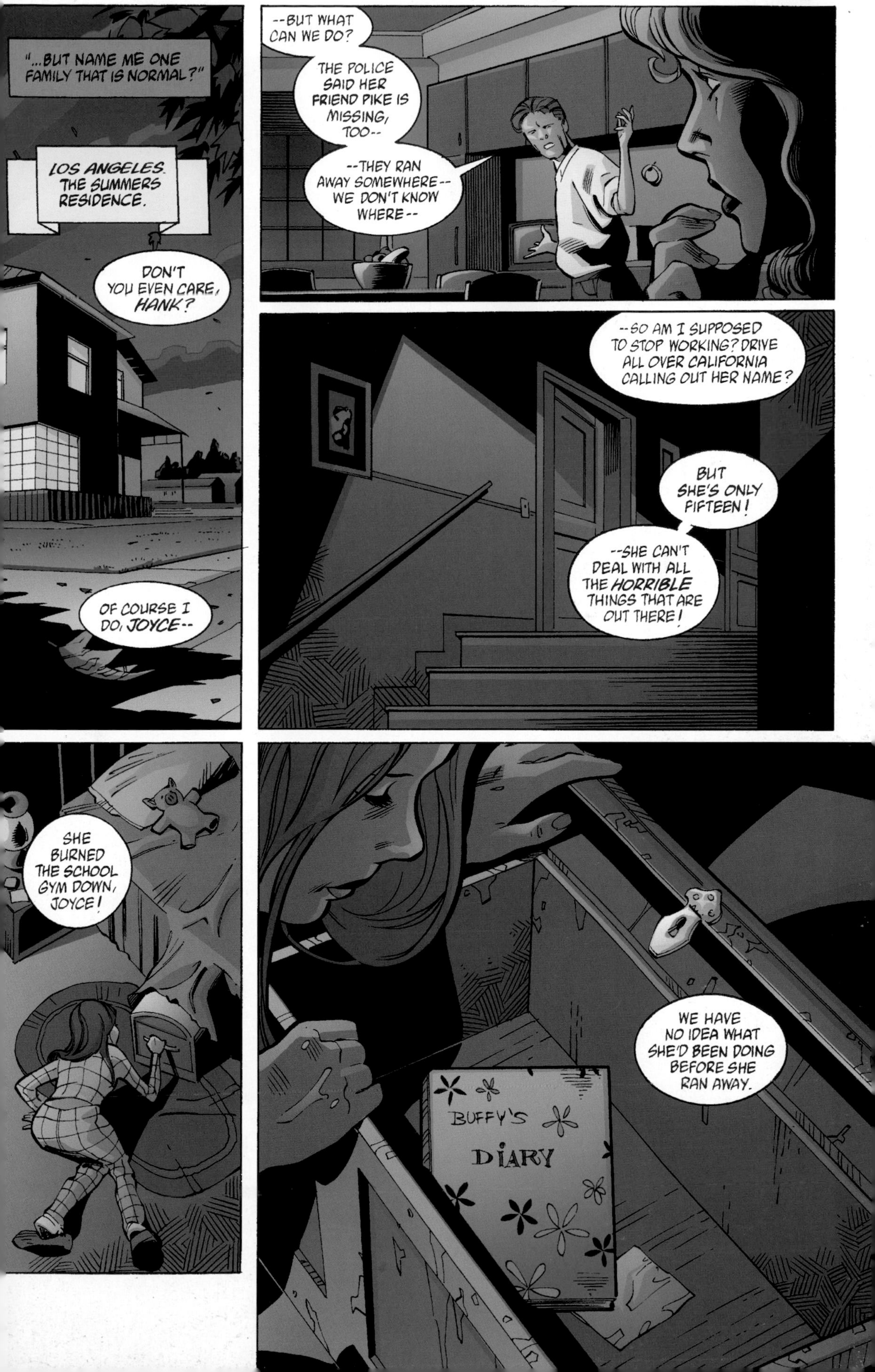
"...BUT NAME ME ONE FAMILY THAT IS NORMAL?"
LOS ANGELES. THE SUMMERS RESIDENCE.
DON'T YOU EVEN CARE, HANK?
OF COURSE I DO, JOYCE--
--BUT WHAT CAN WE DO?
THE POLICE SAID HER FRIEND PIKE IS MISSING, TOO--
--THEY RAN AWAY SOMEWHERE-- WE DON'T KNOW WHERE--
--SO AM I SUPPOSED TO STOP WORKING? DRIVE ALL OVER CALIFORNIA CALLING OUT HER NAME?
BUT SHE'S ONLY FIFTEEN!
--SHE CAN'T DEAL WITH ALL THE HORRIBLE THINGS THAT ARE OUT THERE!
SHE BURNED THE SCHOOL GYM DOWN, JOYCE!
WE HAVE NO IDEA WHAT SHE'D BEEN DOING BEFORE SHE RAN AWAY.
BUFFY'S DIARY

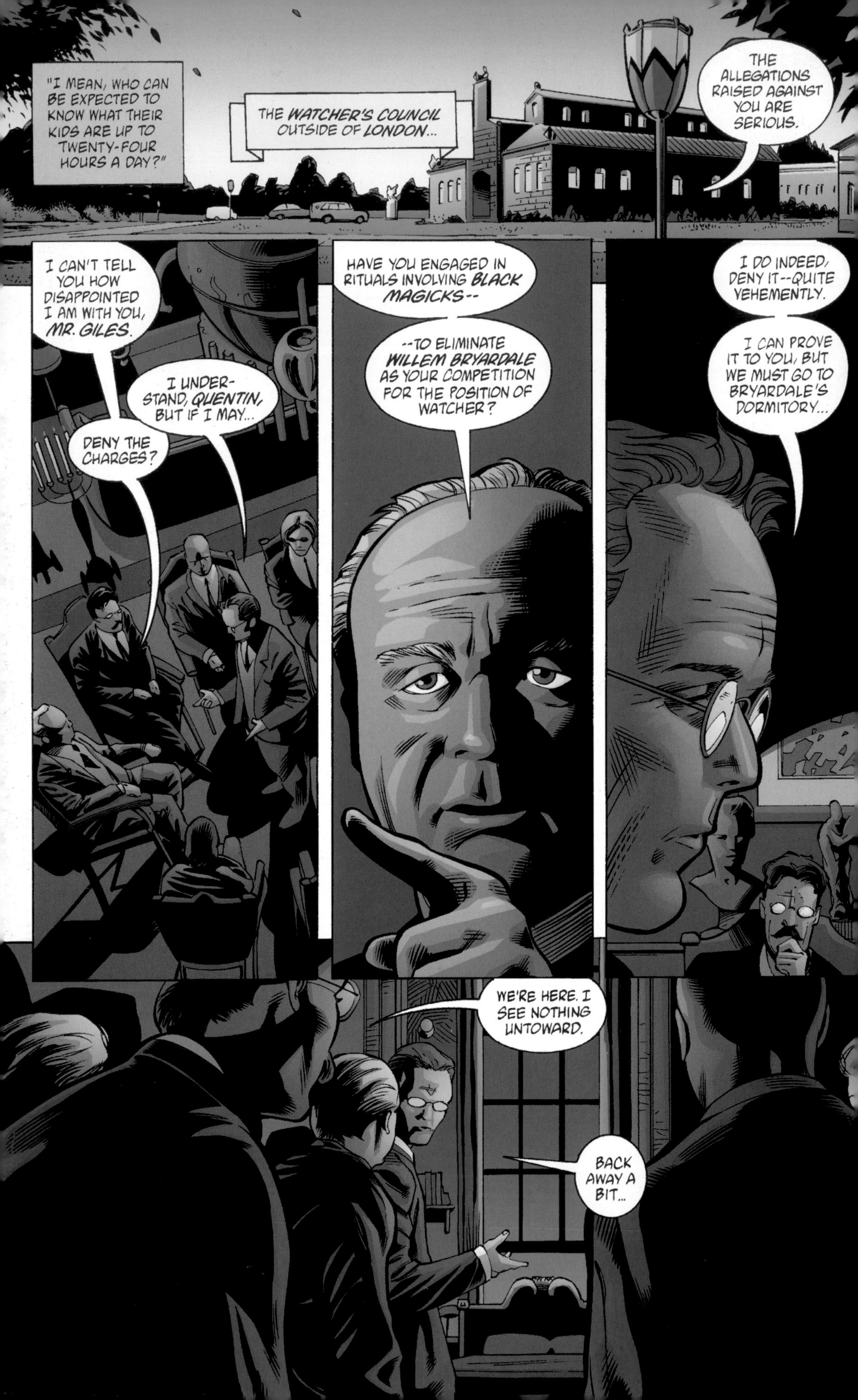
"I MEAN, WHO CAN BE EXPECTED TO KNOW WHAT THEIR KIDS ARE UP TO TWENTY-FOUR HOURS A DAY?"
THE WATCHER'S COUNCIL OUTSIDE OF LONDON...
THE ALLEGATIONS RAISED AGAINST YOU ARE SERIOUS.
I CAN'T TELL YOU HOW DISAPPOINTED I AM WITH YOU, MR. GILES.
I UNDERSTAND, QUENTIN, BUT IF I MAY...
DENY THE CHARGES?
HAVE YOU ENGAGED IN RITUALS INVOLVING BLACK MAGICKS--
--TO ELIMINATE WILLEM BRYARDALE AS YOUR COMPETITION FOR THE POSITION OF WATCHER?
I DO INDEED, DENY IT--QUITE VEHEMENTLY.
I CAN PROVE IT TO YOU, BUT WE MUST GO TO BRYARDALE'S DORMITORY...
WE'RE HERE. I SEE NOTHING UNTOWARD.
BACK AWAY A BIT...

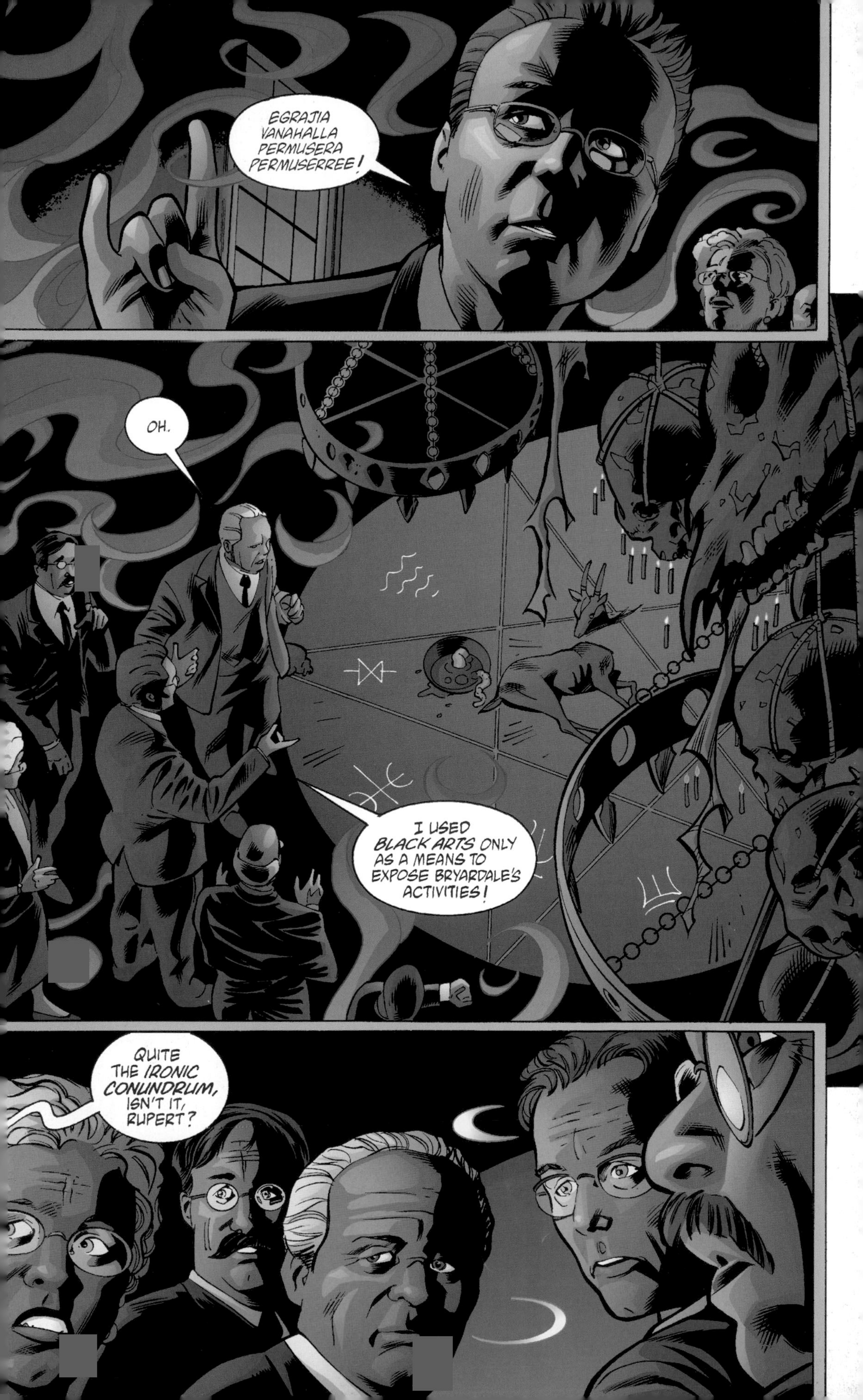
EGRAJIA VANAHALLA PERMUSERA PERMUSERREE!
OH.
I USED *BLACK ARTS* ONLY AS A MEANS TO EXPOSE BRYARDALE'S ACTIVITIES!
QUITE THE *IRONIC CONUNDRUM,* ISN'T IT, RUPERT?

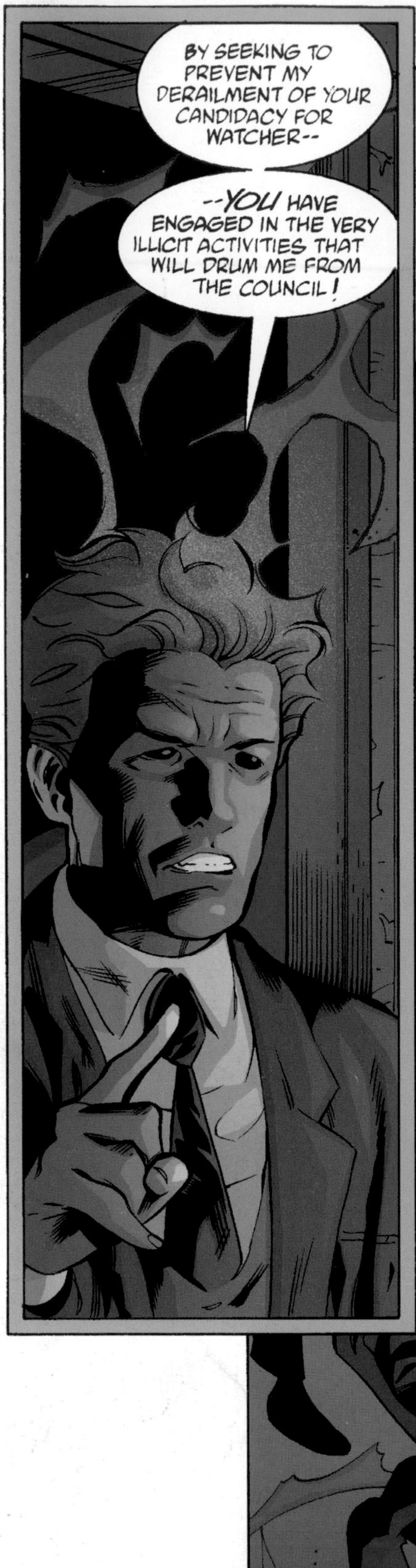
BY SEEKING TO PREVENT MY DERAILMENT OF YOUR CANDIDACY FOR WATCHER--
--YOU HAVE ENGAGED IN THE VERY ILLICIT ACTIVITIES THAT WILL DRUM ME FROM THE COUNCIL!
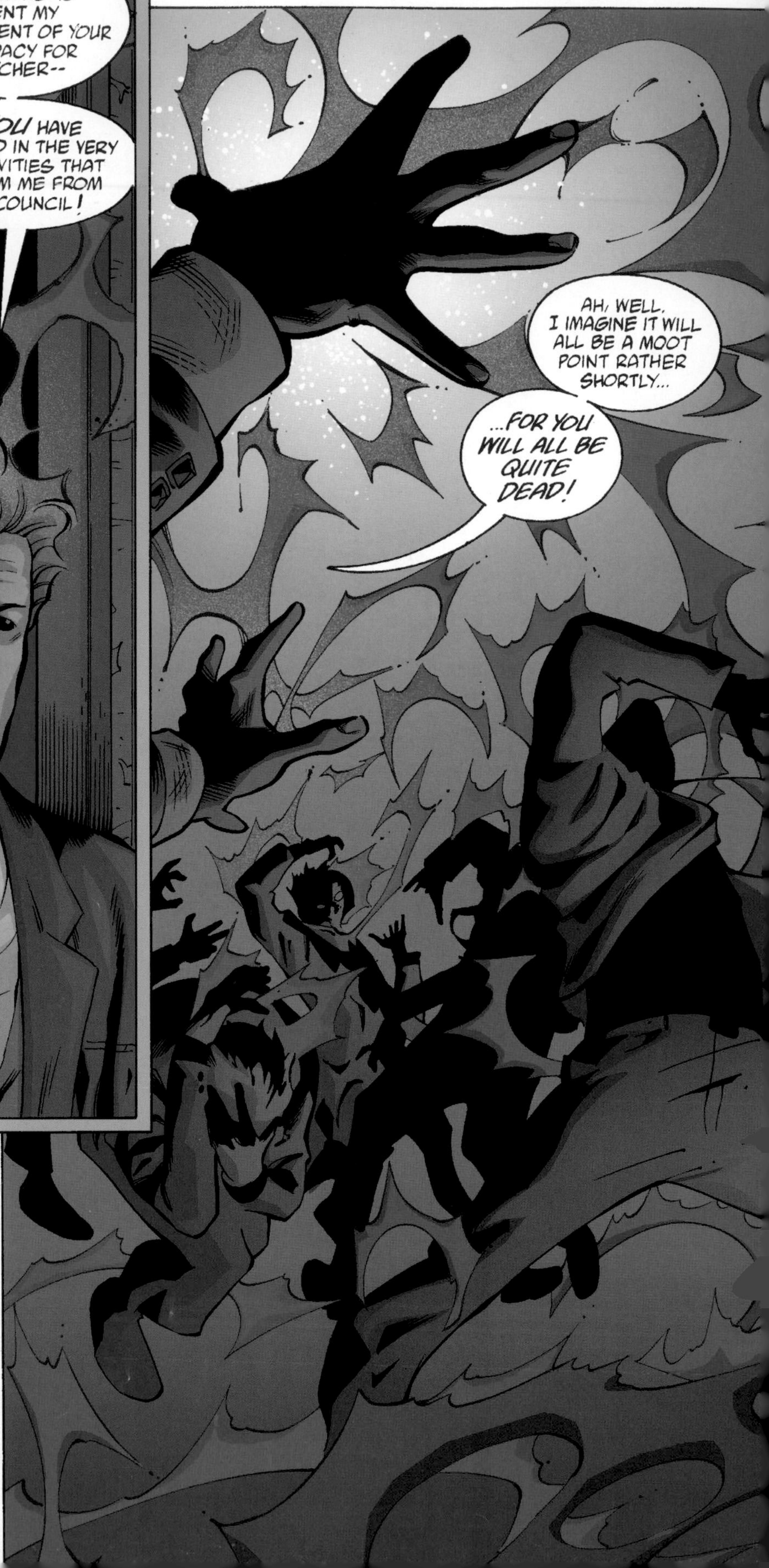
AH, WELL. I IMAGINE IT WILL ALL BE A MOOT POINT RATHER SHORTLY...
...FOR YOU WILL ALL BE QUITE DEAD!

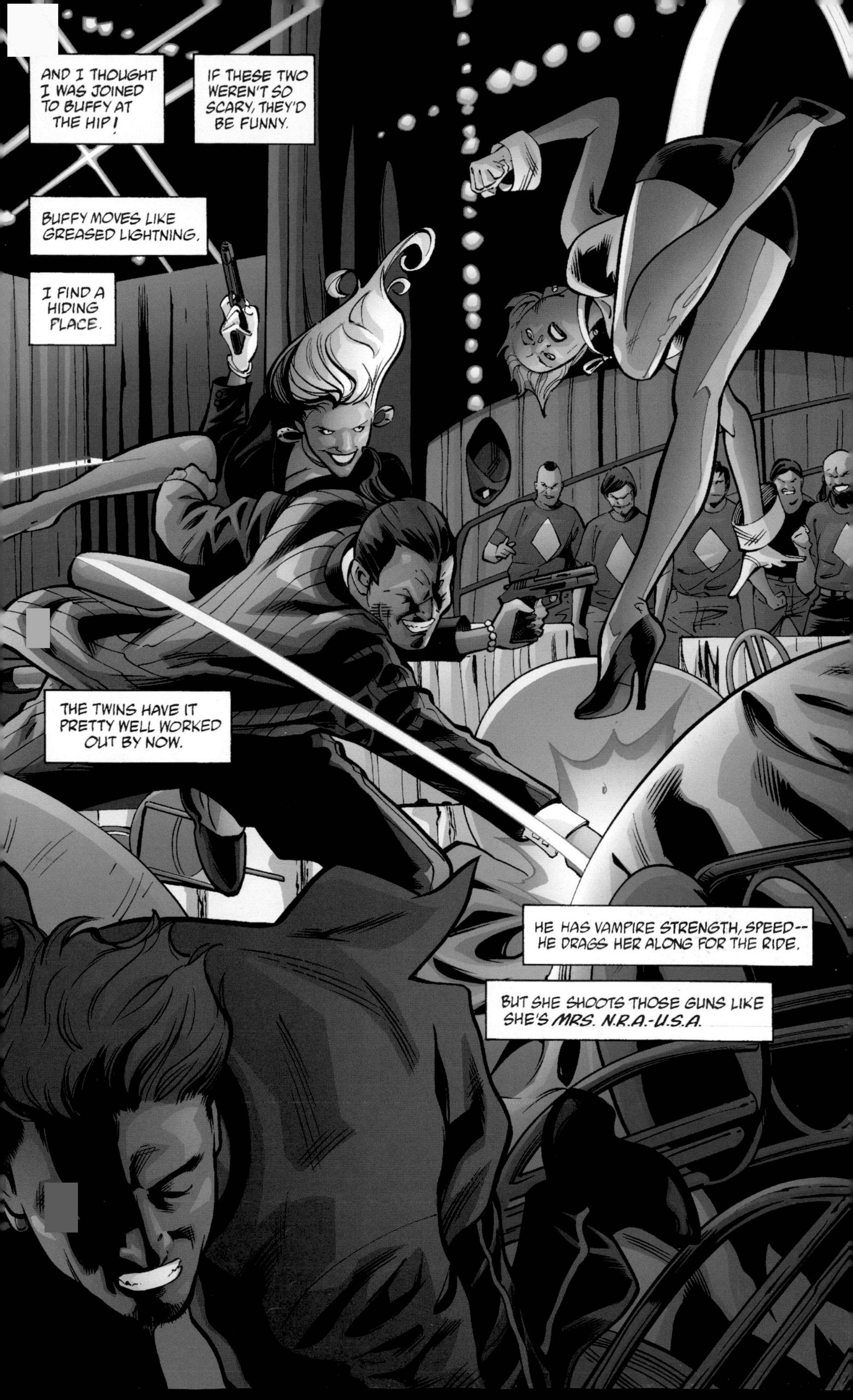
AND I THOUGHT I WAS JOINED TO BUFFY AT THE HIP!
IF THESE TWO WEREN'T SO SCARY, THEY'D BE FUNNY.
BUFFY MOVES LIKE GREASED LIGHTNING.
I FIND A HIDING PLACE.
THE TWINS HAVE IT PRETTY WELL WORKED OUT BY NOW.
HE HAS VAMPIRE STRENGTH, SPEED-- HE DRAGS HER ALONG FOR THE RIDE.
BUT SHE SHOOTS THOSE GUNS LIKE SHE'S *MRS. N.R.A.-U.S.A.*

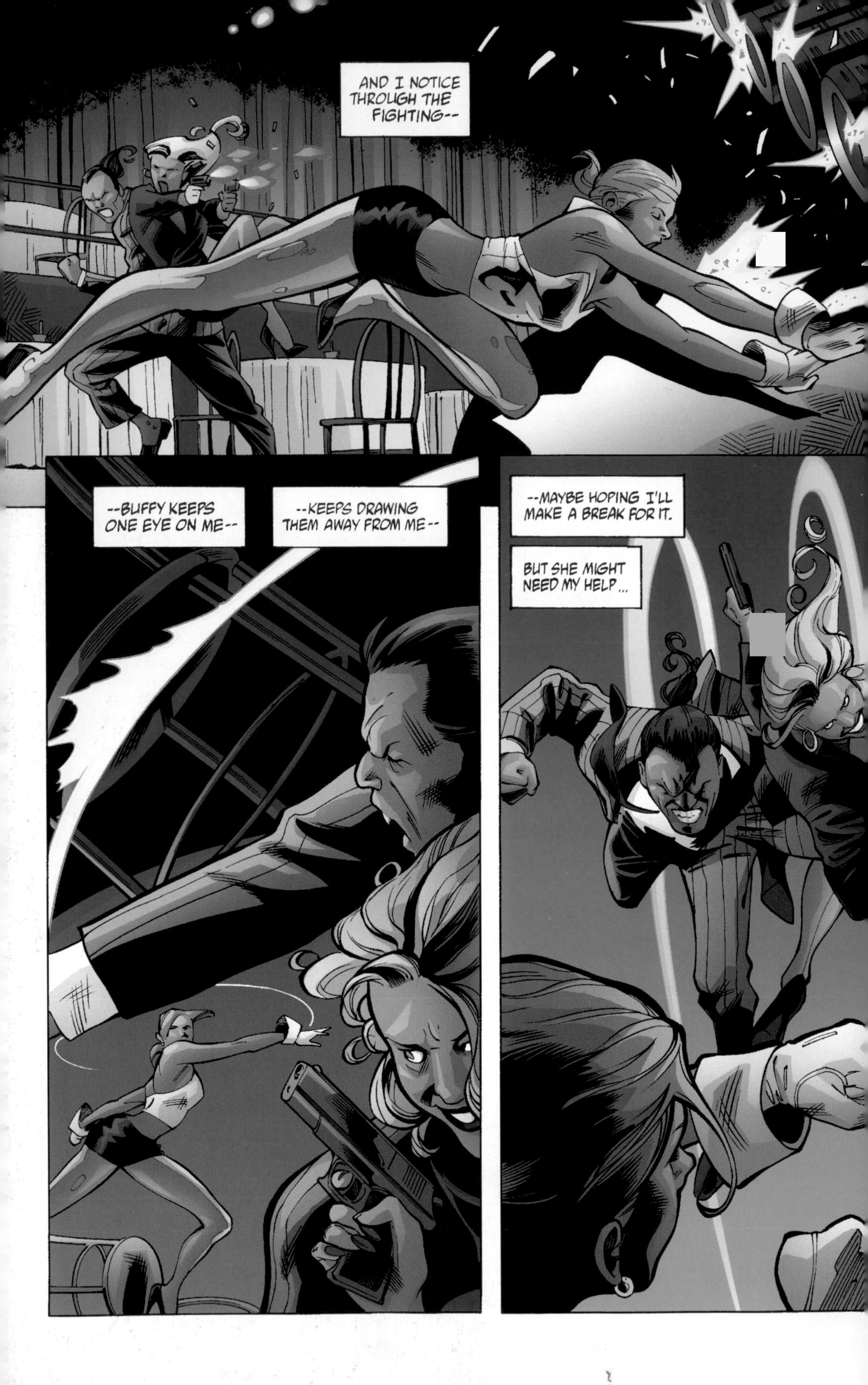
AND I NOTICE THROUGH THE FIGHTING--
--BUFFY KEEPS ONE EYE ON ME--
--KEEPS DRAWING THEM AWAY FROM ME--
--MAYBE HOPING I'LL MAKE A BREAK FOR IT.
BUT SHE MIGHT NEED MY HELP...

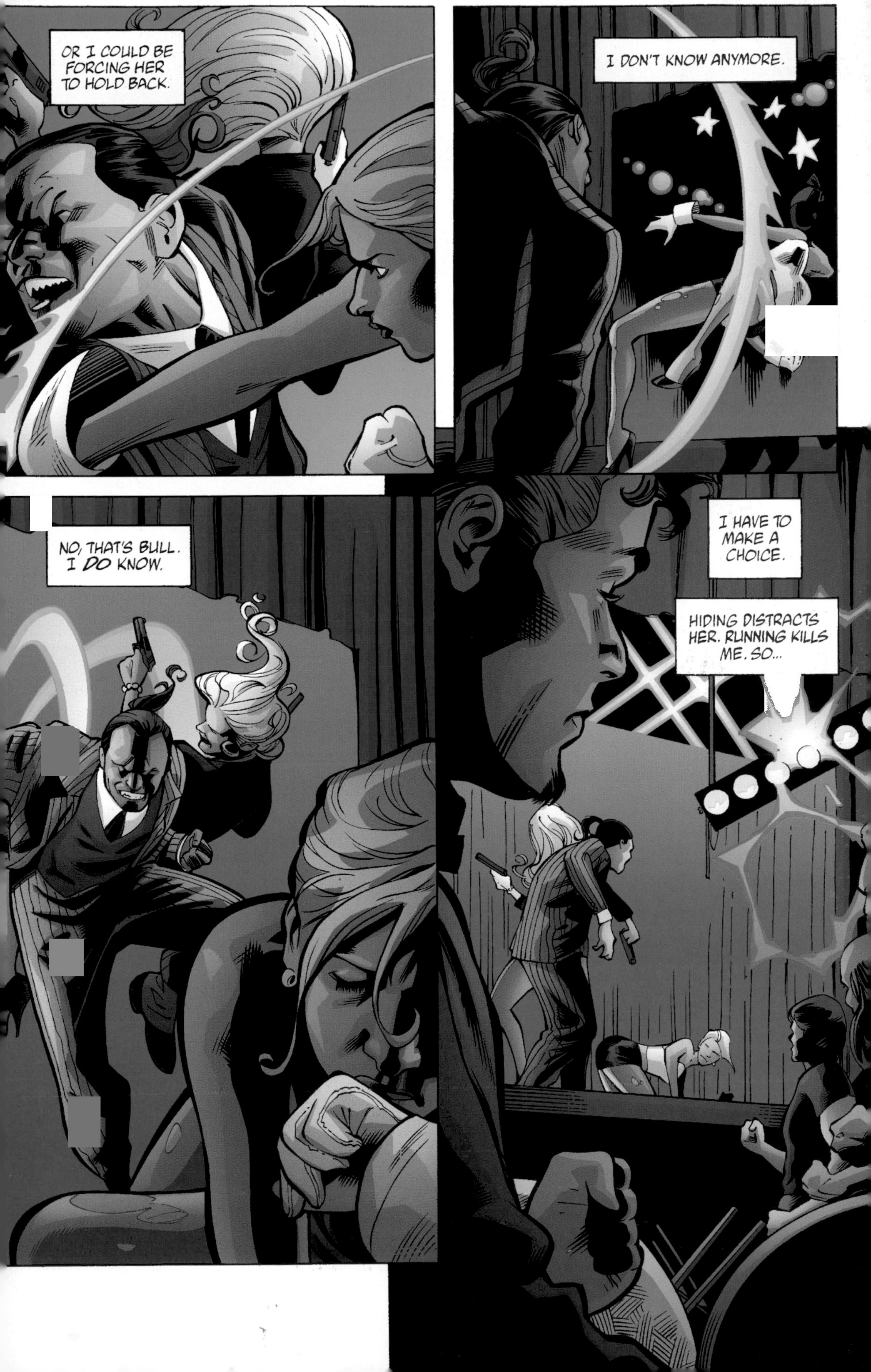
OR I COULD BE FORCING HER TO HOLD BACK.
I DON'T KNOW ANYMORE.
NO, THAT'S BULL. I DO KNOW.
I HAVE TO MAKE A CHOICE.
HIDING DISTRACTS HER. RUNNING KILLS ME. SO...

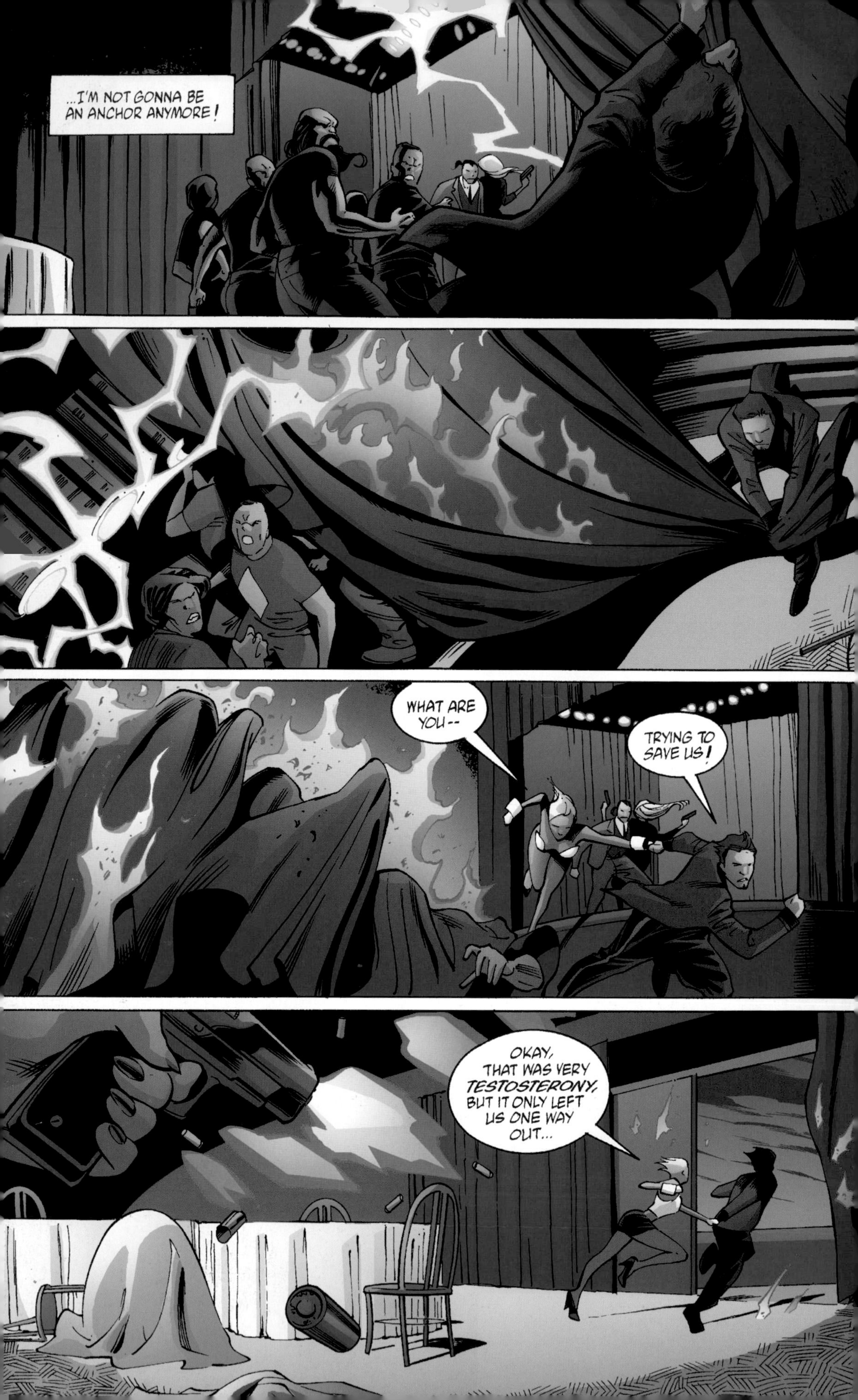
...I'M NOT GONNA BE AN ANCHOR ANYMORE!
WHAT ARE YOU--
TRYING TO SAVE US!
OKAY, THAT WAS VERY *TESTOSTERONY*, BUT IT ONLY LEFT US ONE WAY OUT...

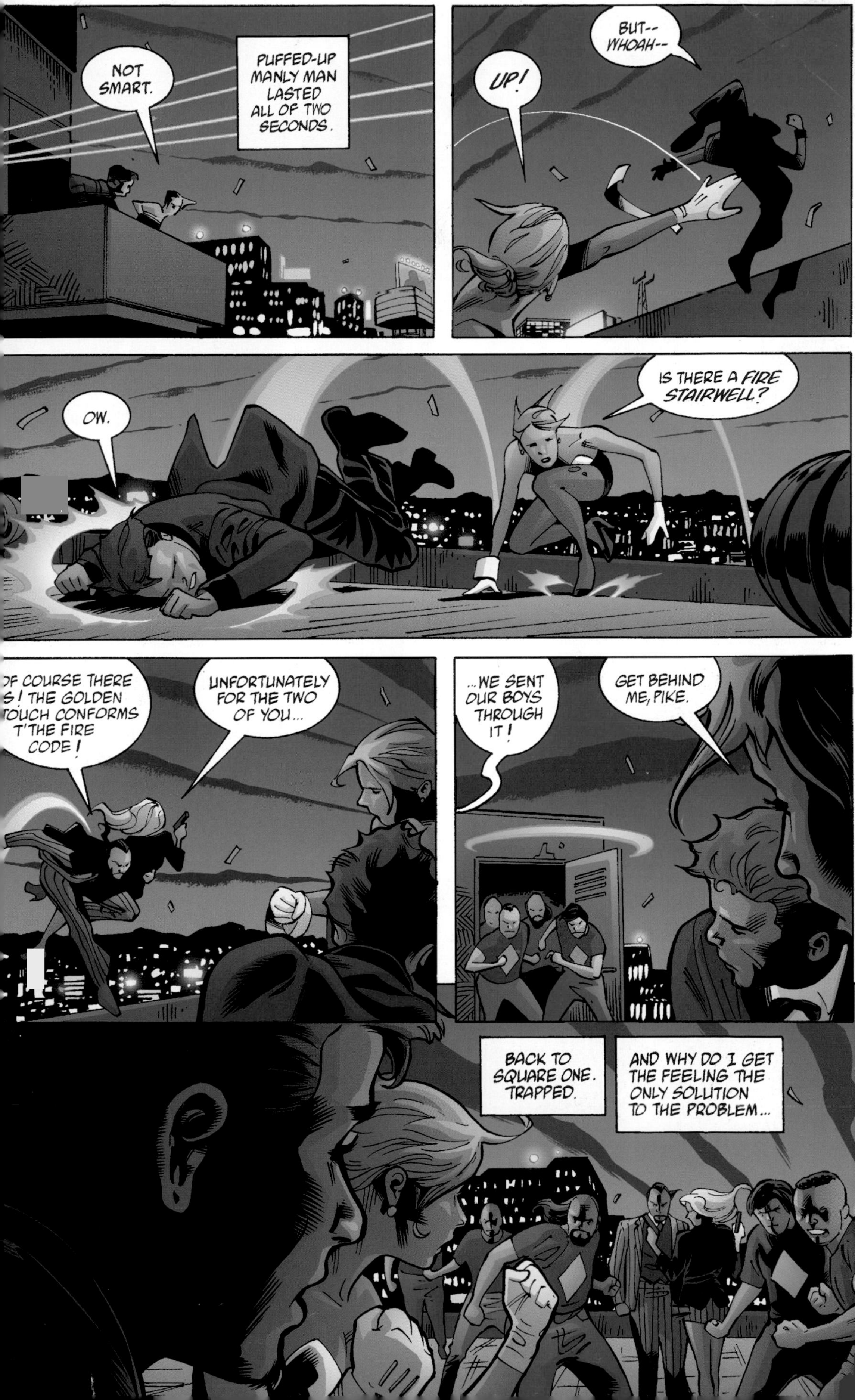
NOT SMART.
PUFFED-UP MANLY MAN LASTED ALL OF TWO SECONDS.
UP!
BUT-- WHOAH--
OW.
IS THERE A FIRE STAIRWELL?
F COURSE THERE S! THE GOLDEN TOUCH CONFORMS T' THE FIRE CODE!
UNFORTUNATELY FOR THE TWO OF YOU...
...WE SENT OUR BOYS THROUGH IT!
GET BEHIND ME, PIKE.
BACK TO SQUARE ONE. TRAPPED.
AND WHY DO I GET THE FEELING THE ONLY SOLUTION TO THE PROBLEM...

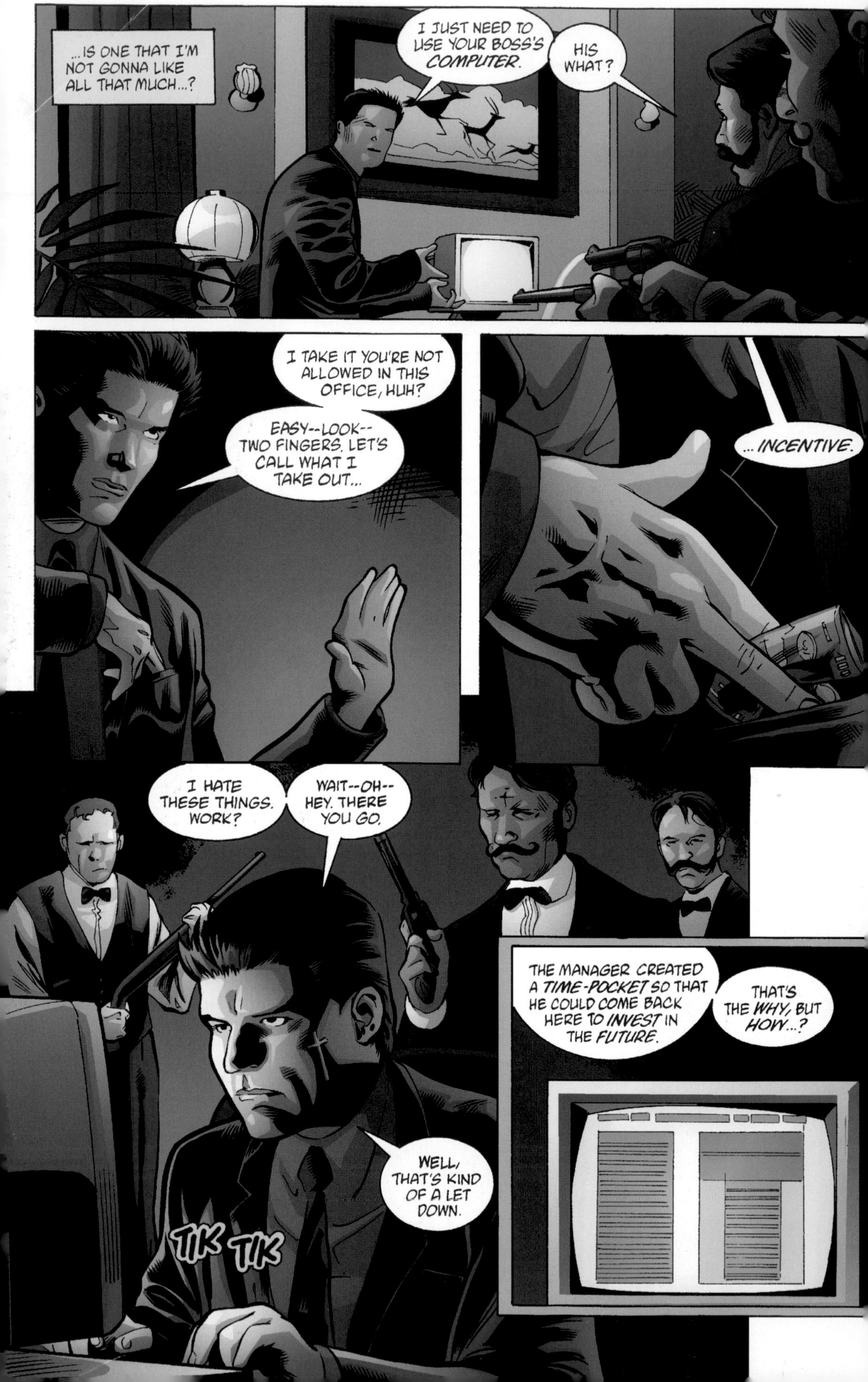
...IS ONE THAT I'M NOT GONNA LIKE ALL THAT MUCH...?
I JUST NEED TO USE YOUR BOSS'S *COMPUTER*.
HIS WHAT?
I TAKE IT YOU'RE NOT ALLOWED IN THIS OFFICE, HUH?
EASY--LOOK-- TWO FINGERS. LET'S CALL WHAT I TAKE OUT...
...*INCENTIVE*.
I HATE THESE THINGS. WORK?
WAIT--OH-- HEY. THERE YOU GO.
WELL, THAT'S KIND OF A LET DOWN.
TIK TIK
THE MANAGER CREATED A *TIME-POCKET* SO THAT HE COULD COME BACK HERE TO *INVEST* IN THE *FUTURE*.
THAT'S THE *WHY*, BUT *HOW*...?

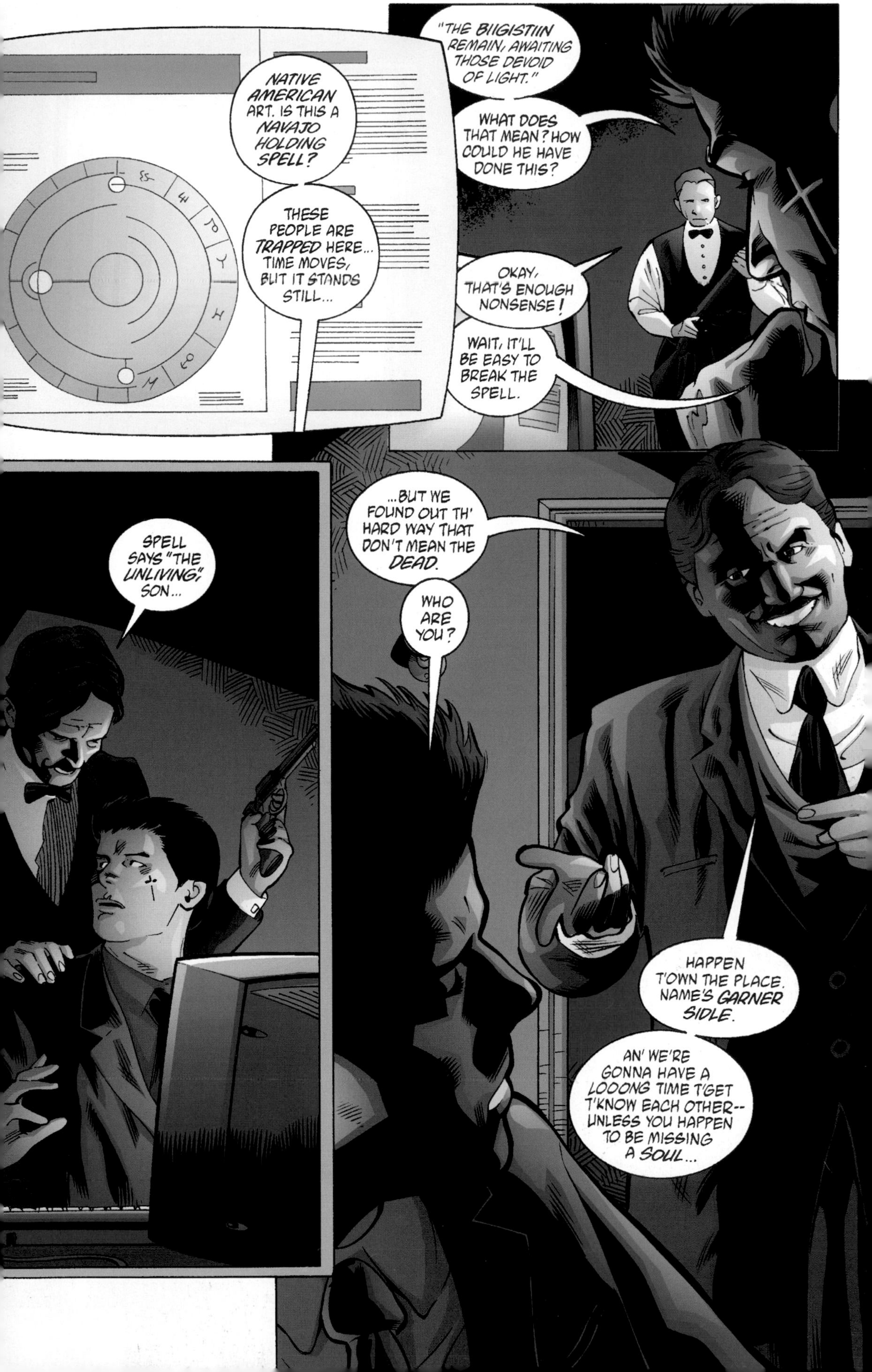
NATIVE AMERICAN ART. IS THIS A NAVAJO HOLDING SPELL?
THESE PEOPLE ARE TRAPPED HERE... TIME MOVES, BUT IT STANDS STILL...
"THE BIIGISTIIN REMAIN, AWAITING THOSE DEVOID OF LIGHT."
WHAT DOES THAT MEAN? HOW COULD HE HAVE DONE THIS?
OKAY, THAT'S ENOUGH NONSENSE!
WAIT, IT'LL BE EASY TO BREAK THE SPELL.
SPELL SAYS "THE UNLIVING," SON...
...BUT WE FOUND OUT TH' HARD WAY THAT DON'T MEAN THE DEAD.
WHO ARE YOU?
HAPPEN T'OWN THE PLACE. NAME'S GARNER SIDLE.
AN' WE'RE GONNA HAVE A LOOONG TIME T'GET T'KNOW EACH OTHER-- UNLESS YOU HAPPEN TO BE MISSING A SOUL...

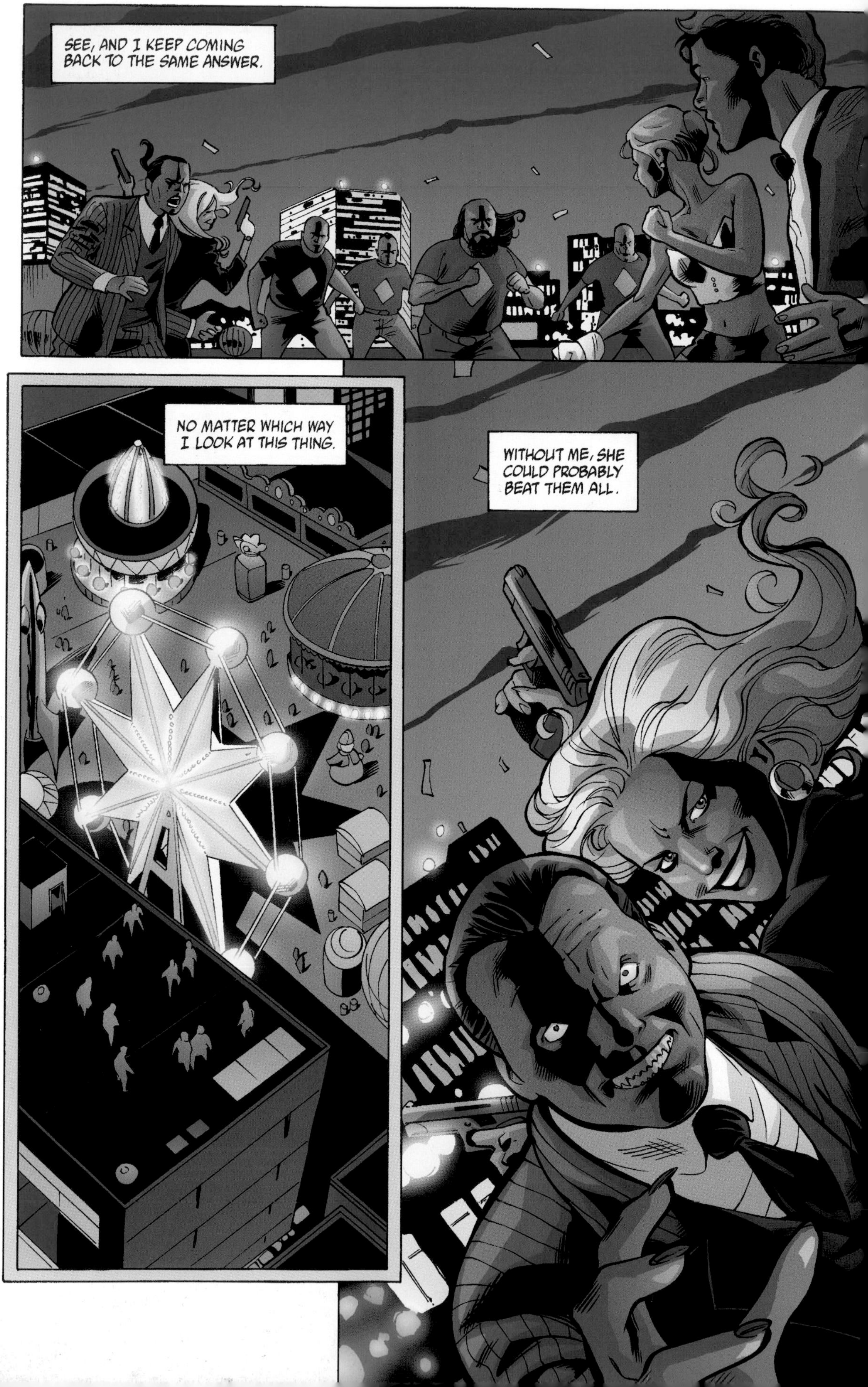
SEE, AND I KEEP COMING BACK TO THE SAME ANSWER.
NO MATTER WHICH WAY I LOOK AT THIS THING.
WITHOUT ME, SHE COULD PROBABLY BEAT THEM ALL.

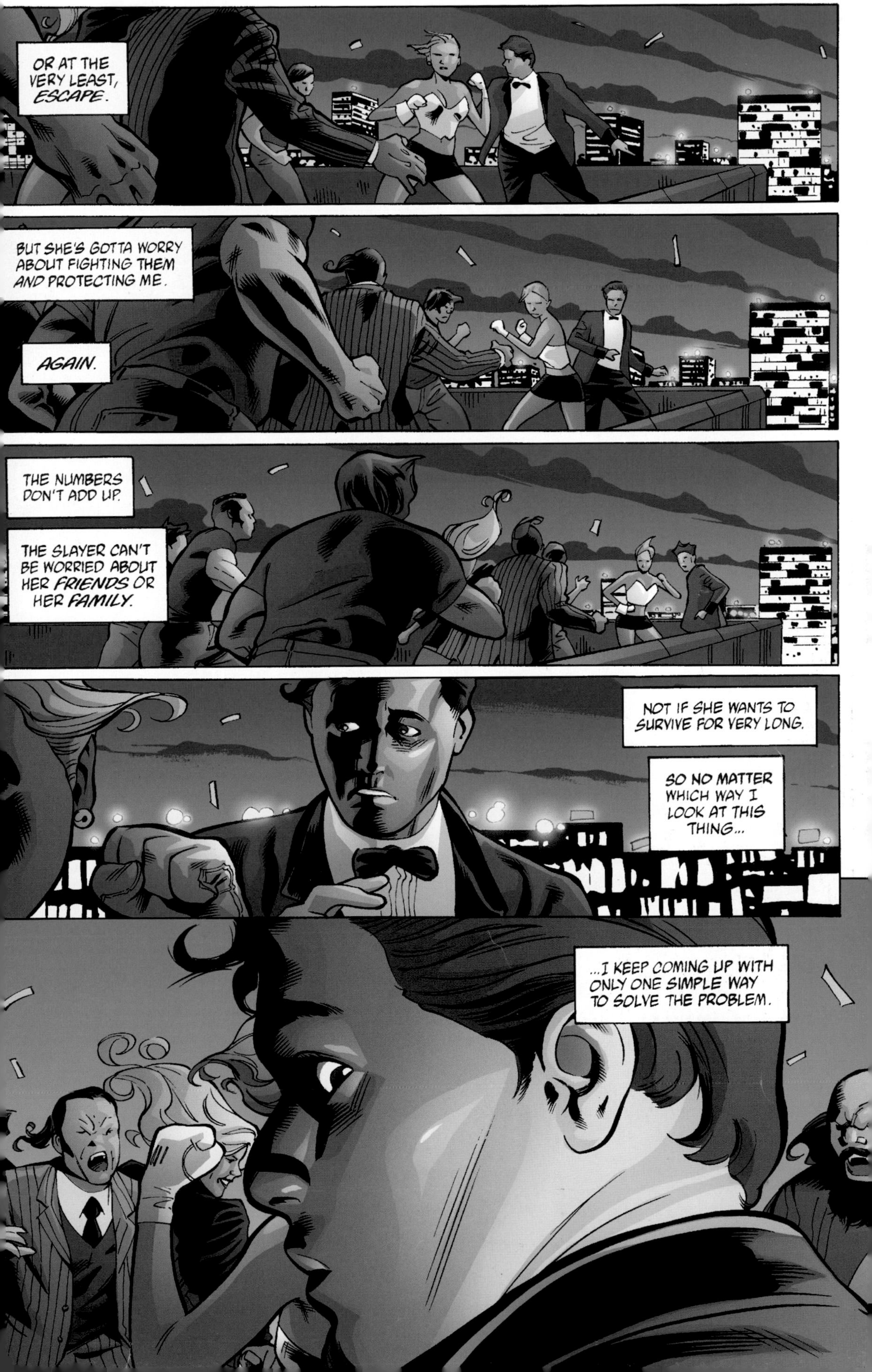
OR AT THE VERY LEAST, ESCAPE.
BUT SHE'S GOTTA WORRY ABOUT FIGHTING THEM AND PROTECTING ME.
AGAIN.
THE NUMBERS DON'T ADD UP.
THE SLAYER CAN'T BE WORRIED ABOUT HER FRIENDS OR HER FAMILY.
NOT IF SHE WANTS TO SURVIVE FOR VERY LONG.
SO NO MATTER WHICH WAY I LOOK AT THIS THING...
...I KEEP COMING UP WITH ONLY ONE SIMPLE WAY TO SOLVE THE PROBLEM.

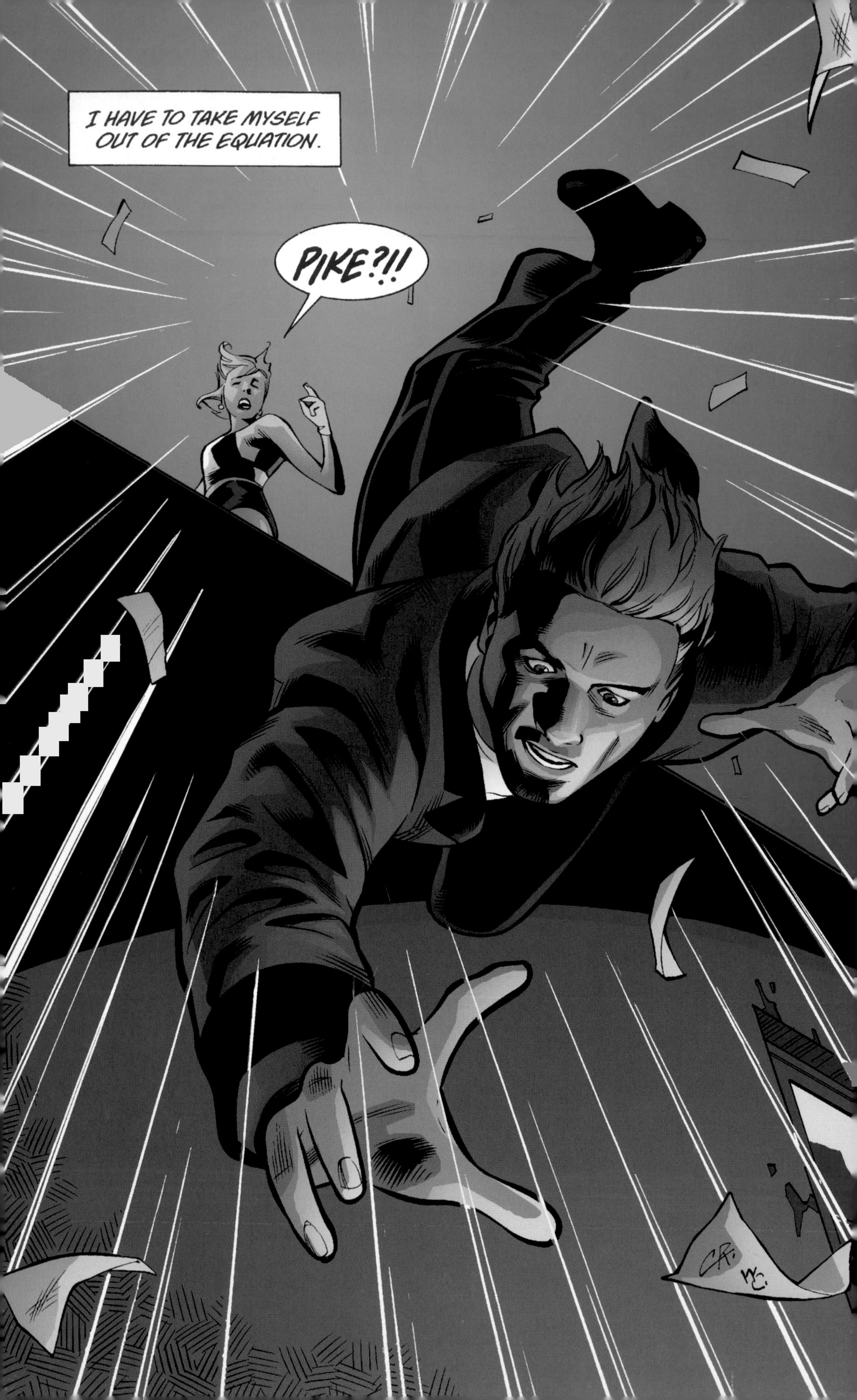
I HAVE TO TAKE MYSELF OUT OF THE EQUATION.
PIKE?!!

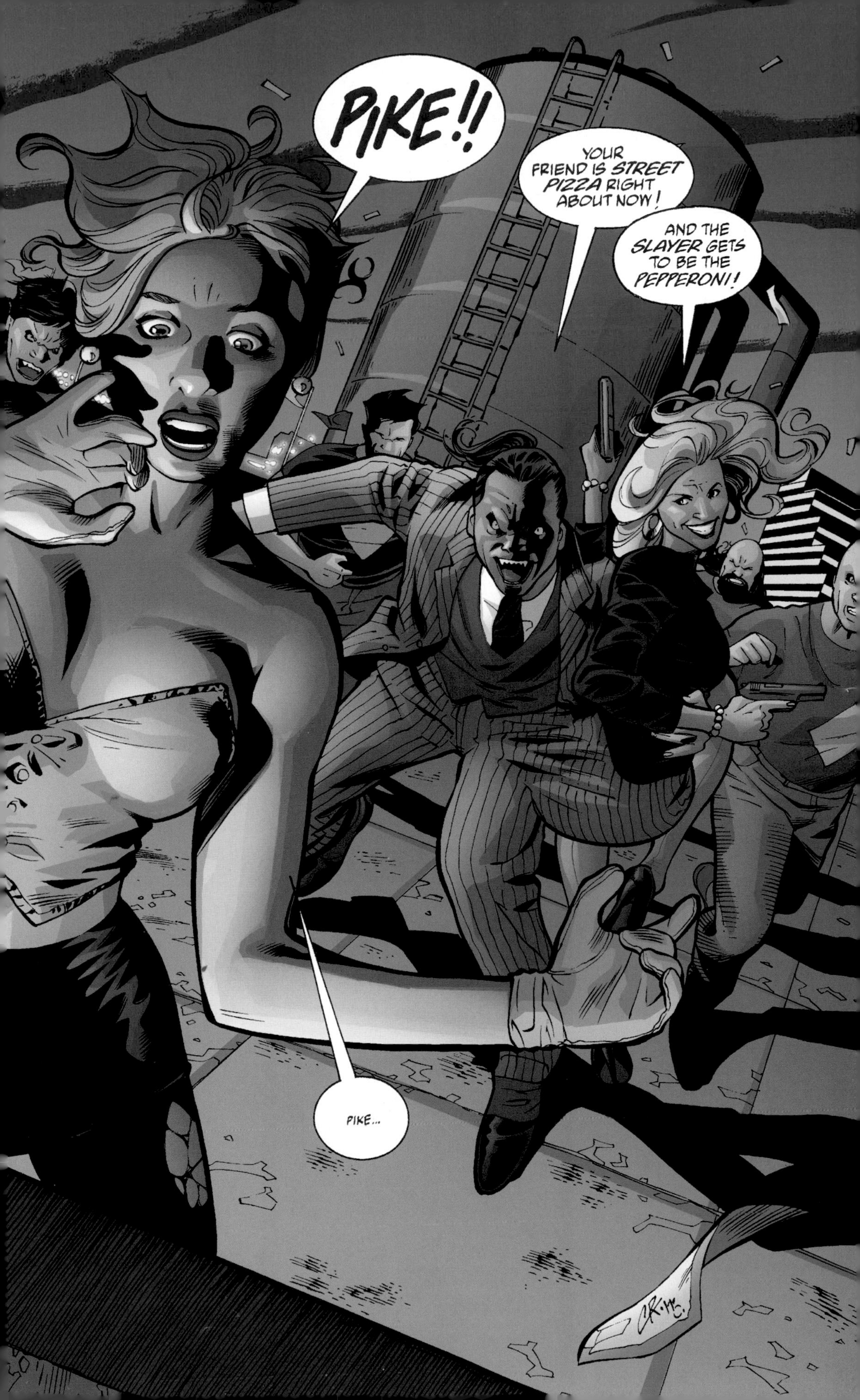
PIKE!!
YOUR FRIEND IS STREET PIZZA RIGHT ABOUT NOW!
AND THE SLAYER GETS TO BE THE PEPPERONI!
PIKE...

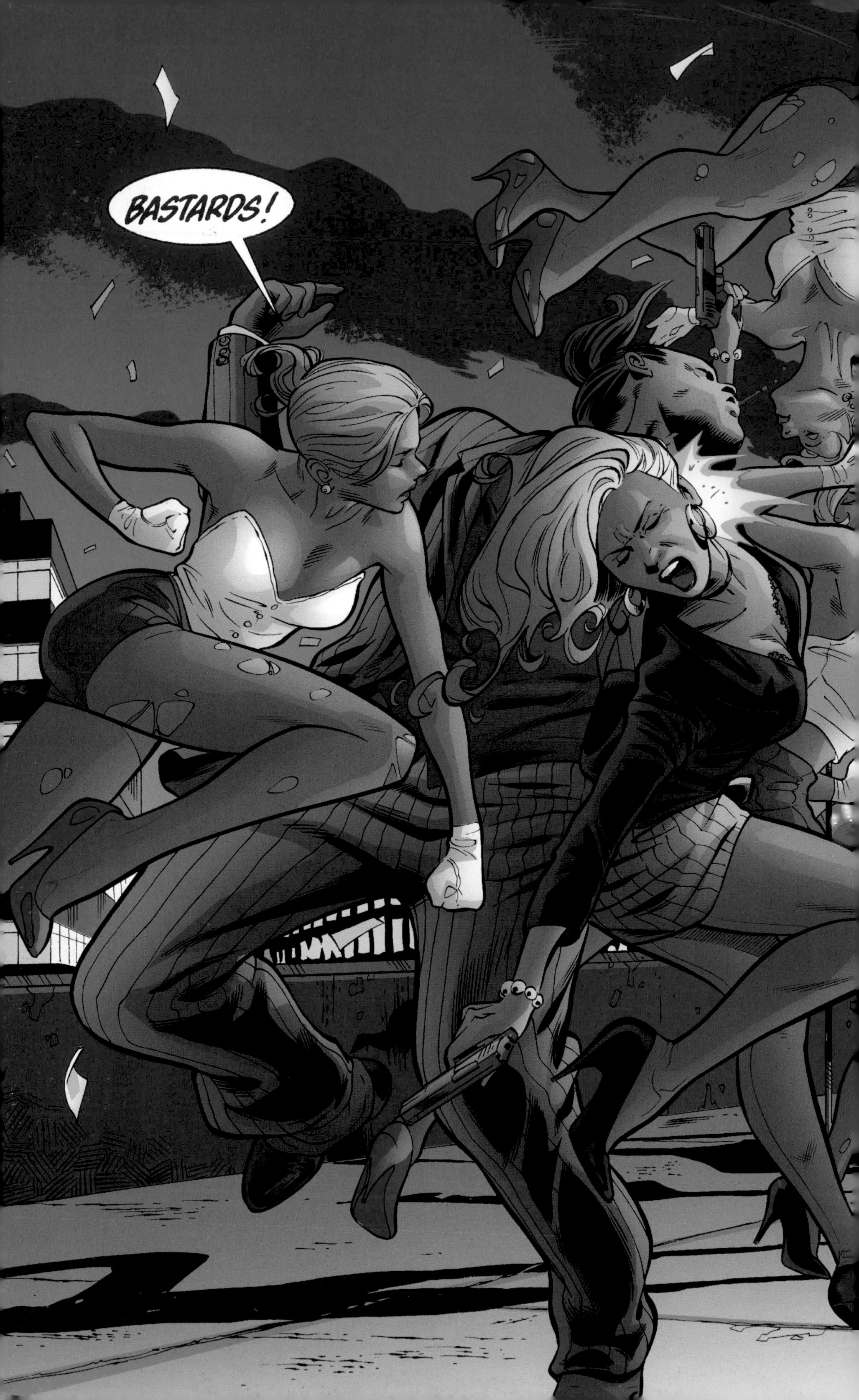
BASTARDS!

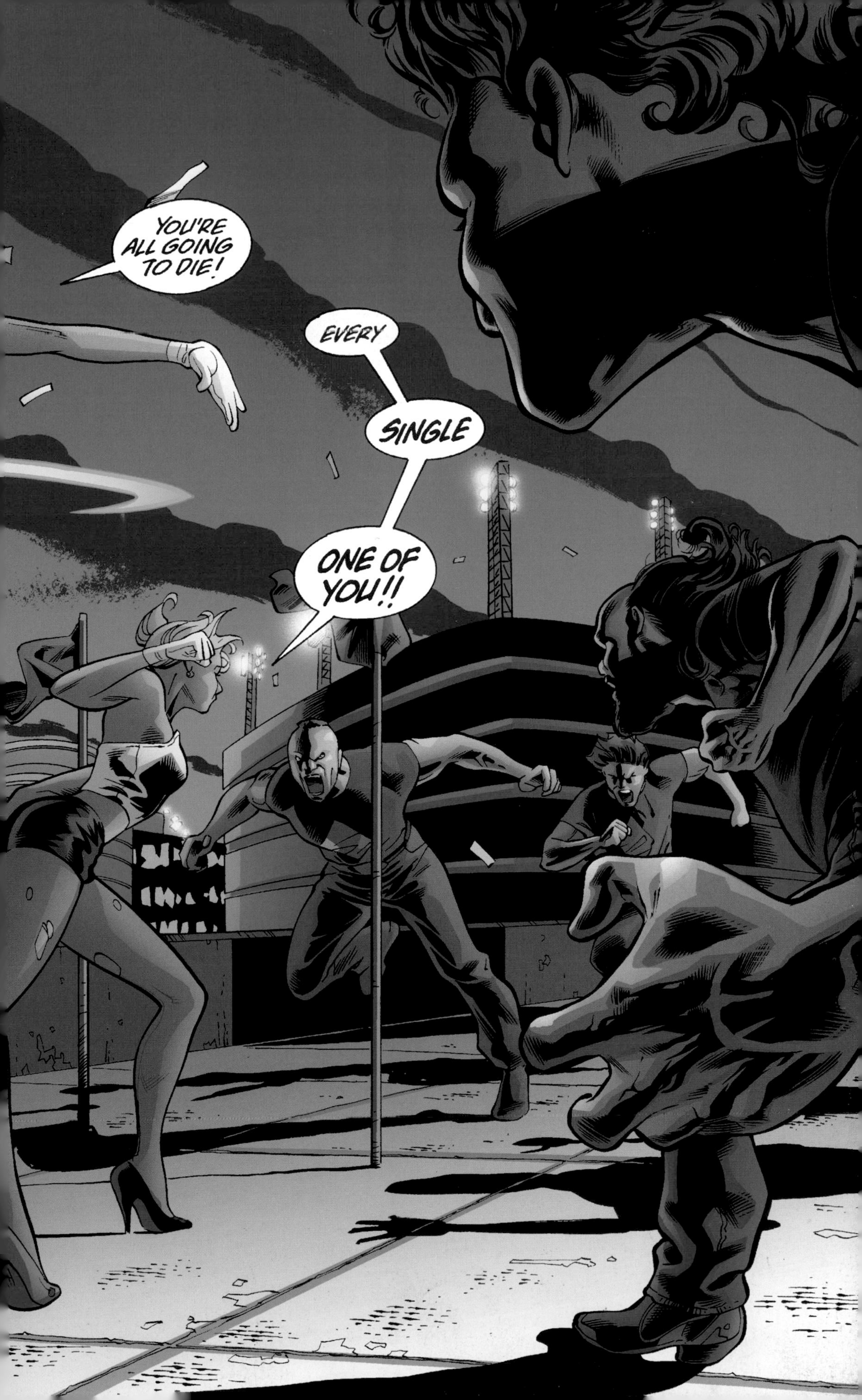
YOU'RE ALL GOING TO DIE!
EVERY
SINGLE
ONE OF YOU!!

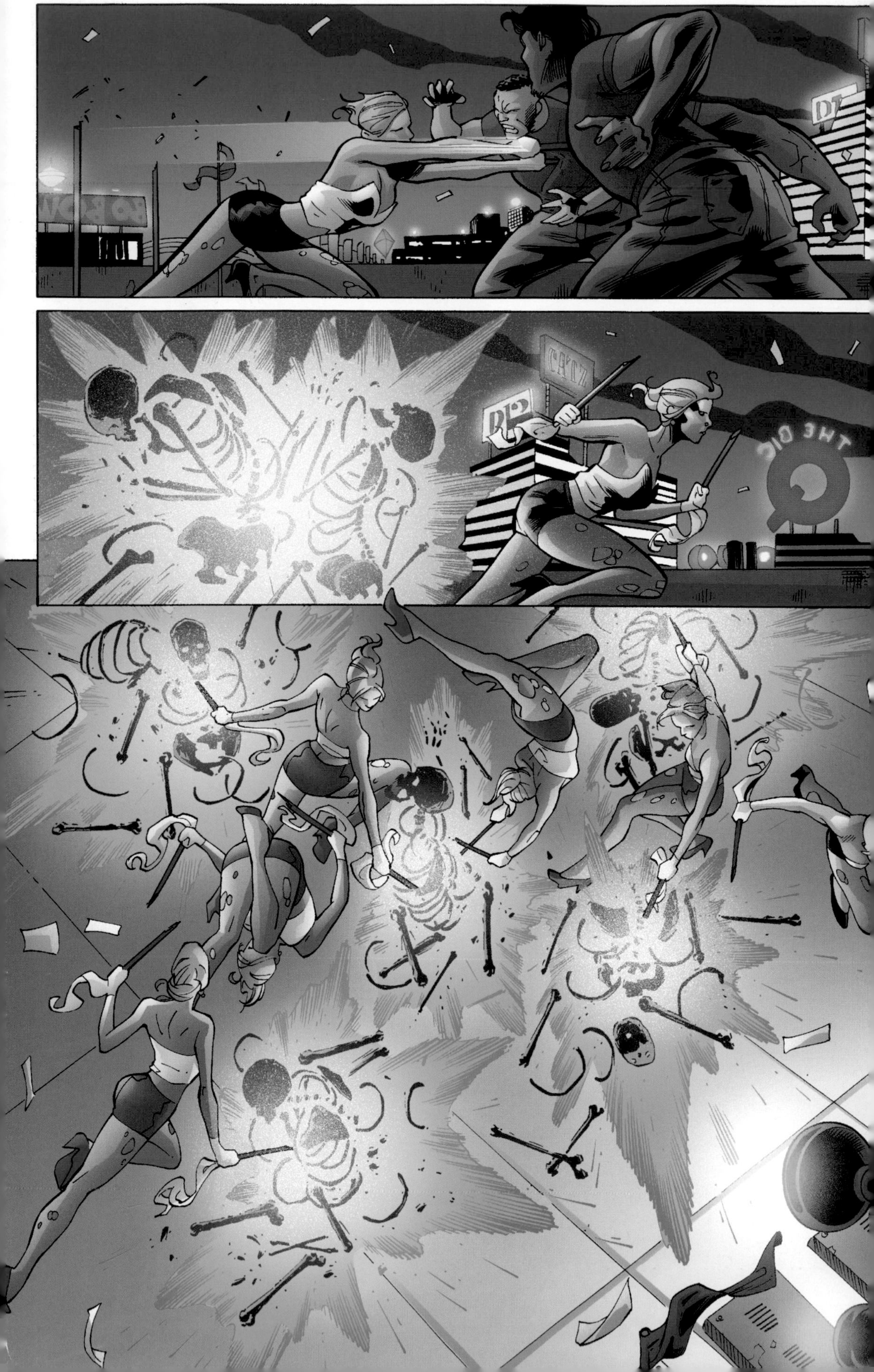

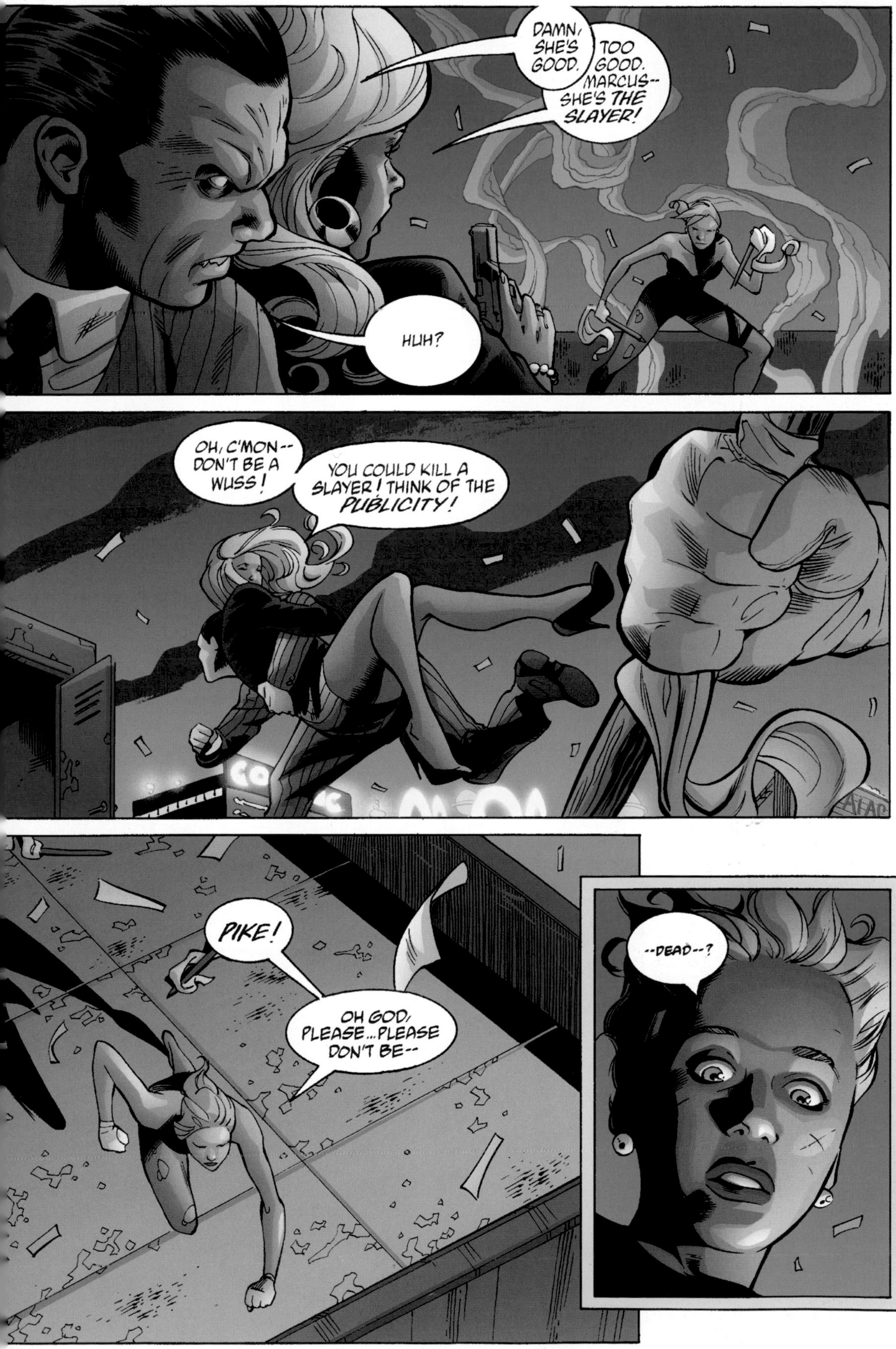

DAMN, SHE'S GOOD.
TOO GOOD. MARCUS-- SHE'S THE SLAYER!
HUH?
OH, C'MON-- DON'T BE A WUSS!
YOU COULD KILL A SLAYER! THINK OF THE PUBLICITY!
PIKE!
OH GOD, PLEASE...PLEASE DON'T BE--
--DEAD--?

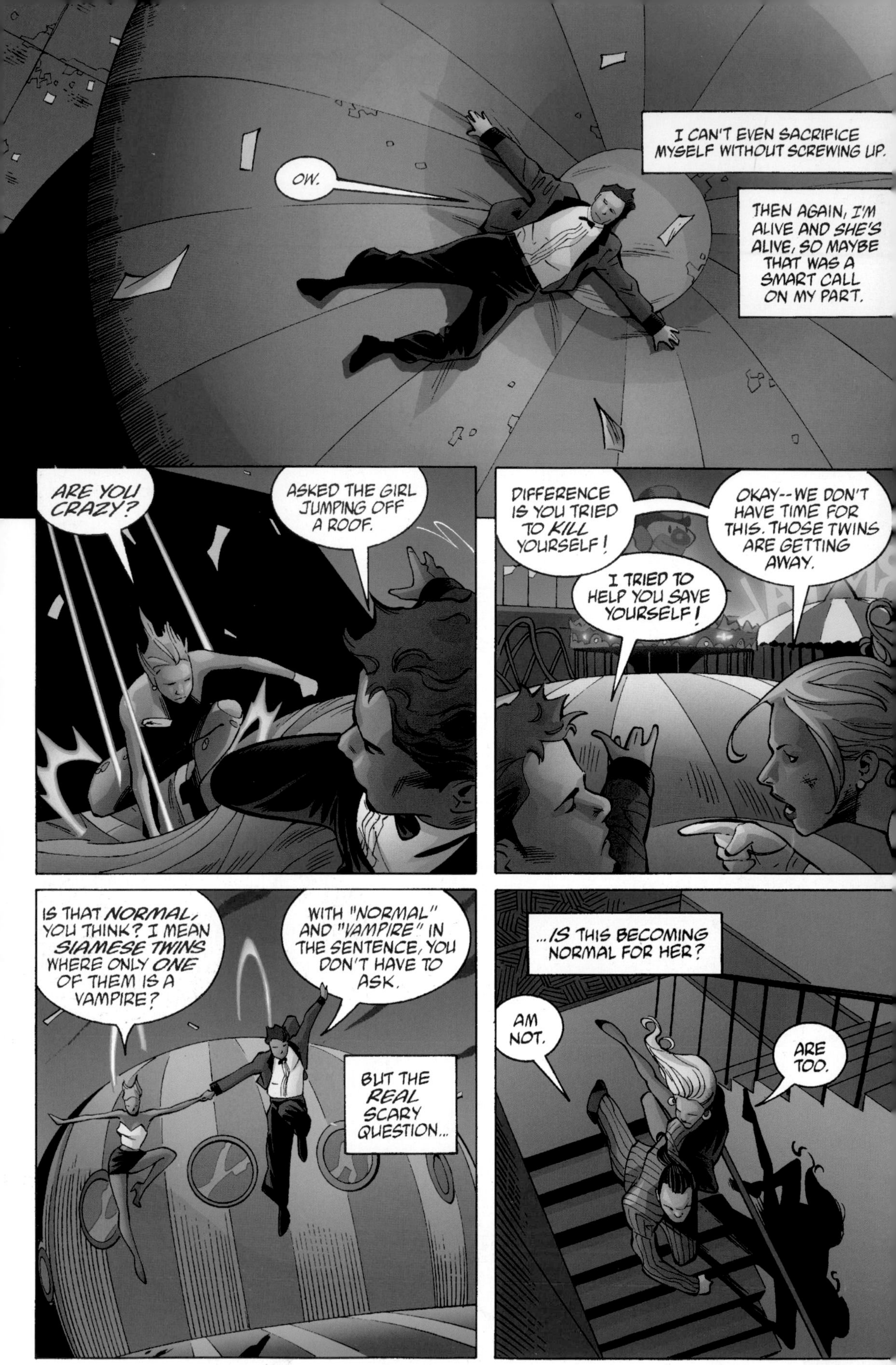
OW.
I CAN'T EVEN SACRIFICE MYSELF WITHOUT SCREWING UP.
THEN AGAIN, I'M ALIVE AND SHE'S ALIVE, SO MAYBE THAT WAS A SMART CALL ON MY PART.
ARE YOU CRAZY?
ASKED THE GIRL JUMPING OFF A ROOF.
DIFFERENCE IS YOU TRIED TO KILL YOURSELF!
I TRIED TO HELP YOU SAVE YOURSELF!
OKAY--WE DON'T HAVE TIME FOR THIS. THOSE TWINS ARE GETTING AWAY.
IS THAT NORMAL, YOU THINK? I MEAN SIAMESE TWINS WHERE ONLY ONE OF THEM IS A VAMPIRE?
WITH "NORMAL" AND "VAMPIRE" IN THE SENTENCE, YOU DON'T HAVE TO ASK.
BUT THE REAL SCARY QUESTION...
...IS THIS BECOMING NORMAL FOR HER?
AM NOT.
ARE TOO.

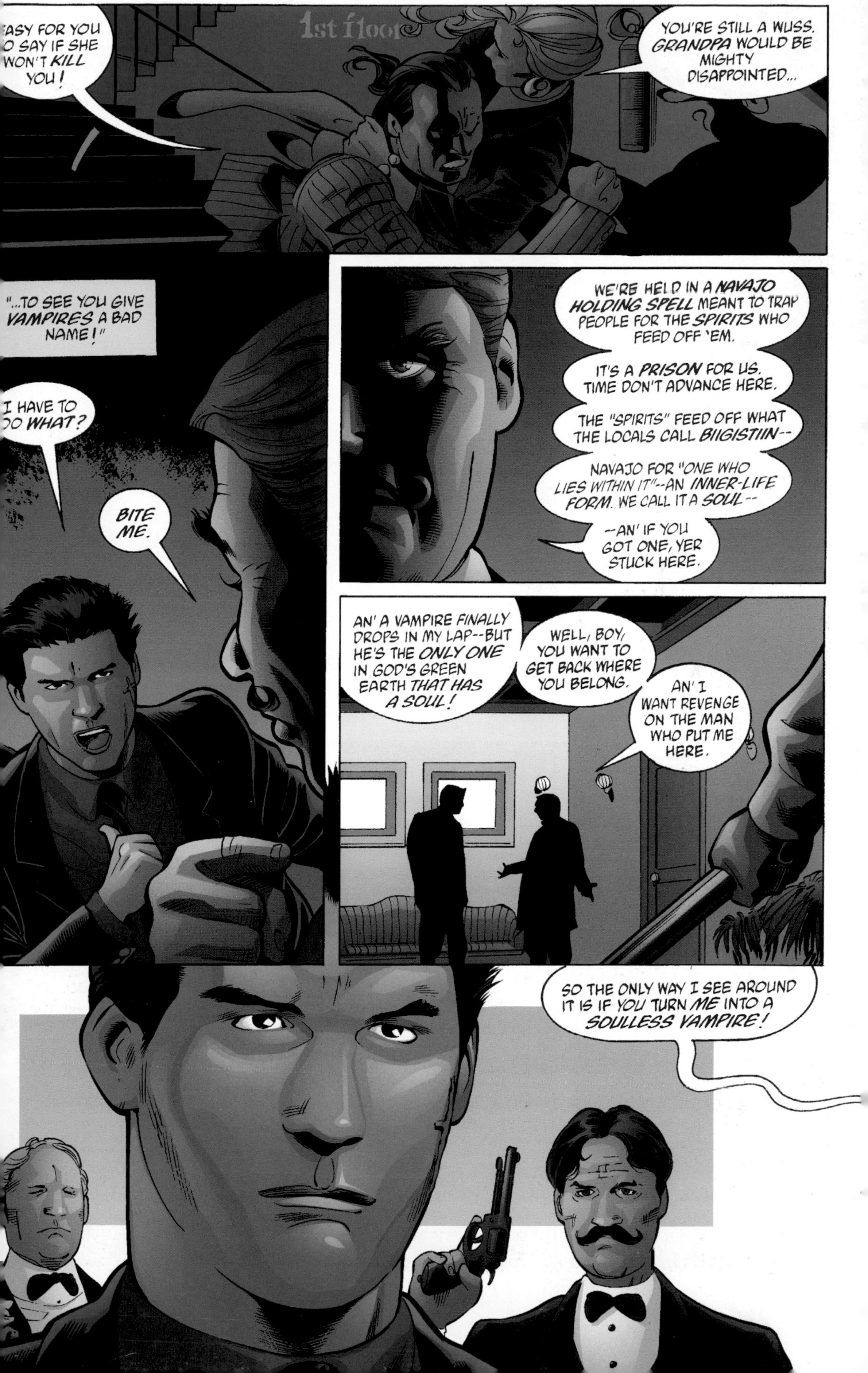
1st floor
EASY FOR YOU TO SAY IF SHE WON'T KILL YOU!
YOU'RE STILL A WUSS. GRANDPA WOULD BE MIGHTY DISAPPOINTED...
"...TO SEE YOU GIVE VAMPIRES A BAD NAME!"
I HAVE TO DO WHAT?
BITE ME.
WE'RE HELD IN A NAVAJO HOLDING SPELL MEANT TO TRAP PEOPLE FOR THE SPIRITS WHO FEED OFF 'EM.
IT'S A PRISON FOR US. TIME DON'T ADVANCE HERE.
THE "SPIRITS" FEED OFF WHAT THE LOCALS CALL BIIGISTIIN--
NAVAJO FOR "ONE WHO LIES WITHIN IT"--AN INNER-LIFE FORM. WE CALL IT A SOUL--
--AN' IF YOU GOT ONE, YER STUCK HERE.
AN' A VAMPIRE FINALLY DROPS IN MY LAP--BUT HE'S THE ONLY ONE IN GOD'S GREEN EARTH THAT HAS A SOUL!
WELL, BOY, YOU WANT TO GET BACK WHERE YOU BELONG.
AN' I WANT REVENGE ON THE MAN WHO PUT ME HERE.
SO THE ONLY WAY I SEE AROUND IT IS IF YOU TURN ME INTO A SOULLESS VAMPIRE!

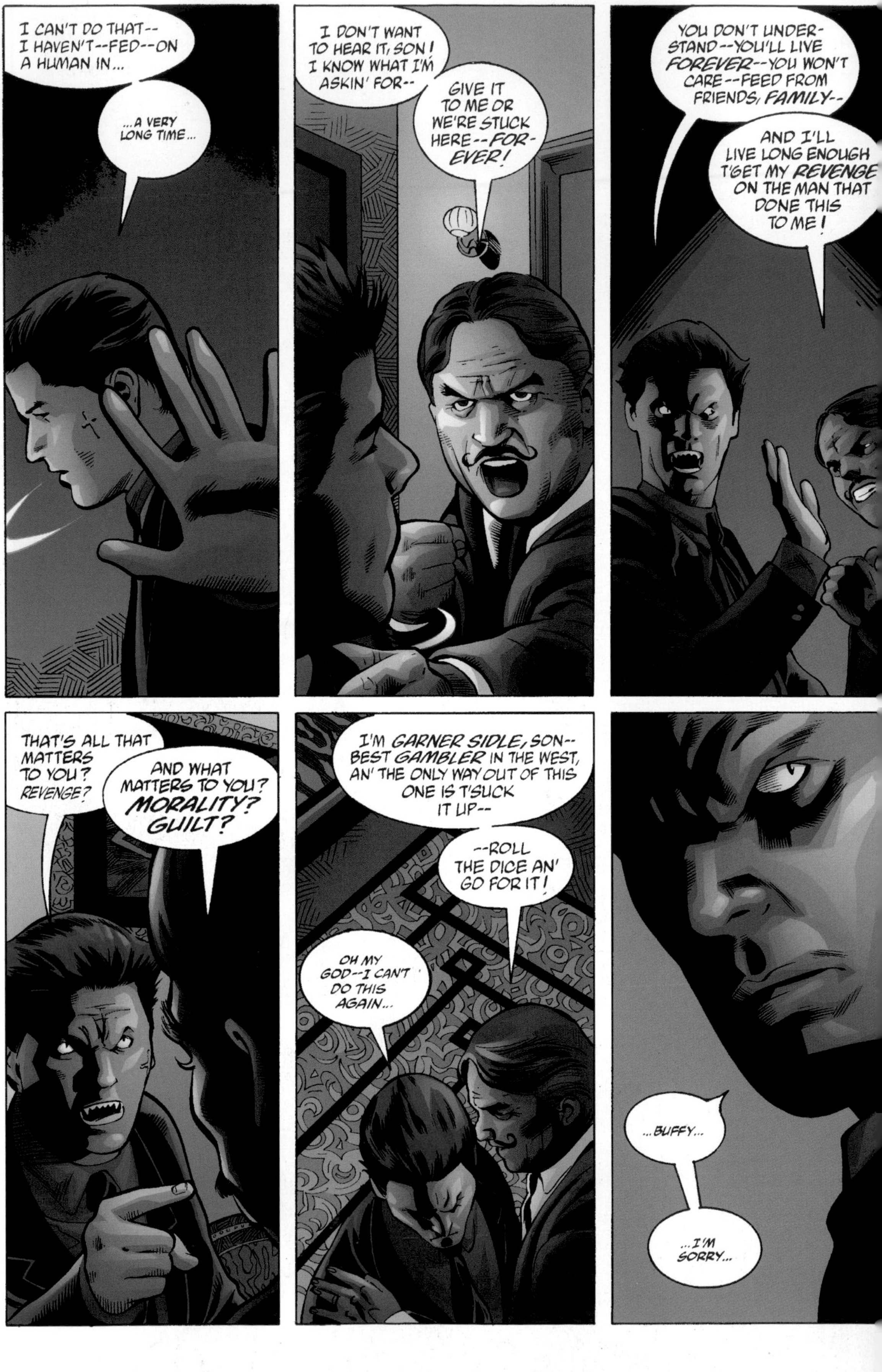
I CAN'T DO THAT-- I HAVEN'T--FED--ON A HUMAN IN...
...A VERY LONG TIME...
I DON'T WANT TO HEAR IT, SON! I KNOW WHAT I'M ASKIN' FOR--
GIVE IT TO ME OR WE'RE STUCK HERE--FOR-EVER!
YOU DON'T UNDER-STAND--YOU'LL LIVE FOREVER--YOU WON'T CARE--FEED FROM FRIENDS, FAMILY--
AND I'LL LIVE LONG ENOUGH T'GET MY REVENGE ON THE MAN THAT DONE THIS TO ME!
THAT'S ALL THAT MATTERS TO YOU? REVENGE?
AND WHAT MATTERS TO YOU? MORALITY? GUILT?
I'M GARNER SIDLE, SON-- BEST GAMBLER IN THE WEST, AN' THE ONLY WAY OUT OF THIS ONE IS T'SUCK IT UP--
--ROLL THE DICE AN' GO FOR IT!
OH MY GOD--I CAN'T DO THIS AGAIN...
...BUFFY...
...I'M SORRY...

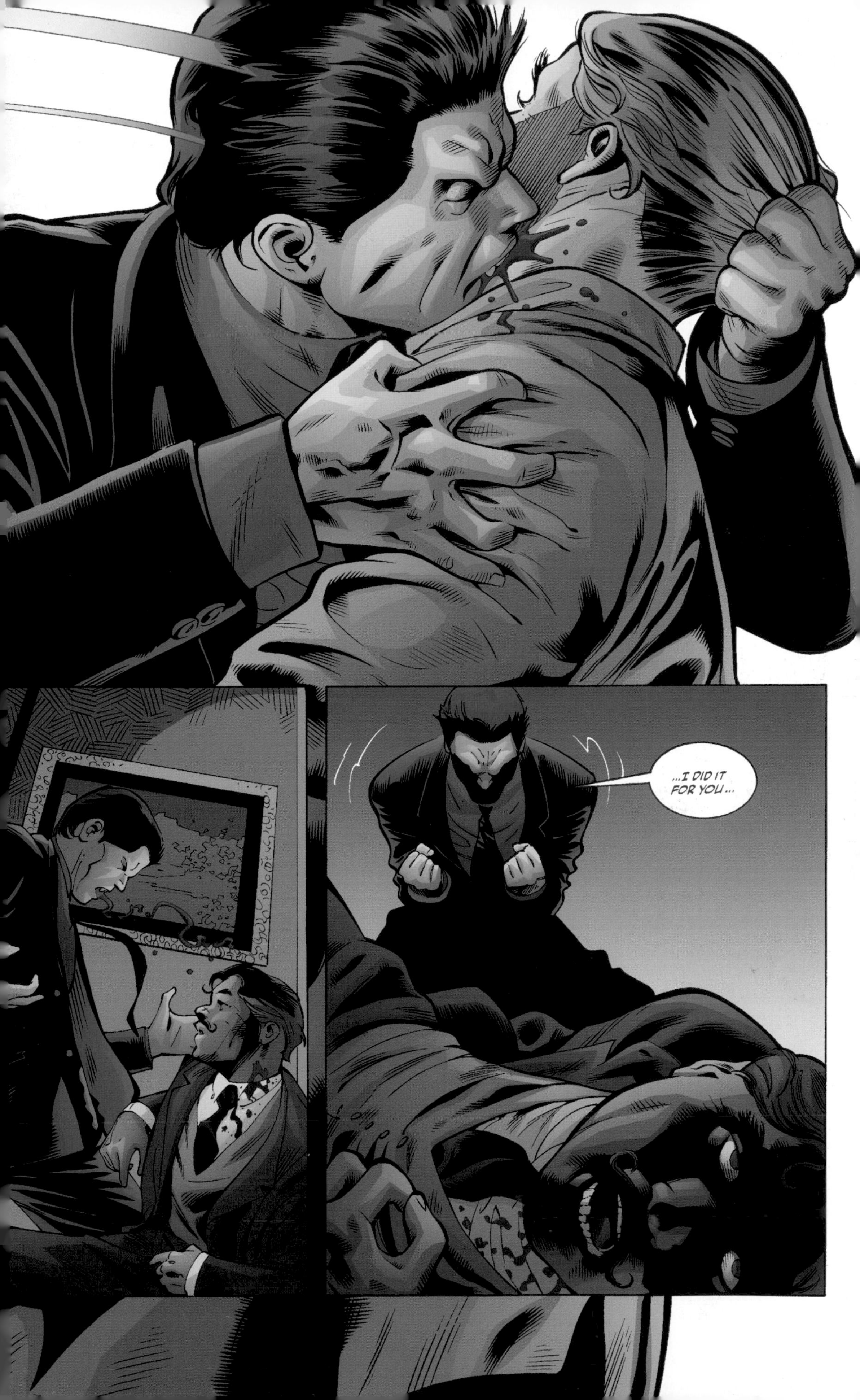
...I DID IT FOR YOU...

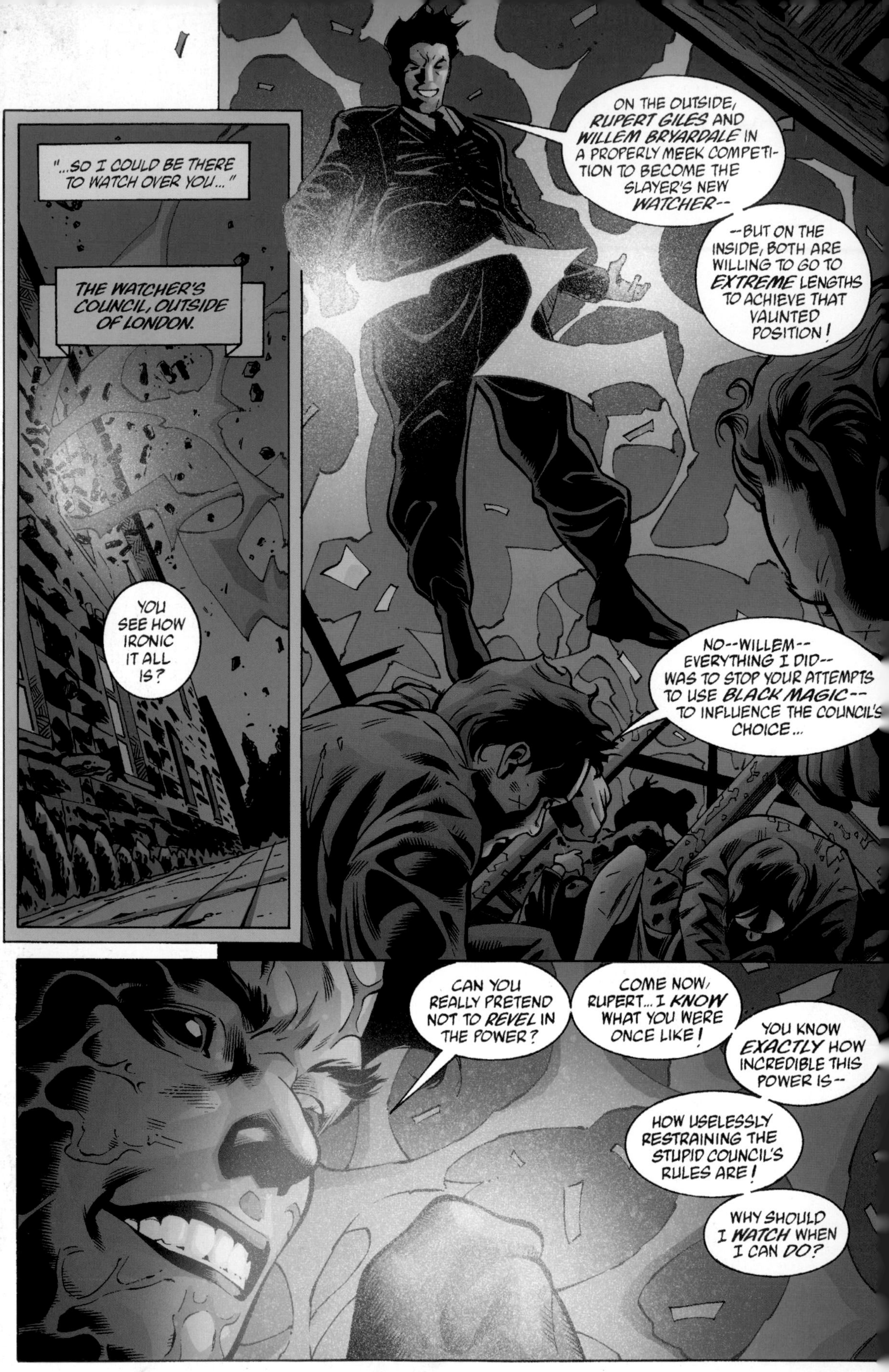
"...SO I COULD BE THERE TO WATCH OVER YOU..."
THE WATCHER'S COUNCIL, OUTSIDE OF LONDON.
YOU SEE HOW IRONIC IT ALL IS?
ON THE OUTSIDE, RUPERT GILES AND WILLEM BRYARDALE IN A PROPERLY MEEK COMPETITION TO BECOME THE SLAYER'S NEW WATCHER--
--BUT ON THE INSIDE, BOTH ARE WILLING TO GO TO EXTREME LENGTHS TO ACHIEVE THAT VAUNTED POSITION!
NO--WILLEM--EVERYTHING I DID--WAS TO STOP YOUR ATTEMPTS TO USE BLACK MAGIC--TO INFLUENCE THE COUNCIL'S CHOICE...
CAN YOU REALLY PRETEND NOT TO REVEL IN THE POWER?
COME NOW, RUPERT... I KNOW WHAT YOU WERE ONCE LIKE!
YOU KNOW EXACTLY HOW INCREDIBLE THIS POWER IS--
HOW USELESSLY RESTRAINING THE STUPID COUNCIL'S RULES ARE!
WHY SHOULD I WATCH WHEN I CAN DO?

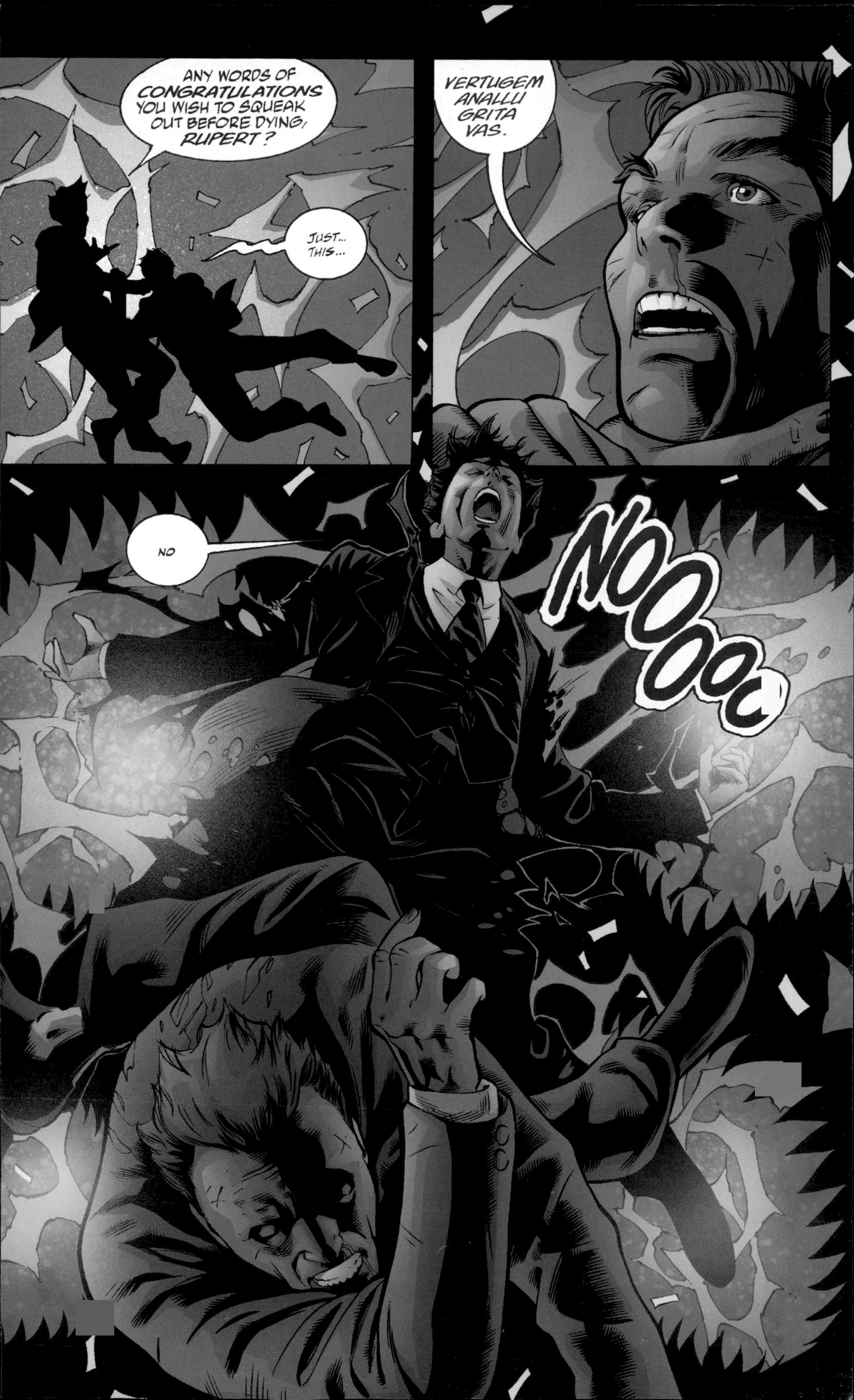
ANY WORDS OF CONGRATULATIONS YOU WISH TO SQUEAK OUT BEFORE DYING, RUPERT?
JUST... THIS...
VERTUGEM ANALLU GRITA VAS.
NO
NOOOOO

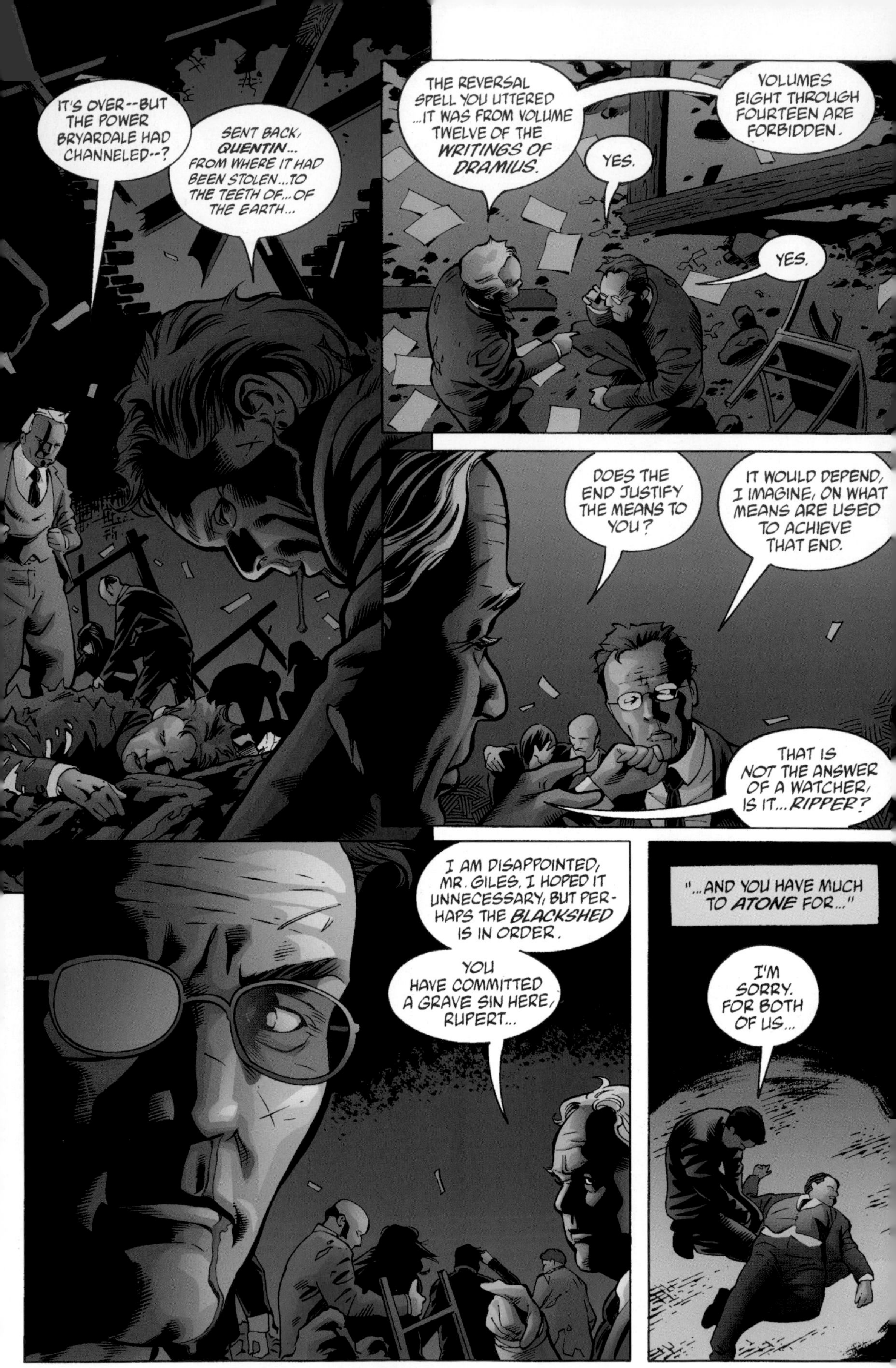
IT'S OVER--BUT THE POWER BRYARDALE HAD CHANNELED--?
SENT BACK, QUENTIN... FROM WHERE IT HAD BEEN STOLEN...TO THE TEETH OF...OF THE EARTH...
THE REVERSAL SPELL YOU UTTERED ...IT WAS FROM VOLUME TWELVE OF THE WRITINGS OF DRAMIUS.
YES.
VOLUMES EIGHT THROUGH FOURTEEN ARE FORBIDDEN.
YES.
DOES THE END JUSTIFY THE MEANS TO YOU?
IT WOULD DEPEND, I IMAGINE, ON WHAT MEANS ARE USED TO ACHIEVE THAT END.
THAT IS NOT THE ANSWER OF A WATCHER, IS IT...RIPPER?
I AM DISAPPOINTED, MR. GILES. I HOPED IT UNNECESSARY, BUT PERHAPS THE BLACKSHED IS IN ORDER.
YOU HAVE COMMITTED A GRAVE SIN HERE, RUPERT...
"...AND YOU HAVE MUCH TO ATONE FOR..."
I'M SORRY. FOR BOTH OF US...

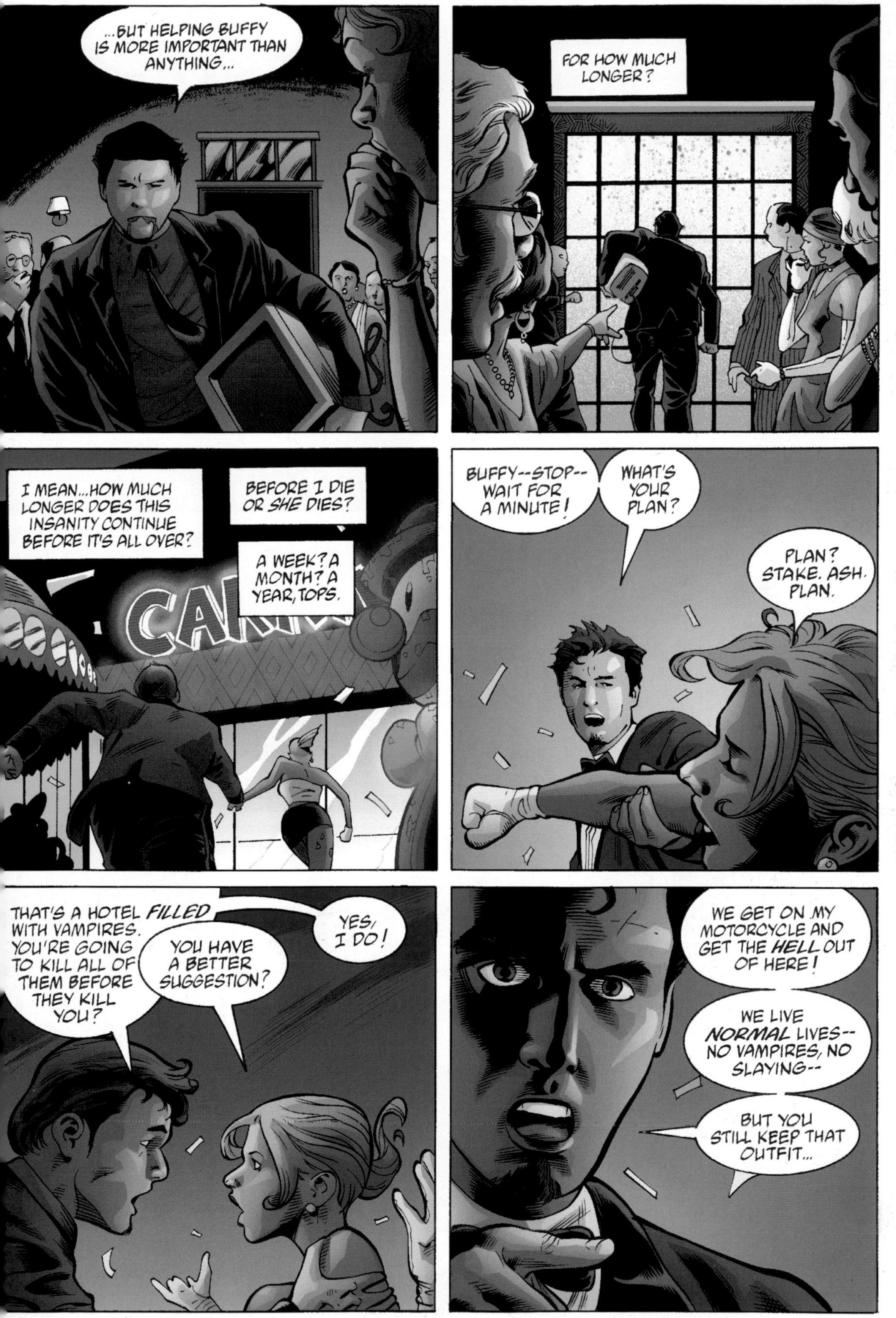
...BUT HELPING BUFFY IS MORE IMPORTANT THAN ANYTHING...
FOR HOW MUCH LONGER?
I MEAN...HOW MUCH LONGER DOES THIS INSANITY CONTINUE BEFORE IT'S ALL OVER?
BEFORE I DIE OR SHE DIES?
A WEEK? A MONTH? A YEAR, TOPS.
BUFFY--STOP--WAIT FOR A MINUTE!
WHAT'S YOUR PLAN?
PLAN? STAKE. ASH. PLAN.
THAT'S A HOTEL FILLED WITH VAMPIRES. YOU'RE GOING TO KILL ALL OF THEM BEFORE THEY KILL YOU?
YOU HAVE A BETTER SUGGESTION?
YES, I DO!
WE GET ON MY MOTORCYCLE AND GET THE HELL OUT OF HERE!
WE LIVE NORMAL LIVES--NO VAMPIRES, NO SLAYING--
BUT YOU STILL KEEP THAT OUTFIT...

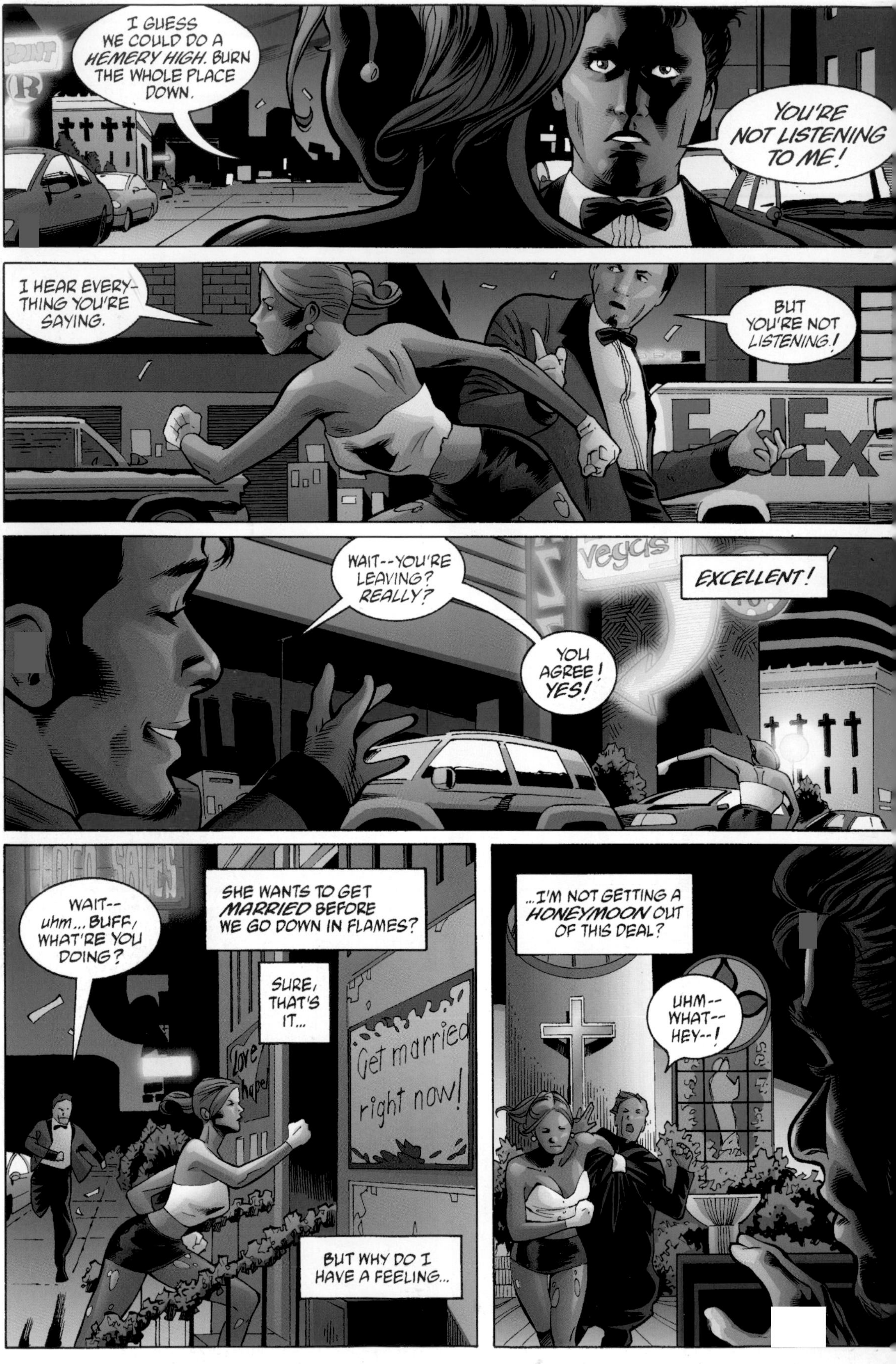
I GUESS WE COULD DO A HEMERY HIGH. BURN THE WHOLE PLACE DOWN.
YOU'RE NOT LISTENING TO ME!
I HEAR EVERYTHING YOU'RE SAYING.
BUT YOU'RE NOT LISTENING!
WAIT--YOU'RE LEAVING? REALLY?
YOU AGREE! YES!
EXCELLENT!
WAIT-- uhm... BUFF, WHAT'RE YOU DOING?
SHE WANTS TO GET MARRIED BEFORE WE GO DOWN IN FLAMES?
SURE, THAT'S IT...
Get married right now!
BUT WHY DO I HAVE A FEELING...
...I'M NOT GETTING A HONEYMOON OUT OF THIS DEAL?
UHM-- WHAT-- HEY--!

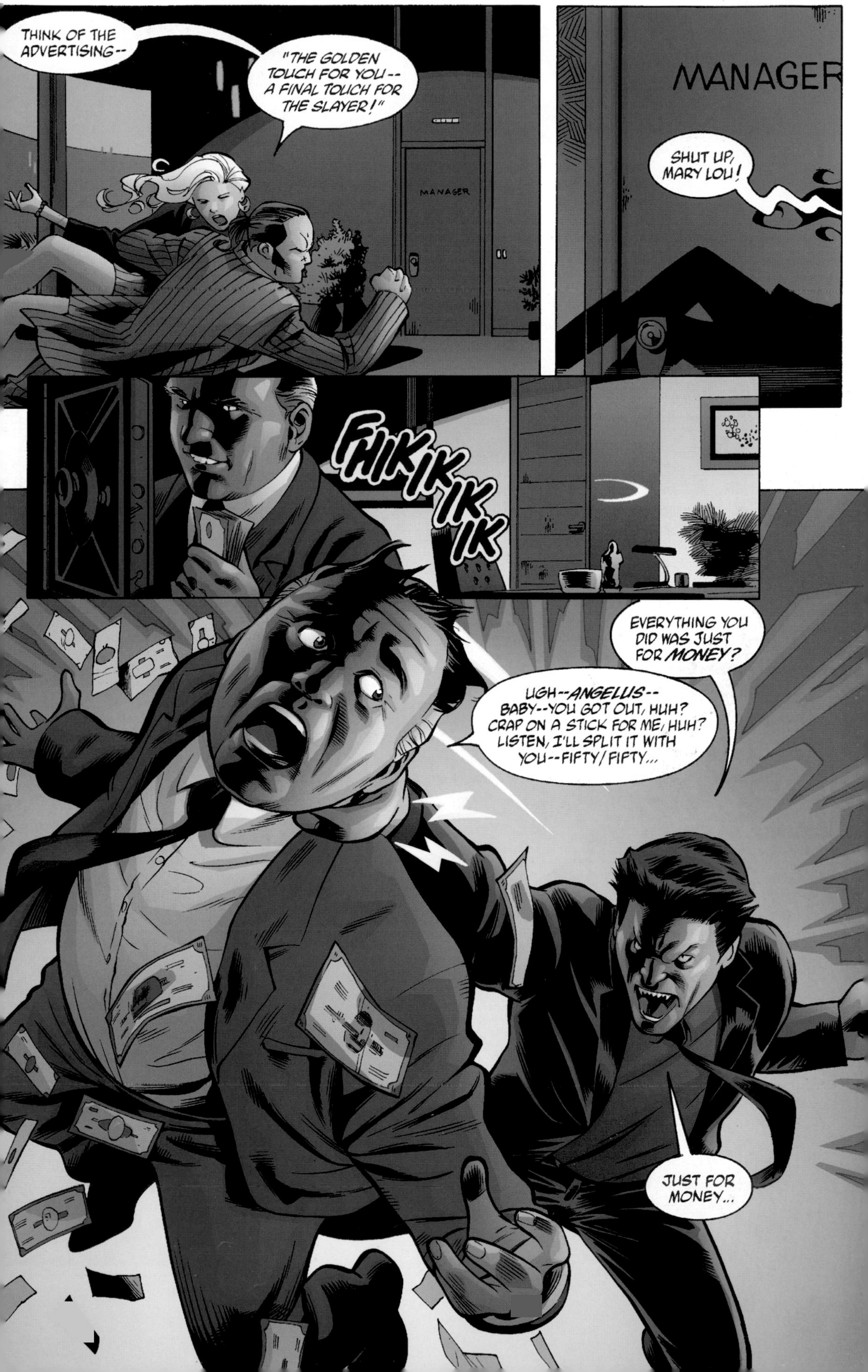
THINK OF THE ADVERTISING--
"THE GOLDEN TOUCH FOR YOU-- A FINAL TOUCH FOR THE SLAYER!"
MANAGER
MANAGER
SHUT UP, MARY LOU!
FHIKIKIKIK
EVERYTHING YOU DID WAS JUST FOR MONEY?
UGH--ANGELUS-- BABY--YOU GOT OUT, HUH? CRAP ON A STICK FOR ME, HUH? LISTEN, I'LL SPLIT IT WITH YOU--FIFTY/FIFTY...
JUST FOR MONEY...

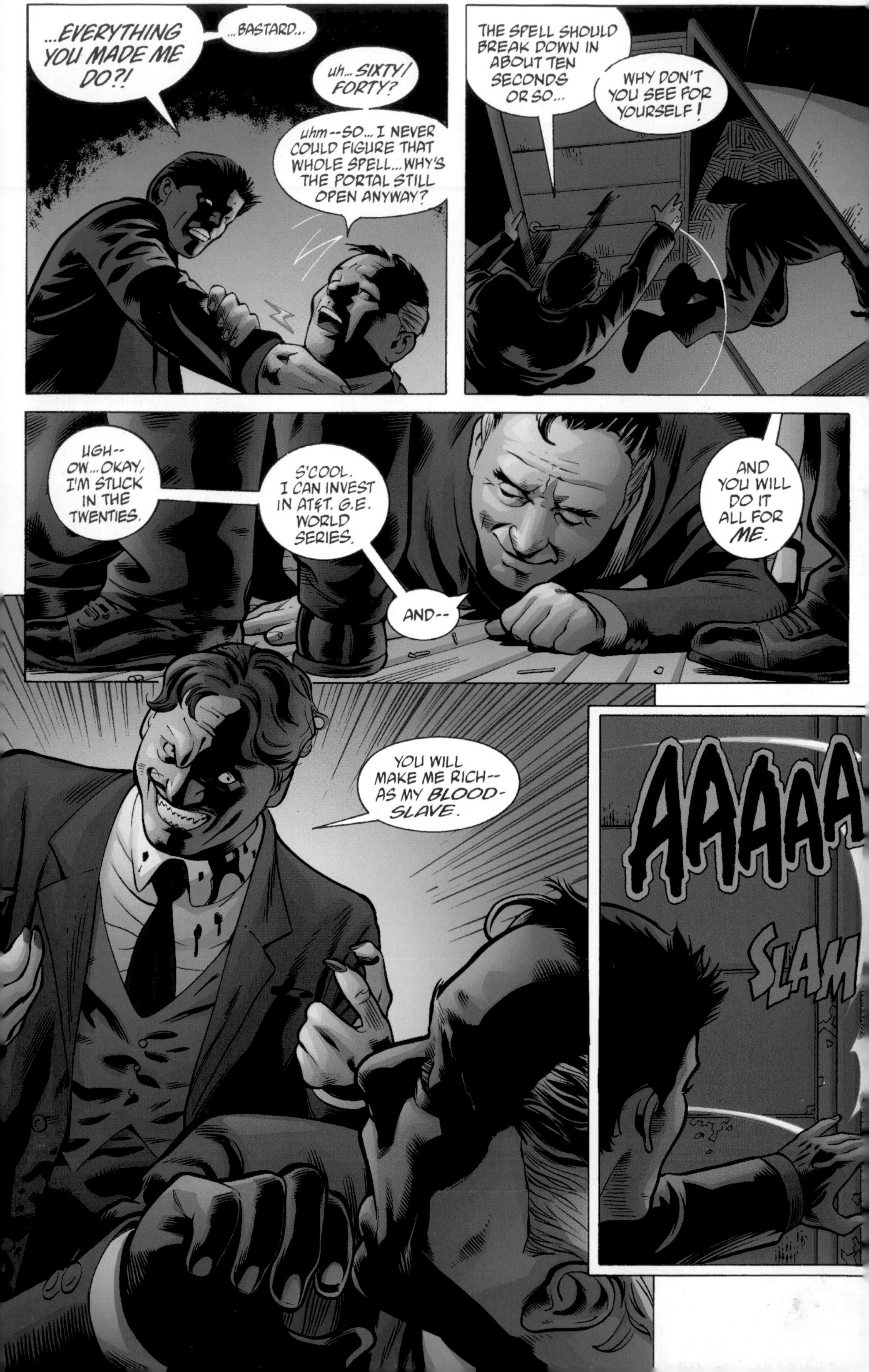
...EVERYTHING YOU MADE ME DO?!
...BASTARD...
uh... SIXTY/ FORTY?
uhm--SO... I NEVER COULD FIGURE THAT WHOLE SPELL...WHY'S THE PORTAL STILL OPEN ANYWAY?
THE SPELL SHOULD BREAK DOWN IN ABOUT TEN SECONDS OR SO...
WHY DON'T YOU SEE FOR YOURSELF!
UGH-- OW...OKAY, I'M STUCK IN THE TWENTIES.
S'COOL. I CAN INVEST IN AT&T. G.E. WORLD SERIES.
AND--
AND YOU WILL DO IT ALL FOR ME.
YOU WILL MAKE ME RICH-- AS MY BLOOD-SLAVE.
AAAAA
SLAM

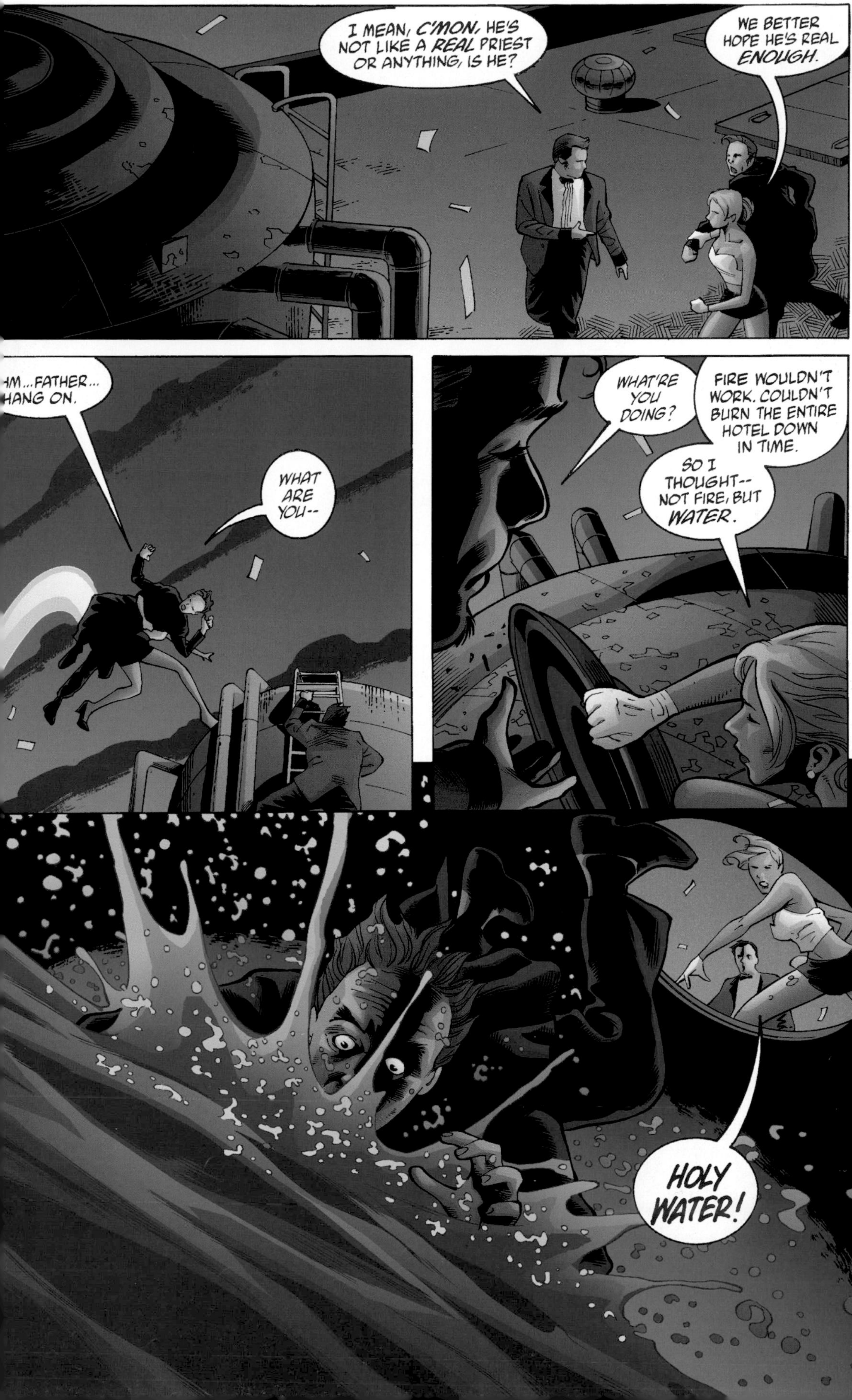
I MEAN, C'MON, HE'S NOT LIKE A REAL PRIEST OR ANYTHING, IS HE?
WE BETTER HOPE HE'S REAL ENOUGH.
HM...FATHER... HANG ON.
WHAT ARE YOU--
WHAT'RE YOU DOING?
FIRE WOULDN'T WORK. COULDN'T BURN THE ENTIRE HOTEL DOWN IN TIME.
SO I THOUGHT-- NOT FIRE, BUT WATER.
HOLY WATER!

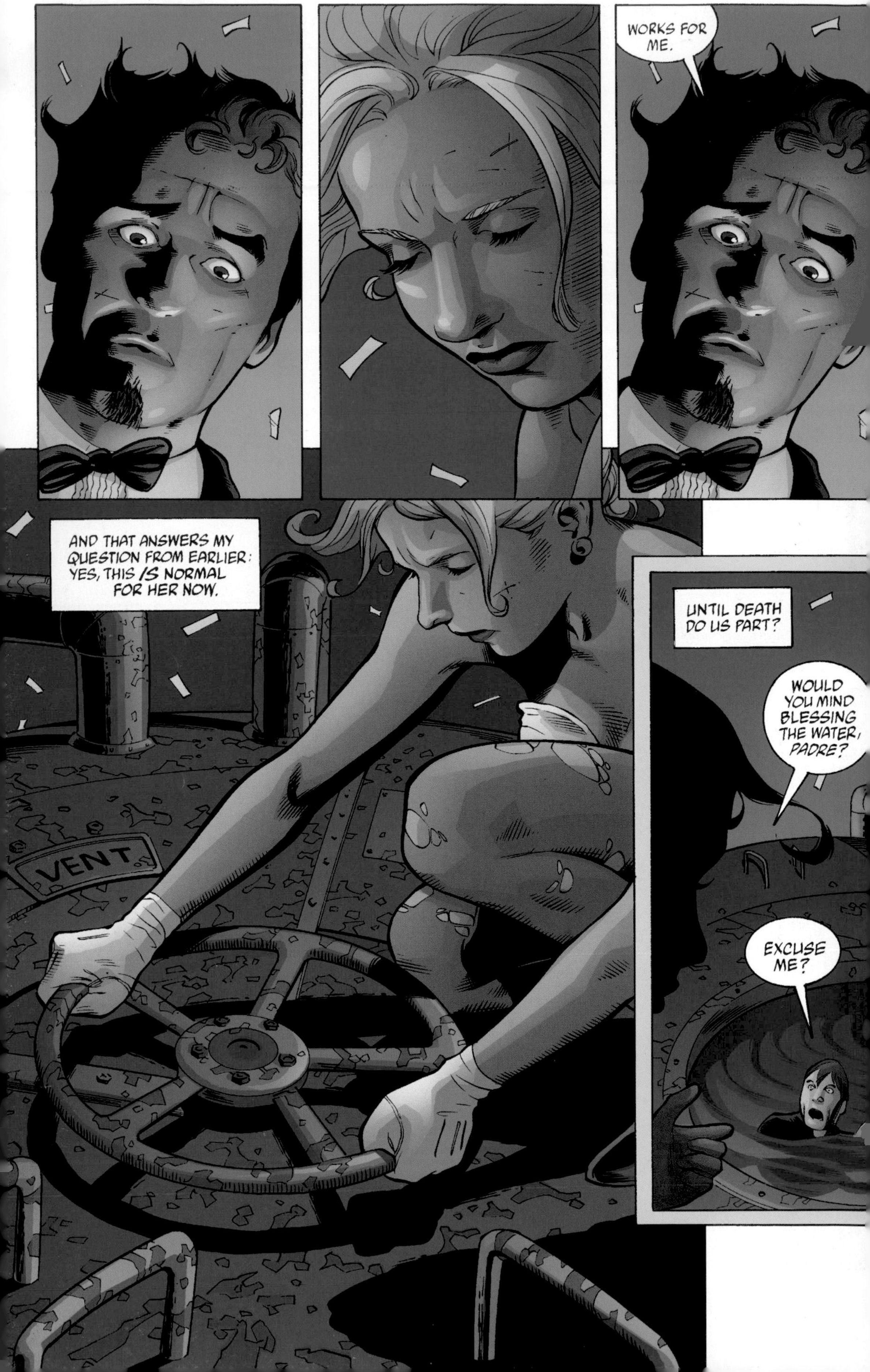
WORKS FOR ME.
AND THAT ANSWERS MY QUESTION FROM EARLIER: YES, THIS IS NORMAL FOR HER NOW.
VENT
UNTIL DEATH DO US PART?
WOULD YOU MIND BLESSING THE WATER, PADRE?
EXCUSE ME?

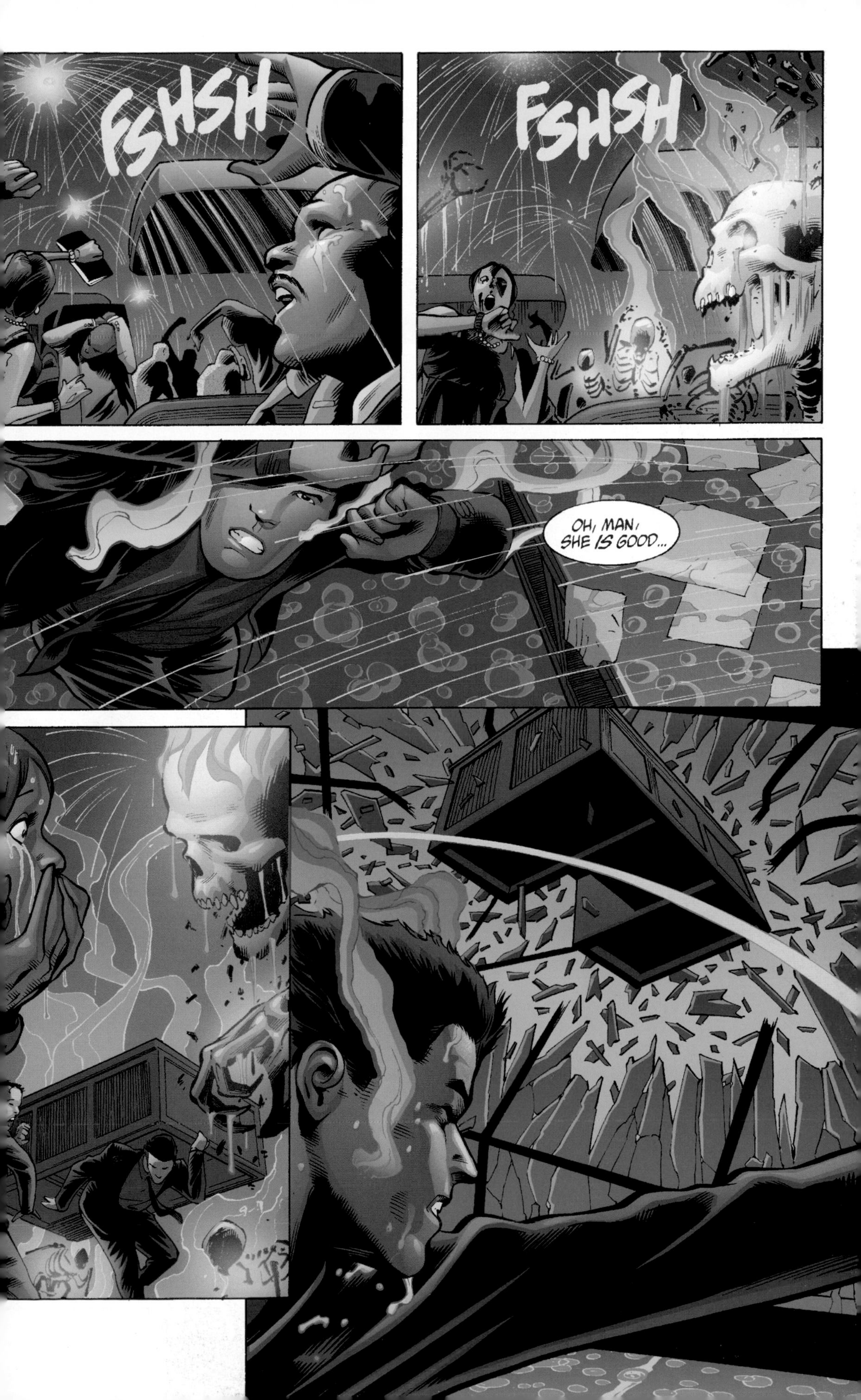
FSHSH
FSHSH
OH, MAN, SHE IS GOOD...

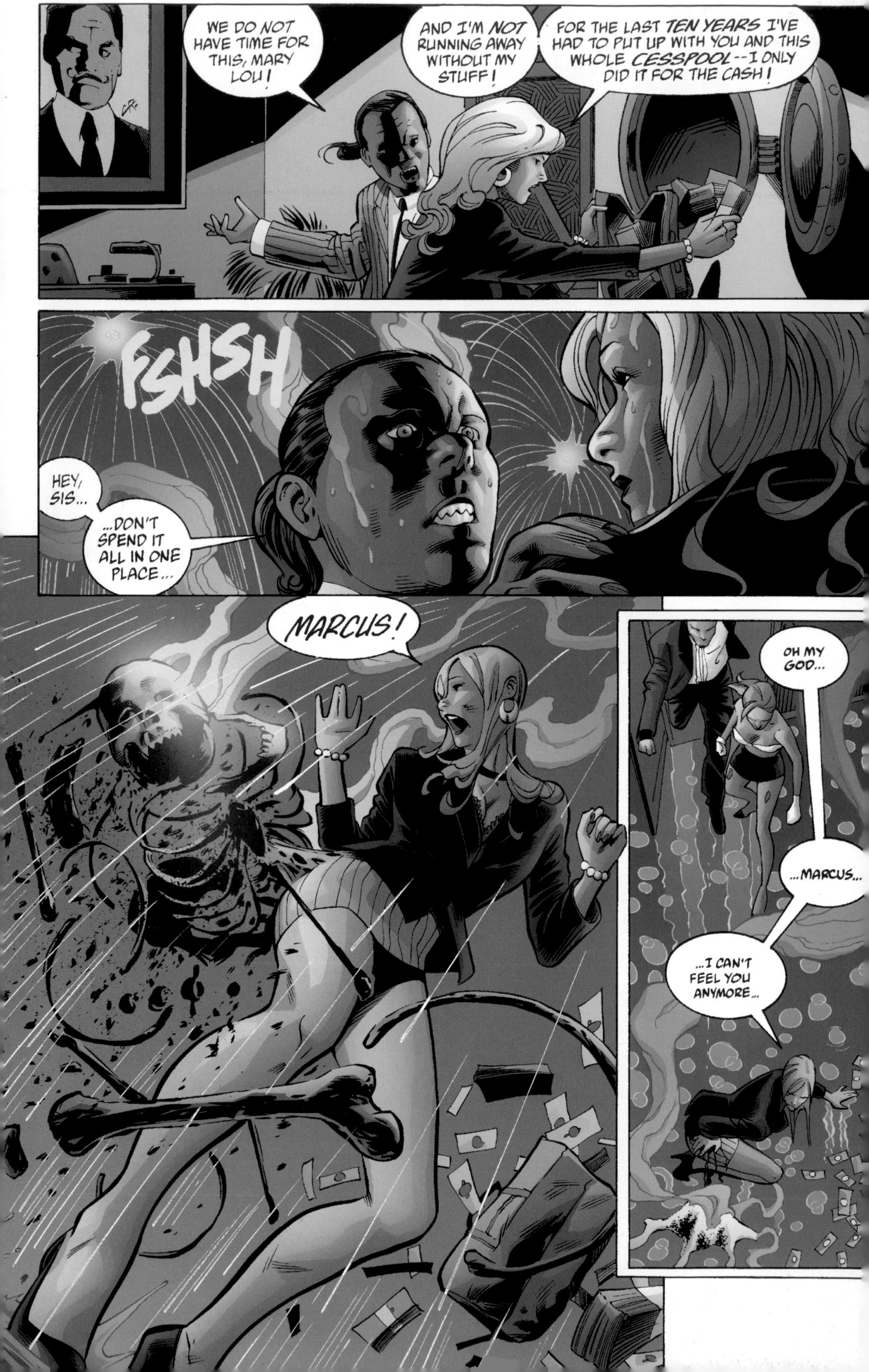
WE DO NOT HAVE TIME FOR THIS, MARY LOU!
AND I'M NOT RUNNING AWAY WITHOUT MY STUFF!
FOR THE LAST TEN YEARS I'VE HAD TO PUT UP WITH YOU AND THIS WHOLE CESSPOOL--I ONLY DID IT FOR THE CASH!
FSHSH
HEY, SIS...
...DON'T SPEND IT ALL IN ONE PLACE...
MARCUS!
OH MY GOD...
...MARCUS...
...I CAN'T FEEL YOU ANYMORE...

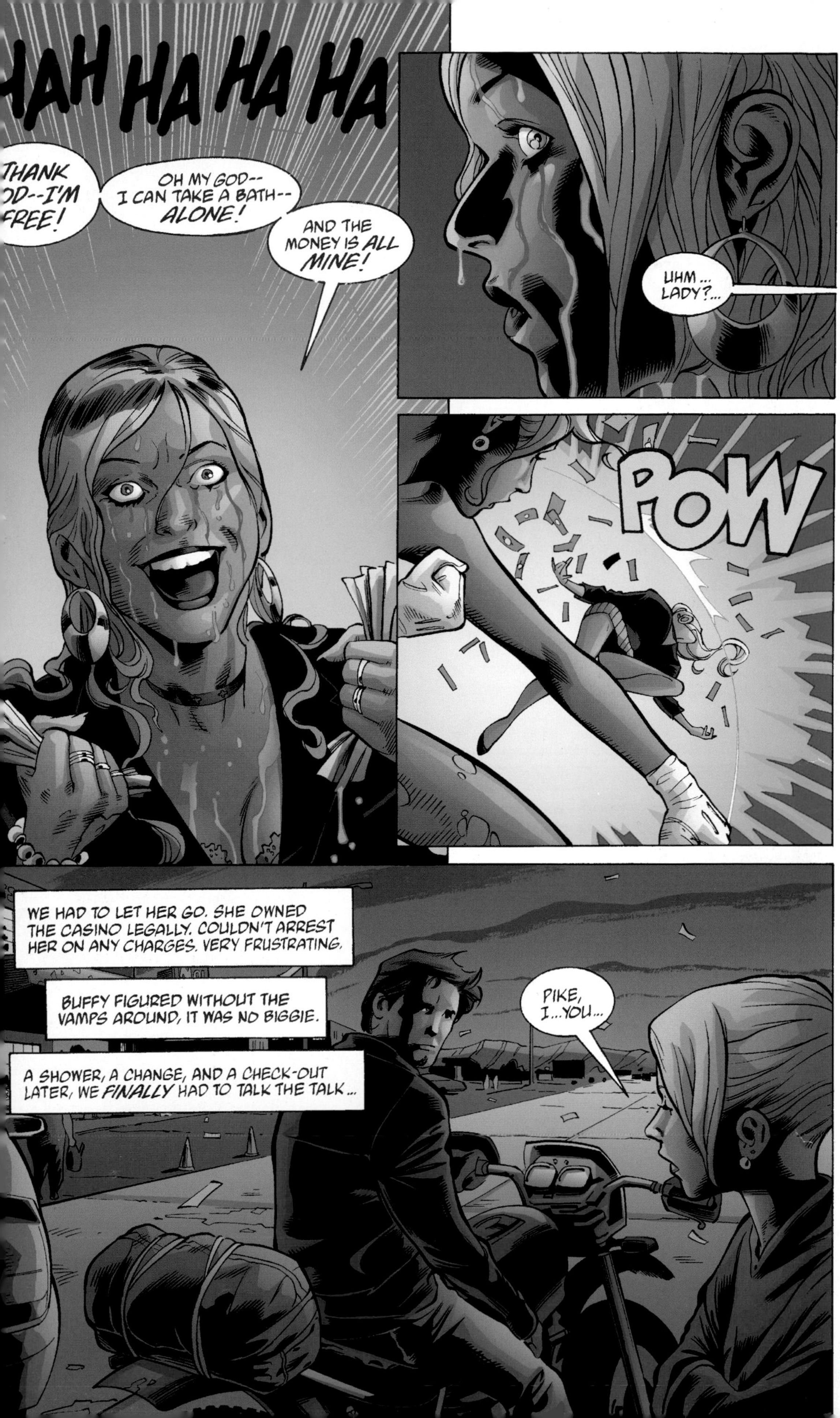
HAH HA HA HA HA
THANK
OD--I'M
FREE!
OH MY GOD--
I CAN TAKE A BATH--
ALONE!
AND THE
MONEY IS ALL
MINE!
UHM...
LADY?...
POW
WE HAD TO LET HER GO. SHE OWNED THE CASINO LEGALLY. COULDN'T ARREST HER ON ANY CHARGES. VERY FRUSTRATING.
BUFFY FIGURED WITHOUT THE VAMPS AROUND, IT WAS NO BIGGIE.
A SHOWER, A CHANGE, AND A CHECK-OUT LATER, WE FINALLY HAD TO TALK THE TALK...
PIKE,
I...YOU...

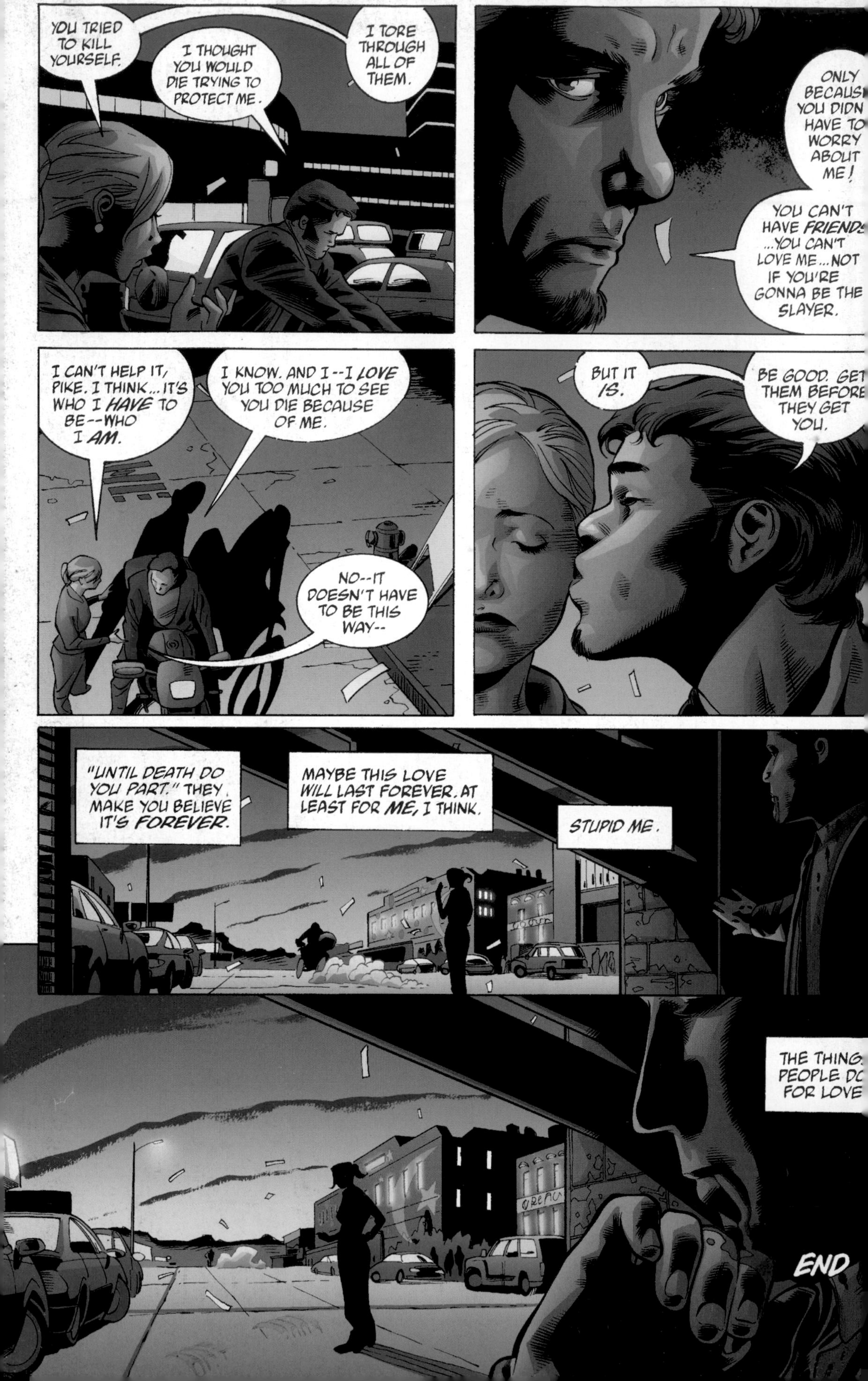

YOU TRIED TO KILL YOURSELF.
I THOUGHT YOU WOULD DIE TRYING TO PROTECT ME.
I TORE THROUGH ALL OF THEM.
ONLY BECAUS YOU DIDN HAVE TO WORRY ABOUT ME!
YOU CAN'T HAVE FRIENDS ...YOU CAN'T LOVE ME...NOT IF YOU'RE GONNA BE THE SLAYER.
I CAN'T HELP IT, PIKE. I THINK... IT'S WHO I HAVE TO BE--WHO I AM.
I KNOW. AND I--I LOVE YOU TOO MUCH TO SEE YOU DIE BECAUSE OF ME.
NO--IT DOESN'T HAVE TO BE THIS WAY--
BUT IT IS.
BE GOOD. GET THEM BEFORE THEY GET YOU.
"UNTIL DEATH DO YOU PART." THEY MAKE YOU BELIEVE IT'S FOREVER.
MAYBE THIS LOVE WILL LAST FOREVER. AT LEAST FOR ME, I THINK.
STUPID ME.
THE THING PEOPLE DO FOR LOVE
END

STAKE OUT THESE ANGEL AND BUFFY THE VAMPIRE SLAYER GRAPHIC NOVELS

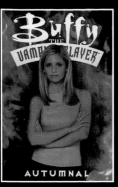

Buffy the Vampire Slayer
Autumnal
Buffy the Vampire Slayer
Bad Blood
Buffy the Vampire Slayer
The Blood of Carthage
Buffy the Vampire Slayer
Crash Test Demons
Buffy the Vampire Slayer
False Memories
Buffy the Vampire Slayer
Food Chain
Buffy the Vampire Slayer
Haunted
Buffy the Vampire Slayer
Note from the Underground
Buffy the Vampire Slayer
Out of the Woodwork
Buffy the Vampire Slayer
Oz
Buffy the Vampire Slayer
Pale Reflections
Buffy the Vampire Slayer
Angel
Buffy the Vampire Slayer
The Remaining Sunlight
Buffy the Vampire Slayer
Ugly Little Monsters
Buffy the Vampire Slayer
Uninvited Guests
Angel
Surrogates

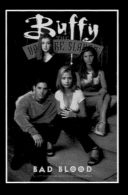

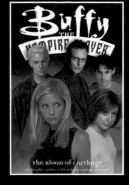

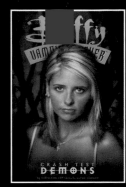

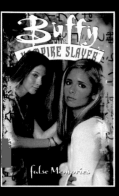

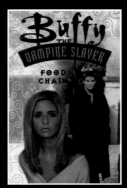

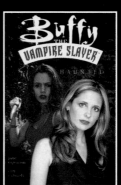

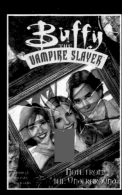

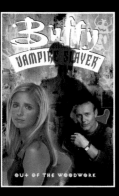

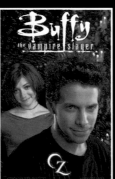

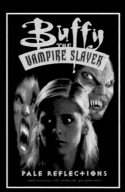

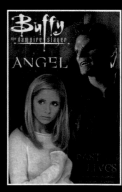

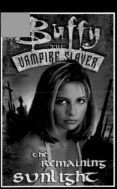

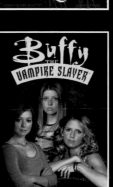

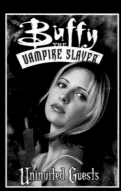

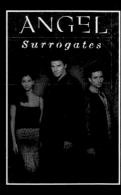

SINK YOUR TEETH INTO THESE *BUFFY THE VAMPIRE SLAYER*™ GRAPHIC NOVELS!

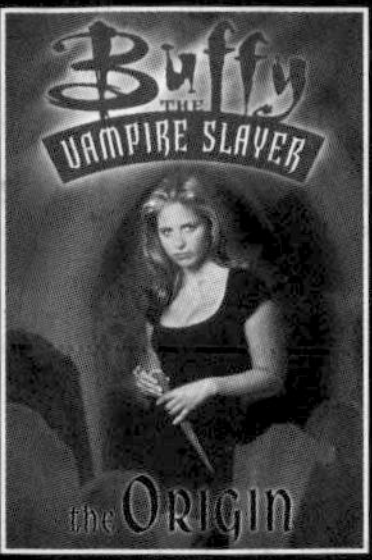
Buffy the Vampire Slayer
the Origin
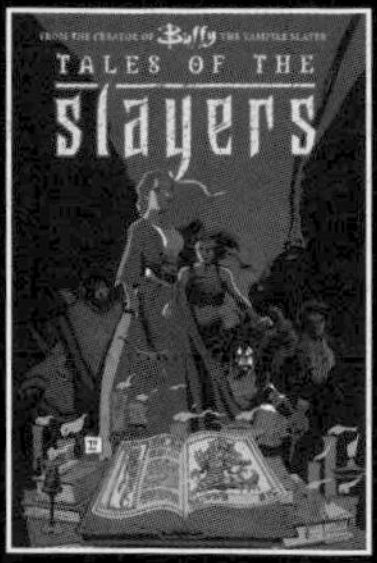
Tales of the Slayers
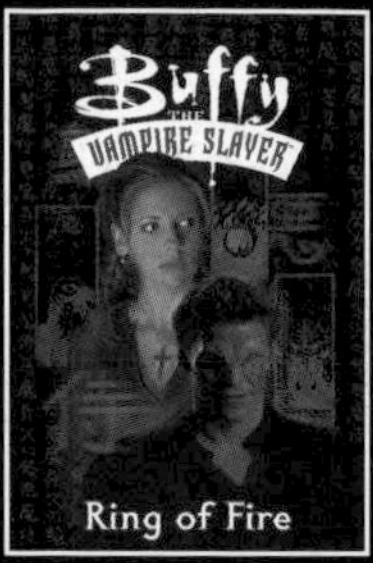
Buffy the Vampire Slayer
Ring of Fire
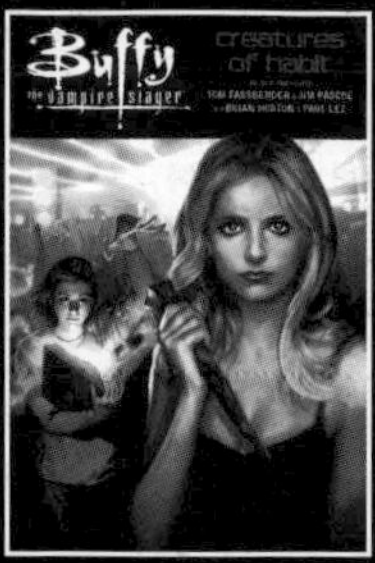
Buffy the vampire slayer
creatures of habit
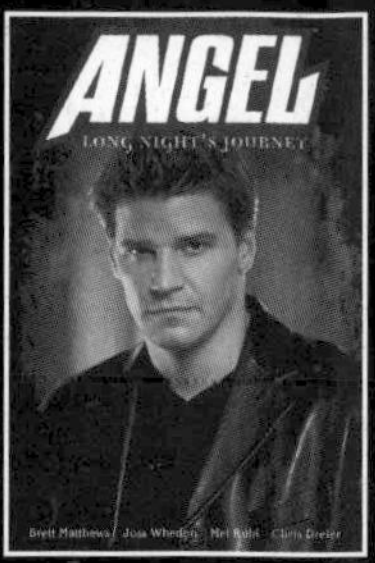
ANGEL
LONG NIGHT'S JOURNEY

BUFFY THE VAMPIRE SLAYER
season one & before

TALES OF THE SLAYERS
Featuring stories from Joss Whedon, Doug Petrie, and Amber Benson!
1-56971-605-6 $14.95

SPIKE AND DRU
Featuring stories from Christopher Golden and Buffy's James Marsters!
1-56971-541-6 $11.95

THE ORIGIN
Based on the screenplay for the original *Buffy the Vampire Slayer* movie!
1-56971-429-0 $9.95

VIVA LAS BUFFY
1-56971-980-2 $12.95

SLAYER INTERRUPTED
1-59307-011-x $12.95

A STAKE TO THE HEART
1-59307-012-8 $12.95

BUFFY THE VAMPIRE SLAYER
season two

RING OF FIRE
Written by Doug Petrie, writer for the *Buffy the Vampire Slayer* TV series!
1-56971-482-7 $9.95

BUFFY THE VAMPIRE SLAYER
season three

THE DUST WALTZ
1-56971-342-1 $9.95

THE REMAINING SUNLIGHT
1-56971-354-5 $9.95

UNINVITED GUESTS
1-56971-436-3 $10.95

SUPERNATURAL DEFENSE KIT
A color hardcover that comes in as slipcase with a "claddagh" ring, a cross, and vial of "holy water"!
1-56971-486-X $19.95

FOOD CHAIN
Featuring a story from Doug Petrie!
1-56971-602-1 $17.95

BAD BLOOD
1-56971-445-2 $9.95

CRASH TEST DEMONS
1-56971-461-4 $9.95

PALE REFLECTIONS
1-56971-475-4 $9.95

HAUNTED
Written by Jane Espenson, writer for the *Buffy the Vampire Slayer* TV series!
1-56971-737-0 $12.95

BUFFY THE VAMPIRE SLAYER
season four

THE BLOOD OF CARTHAGE
1-56971-534-3 $12.95

OZ
1-56971-569-6 $9.95

AUTUMNAL
1-56971-554-8 $9.95

PAST LIVES
1-56971-552-1 $9.95

OUT OF THE WOODWORK
1-56971-738-9 $12.95

WILLOW & TARA
Stories from Christopher Golden and *Buffy*'s Amber Benson!
1-56971-905-5 $9.95

BUFFY THE VAMPIRE SLAYER
season five

FALSE MEMORIES
1-56971-736-2 $12.95

UGLY LITTLE MONSTERS
1-56971-750-8 $12.95

DEATH OF BUFFY
1-56971-748-6 $15.95

BUFFY THE VAMPIRE SLAYER
season six

CREATURES OF HABIT
(Graphic Story Album)
1-56971-563-7 $17.95

NOTE FROM THE UNDERGROUND
1-56971-888-1 $14.95

ANGEL

THE HOLLOWER
1-56971-450-9 $9.95

SURROGATES
1-56971-491-6 $9.95

EARTHLY POSSESSIONS
1-56971-533-5 $9.95

STRANGE BEDFELLOWS
1-56971-753-2 $12.95

HUNTING GROUND
1-56971-547-5 $9.95

AUTUMNAL
1-56971-559-9 $9.95

LONG NIGHT'S JOURNEY
Written by Brett Matthews and series creator Joss Whedon!
1-56971-752-4 $12.95

DARK HORSE COMICS
darkhorse.com

Available at your local comics shop or bookstore!

To find a comics shop in your area, call 1-888-266-4226
For more information or to order direct:
• On the web: www.darkhorse.com • Email: mailorder@darkhorse.com
•Phone: 1-800-962-0052 Mon.-Sat. 9 A.M. to 5 P.M. Pacific Time
*Prices and availability subject to change